CW00958292

ROTH FAMILY FOUNDATION

*Music in America Imprint*

Michael P. Roth

and Sukey Garcetti

have endowed this

imprint to honor the

memory of their parents,

Julia and Harry Roth,

whose deep love of music

they wish to share

with others.

*Leonard Bernstein*

# Leonard Bernstein

*The Political Life of an American Musician*

## Barry Seldes

UNIVERSITY OF CALIFORNIA PRESS

*Berkeley   Los Angeles   London*

MASS: A THEATRE PIECE FOR SINGERS, PLAYERS AND DANCERS
© Copyright 1971 by Amberson Holdings LLC and Stephen Schwartz
Leonard Bernstein Music Publishing Company LLC, Publisher
Boosey & Hawkes, Inc., Sole Agent
Reprinted by permission

KADDISH (SYMPHONY NO. 3)
© Copyright 1963, 1967 by Amberson Holdings LLC, Copyright renewed.
Leonard Bernstein Music Publishing Company LLC, Publisher
Boosey & Hawkes, Inc., Sole Agent
Reprinted by permission.

University of California Press, one of the most distinguished university
presses in the United States, enriches lives around the world by advancing
scholarship in the humanities, social sciences, and natural sciences. Its
activities are supported by the UC Press Foundation and by philanthropic
contributions from individuals and institutions. For more information, visit
www.ucpress.edu.

University of California Press
Berkeley and Los Angeles, California

University of California Press, Ltd.
London, England

© 2009 by The Regents of the University of California
Library of Congress Cataloging-in-Publication Data
Seldes, Barry.
    Leonard Bernstein : the political life of an American musician /
Barry Seldes.
        p.    cm.
    Includes bibliographical references and index.
    ISBN: 978-0-520-25764-1 (cloth : alk. paper)
    1. Bernstein, Leonard, 1918–1990—Political activity.    2. Bernstein,
Leonard, 1918–1990—Political and social views.    3. Musicians—United
States—Political activity.    I. Title.
    ML410.B566S45    2009
    780.92—dc22
    [B]                                                    2008040829

Manufactured in the United States of America

18   17   16   15   14   13   12   11   10   09
10   9   8   7   6   5   4   3   2   1

This book is printed on Natures Book, which contains 50% post-consumer
waste and meets the minimum requirements of ANSI/NISO Z39.48–1992
(R 1997) (*Permanence of Paper*).

*To the memory of*
*Gertrude Seldes (1912–1983)*
*Nathan Seldes (1909–1979)*

You have a . . . task. . . . It is to establish from all these freewheeling personalities within your States a tie that shall be as a blood-bond. Their lives are of many moods and colors. Build them into a great Cathedral. Their voices are unconscious and spontaneous and discordant. Compose from them a symphony.

Romain Rolland, "America and the Arts"

The fatal shortcoming of nine-tenths of the music produced in America is its utter innocence of any vital relationship to the community.

Paul Rosenfeld, "The American Composer"

The objective conditions necessary to the realization of a work of art are, as we know, a highly complex phenomenon, involving one's public, the possibility of contact with it, the general atmosphere, and above all freedom from involuntary subjective control.

Czeslaw Milosz, *The Captive Mind*

# CONTENTS

# ILLUSTRATIONS

# ACKNOWLEDGMENTS

My colleagues at Rider University granted me research fellowships and a sabbatical from teaching in order to finish this book. I am very grateful to editor Mary Francis, who has overseen the book's publication, assistant editor Kalicia Pivirotto, production editors Mary Severance and Elizabeth Berg, and copy editor Adrienne Harris for their professionalism and generosity of spirit.

Mark Eden Horowitz, the archivist of the Bernstein Collection at the Library of Congress, gave me invaluable assistance in locating documents and answered myriad questions about the collection. Marie Carter of the Bernstein office was very kind in granting me permission to photocopy and then quote from documents in the Bernstein Collection. I also thank the staff of the Performing Arts Reading Room of the Library of Congress for their help. I thank the American Civil Liberties Union of Southern California for making available to me a copy of the FBI Bernstein dossier. Alexander Bernstein, Burton Bernstein, Margaret Carlson, and Stephen Wadsworth were most gracious in granting me interviews. I am grateful to Barbara Haws and her colleagues at the New York Philharmonic Archive, the staff at the Ford Foundation Archive, and Mark Rozenzweig of the Reference Center for Marxist Studies for their guidance and assistance in helping me pursue lines of research in their respective collections.

I wish to thank Maryke Seldes for her translation work. My debt to her for support over the years is enormous.

I owe a great debt of gratitude to a number of colleagues and friends. Barbara Heyman was painstaking in her reading of the text, provided much critical commentary, gave me counsel, and otherwise helped me ready the manuscript for submission. James Poivan and Barry Malzberg read earlier versions of the manuscript: their suggestions helped me shape the book's argument. Alan Lesitsky, who also read the manuscript and offered important commentary, supplied me a specialist discographer's help. Lindsey Christiansen and J. J. Penna read the manuscript and corrected a number of infelicities, musical and otherwise.

Steven Allen, James Dickinson, Joseph Gowaskie, Linda Materna, Jonathan Mendilow, Ilan Peleg, Gerald Pomper, and Frank Rusciano read various parts of the text and offered me critical advice. Richard Swain was very helpful to me in the early stages of researching this book.

My son, Alex, and his bride, Sabre Mrkva, have given me great cheer. Linda Materna continues to find innumerable ways to support my work and my life.

# Introduction

On the morning of May 14, 1959, an excited crowd of thousands gathered at Broadway and West 64th Street to witness ground-breaking ceremonies for the Lincoln Center for the Performing Arts. The day was a glorious one for New Yorkers, for their new complex—concentrating in one place the city's world-class dance, orchestral, and operatic ensembles and a new repertory theater—would be proof visible of New York's cultural ascendancy. In the words of urban-planning czar Robert Moses, Lincoln Center would make the city the "World Center of the Performing Arts," a complement to its place as "World Political Capital."[1]

Festivities began at 11 A.M. with master of ceremonies Leonard Bernstein leading the New York Philharmonic in a performance of Aaron Copland's *Fanfare for the Common Man.* Bernstein then introduced the guest of honor, President Eisenhower, who thanked the artists and praised the many people within government, labor, business, and charitable foundations who had worked to make Lincoln Center possible. He predicted that the "increasing interest in America in cultural matters" would "influence . . . peace and understanding throughout the world." The president then dug up a shovelful of earth to inaugurate construction of the center's first building, Philharmonic Hall, and turned to shake Bernstein's hand.[2]

This handshake was a fitting way to celebrate the partnership between American political aspiration and high culture. For some years, Bernstein had been a cultural ambassador for the United States. He had toured Latin America with the New York Philharmonic in 1958 and, at the behest of the State Department, was about to go on tour to the Soviet Union, a trip that had great significance in the administration's quest for a thaw in the otherwise glacial Cold War. If anyone fit E. B. White's idea of the immigrant to the city who greatly enhances its life and culture, it was Leonard Bernstein. Born in Boston in 1918 and arriving in New York in 1941, soon to become a champion of American music, he was the composer of the great New York ballet *Fancy Free* and the New York musicals *On the Town* (1944), *Wonderful Town* (1953), and *West Side Story* (composed in 1957 and just coming to the end of its great Broadway run at the time of the Lincoln Center groundbreaking), and he had been the principal conductor of the New York Philharmonic in 1957 and music director since 1958. He was a Columbia Records star performer; a gifted television educator; a celebrity much photographed and lionized by *Time, Life,* and other mass-circulation magazines; and a man at home in both highbrow and middle-brow worlds. Now, on this day of celebration, the already formidable Bernstein, the most magisterial of New York's creative and performing artists, was receiving the president's personal recognition as the sovereign of this new center for the performing arts.

Yet this seemingly unambiguously celebratory day had interesting ironies, known only by Bernstein and a few others. For example, as the maestro gave the downbeat to the Philharmonic's brass section to begin Copland's *Fanfare,* only a tiny minority of the onlookers were likely aware, as Bernstein certainly was, that only six years before, in 1953, Eisenhower had banned a performance of Copland's *Lincoln Portrait* at his inauguration because Copland was a supporter of left-wing causes. Did the crowd know that President Truman, in February 1950, had banned Bernstein's music from overseas State Department libraries and functions? Or that in 1953, Eisenhower's State Department had revoked Bernstein's passport on the grounds that the maestro was a security risk, returning it only after

Bernstein, his conducting career on the verge of wreckage, agreed to sign an affidavit confessing to political sins? These darker events were certainly in Bernstein's mind, and perhaps Eisenhower's, as the two Olympians shook hands in joint celebration.

Such were the paradoxes and ironies of that day: the fanfare, waving flags, and hearty handshakes masking a closely guarded tale of presidentially authorized censorship, intimidation, and humiliation. This tale, and other aspects of Bernstein's political life—his blacklisting by CBS in 1950, his later removal from the blacklist, and his return to the podium of the New York Philharmonic as principal conductor and then music director—is the one I tell in these pages. The narrative shows how closely intertwined were Bernstein's political life, philosophic outlook, and music as they developed within the larger contours and contradictions of American political life from the 1930s to his death in 1990.

No one has written this narrative until now. In fact, those who have written about Bernstein have tended to avoid thematic discussion of his political life. This gap is unfortunate, because Bernstein was highly political. He was inevitably responsive to developments in the political and moral climate; his choice of texts to set to music often revealed his political concerns. To ignore the impact of political forces upon Bernstein is to miss out on much of what enlivened and motivated him. This book, which draws on materials in the Leonard Bernstein Collection at the Library of Congress and hundreds of pages in the FBI's Bernstein dossier, much for the first time, offers a new and, I hope, fuller understanding of Bernstein's life, art, and times. That the perspective herein differs markedly from those of other biographies will be evident immediately.[3] Whereas I see Bernstein's political, philosophical, and musical lives as all of a piece, Bernstein's first biographer, Joan Peyser, writing in 1987, offers some summary passages about Bernstein's political activity in the 1940s and attributes his activism to prolonged immaturity, which he grew out of and which bore no relationship to his musical career. Humphrey Burton, who directed many of the films of Bernstein's concerts for Deutsche Grammophon and apparently knew him well, sees Bernstein's political life as a collection of occasional and momentary events that had no connection to his work as composer and conductor. Meryle Secrest devotes two pages of her book to Bernstein's left-wing political life in the 1940s, but like her predecessors Peyser and Burton, she does not examine the deeper effects of his politics on his mind-set.[4] Record producer Paul Myers, to whom I will return shortly, concludes that Bernstein was largely apolitical.

This general failure to deal comprehensively with Bernstein's lifelong political thought is readily explainable. Peyser wrote her book with Bernstein's cooperation but apparently did not gain access to the Bernstein papers and was explicitly denied access to the FBI files that the Bernstein Office obtained under the Freedom of Information Act. Without such permission, Peyser was unable to obtain access to the FBI files while Bernstein was alive.[5] Secrest suffered the same limitations that Peyser did. Burton certainly had access to Leonard Bernstein's papers, but whether he had access to the FBI file is not clear.

Upon Bernstein's death in 1990, the FBI removed restrictions on access to his dossier. In 1994, the Southern California American Civil Liberties Union obtained the collection under the Freedom of Information Act and kindly supplied me with a copy.[6] The Bernstein papers went to the Library of Congress and began to become available to researchers in 1997.[7] The writer who fails to delve into these papers misses critically important dimensions of Bernstein's life and character. Paul Myers, who was a confidant of Bernstein's from 1982 to Bernstein's death in 1990, apparently wrote his wonderful memoir of his association with Bernstein without consulting the Bernstein archive or the FBI dossier, because he writes, "For the most part Bernstein remained remarkably apolitical throughout his life." Myers does move from this rigid stance to remark, "Bernstein was a loyal Democrat and frequently lent his name to social causes. In the paranoia that reflected the dark era of McCarthyism, he could easily have been branded a 'Lefty' or fellow-traveler, but he seldom participated in genuine left-wing politics."[8] Myers's assessment of Bernstein's political life thus approaches the assessments of other biographers.

In this book, I dispel the idea that Bernstein was apolitical or only occasionally political. Deep study of the archival documents, and the other sources they illuminate, reveals Bernstein as a politically engaged man. One comes to see that his political commitments and activities were highly important to him, that he was victimized because of them, and that they often played a significant role in his artistic career. For example, with heretofore-unanalyzed documentation in hand, I have been able to expand upon critic Norman Lebrecht's explanation of Bernstein's troubled conducting career in the early 1950s. Lebrecht sees the Red Scare climate of fear and intimidation as the reason for Bernstein's supposed "unemployability": the maestro was absent from the Philharmonic's podium from the 1951–52 to the 1955–56 seasons, was hired by the Philharmonic's board to share conducting duties with Dimitri Mitropoulos in the fall 1957 season and become music director in 1958. Lebrecht notes that Bernstein "came onto the market during the McCarthy witch-hunt when his leftist sympathies, homoerotic inclinations and racial origins rendered him virtually unemployable in America."[9] But Bernstein was still Jewish in 1956, and if his marriage in 1951 and birth of his first child, Jamie, in 1952 had not removed the taint of homoeroticism, why did they do so in 1956? As for Bernstein's leftist politics, Lebrecht offers no evidence to indicate why in 1956 the Philharmonic board no longer felt that Bernstein's politics were an impediment to hiring him. In short, Lebrecht does not indicate why the board, having shunned Bernstein in the early 1950s because he was Jewish or gay or a left-winger, would hire Bernstein in 1956, when McCarthyism was still in full sway. Certainly, the board was going through a major change with the departure of Arthur Judson, who had been Bernstein's manager; was aware of Bernstein's politics, his homoeroticism, and his Jewish ethnicity and religion. But a careful inquiry into the historical record, now informed by material in the Bernstein Collection and the Bernstein FBI dossier, indicates that the shifting dynamics and imperatives in domestic and international cultural Cold War politics, not changes in the board's composition, prompted board members to invite Bernstein to become principal conductor and music director of the New York Philharmonic.

The archival documentation supports the contention that Bernstein's political commitments were lifelong: he never grew out of them. Depending on events, his involvement may have been stronger now, weaker later, dormant and then active, but Bernstein was always a man of the political Left. In fact, by understanding his responses to the political climate, we can deepen our grasp of his motivations for composing such works as his 1962 *Kaddish* Symphony, his 1971 *Mass,* and his 1977 *Songfest.* We can say much the same about Bernstein's attachment to Gustav Mahler's music. Our understanding of Bernstein's reasons for championing Mahler and promoting the so-called Mahler boom will grow as we chart Bernstein's responses to the political and cultural ethos from which the boom sprang forth.

The first six chapters in this book, organized by decade, discuss Bernstein's political life and its effects on his career from the 1930s to the 1980s. In the last chapter, I bring up a matter close to Bernstein's heart and his greatest artistic disappointment: his self-admitted failure to compose a work of the greatest significance that would be his legacy to the world. I suggest that Bernstein's inability to do so has something to do with the interplay between his creative aspirations and the dynamics of American political culture, which may have stultified or helped stultify his ambitions.

This book, then, is about Leonard Bernstein at the crossroads of politics and the arts from the late 1930s, when he entered Harvard University, to his death in 1990. I do not aim to offer a full biography here. Hermann Broch apparently told Hannah Arendt that her biography of Rahel Vernhagen suffered for lack of the sexual perspective: "I want to know not only who slept with whom but also the address and date."[10] I am afraid that anyone who has similar hopes will be disappointed with this work, for I offer no such names, addresses, and dates. I do think, however, that the reader will find the political perspective on Bernstein's life of profound interest.

I must confess my disappointment with the sparse quantity of "confessional" material necessary for a more complete recording of Bernstein's interior life. I would like to know more about his emotional reactions to the threats and dangers visited upon him during the Cold War years and to have access to the introspective musings and crises of conscience that form the stuff of great psychological biography. To come into the Music (now the Performing Arts) Reading Room of the Library of Congress and find over one thousand boxes of correspondence, writings, and personal business papers gladdens the researcher's heart. To discover that precious few of the letters are from Bernstein, and that still fewer provide revelations of his inner life, disheartens. When, one day, I received an e-mail from Mark Eden Horowitz, the curator of the Leonard Bernstein Collection, reporting that he had uncovered some letters from Bernstein to his sister, Shirley, and that at least one, from 1951, was written as Bernstein anticipated a subpoena from a congressional investigating committee, I felt a flush of anticipation. In fact, I did find in that letter a Bernstein in dread, a far cry from the ever-effusive extrovert of most depictions. However, this letter stands as the exception proving the rule—few other documents reveal Bernstein's reactions to his plight during the Red Scare repression. Nonetheless, I found enough material in other letters, writings, and personal business papers to form an understanding of Bernstein's world during that era and beyond.

My goal, then, is to reconstruct the political man. The Leonard Bernstein who emerges in these pages is a man who, to use an expression of Bertolt Brecht's, lived through dark times.[11] He was scarred and shaped by them. Unless we comprehend Bernstein's life as he lived it within the turmoil of political forces, our image of him will remain foreshortened, a distortion of reality. So too will our understanding of significant aspects of American culture during the Cold War years and beyond.

# CHAPTER ONE

# Young American

## *Bernstein at Harvard*

In 1982, at the age of sixty-four, Leonard Bernstein included in his collection of his writings, *Findings,* some essays from his younger days that prefigured significant elements of his later adult life and career. The first, "Father's Books," written in 1935 when he was seventeen, is about his father and the Talmud. Throughout his life, Bernstein was ever mindful that he was a Jew; he composed music on Jewish themes and in later years referred to himself as a "rabbi," a teacher with a penchant to pass on scholarly learning, wisdom, and lore to orchestral musicians.[1] Moreover, Bernstein came to adopt an Old Testament prophetic voice for much of his music, including his first symphony, *Jeremiah,* and his third, *Kaddish.* The second essay, "The Occult," an assignment for a freshman composition class at Harvard that he wrote in 1938 when he was twenty years old, was about meeting Dimitri Mitropoulos, who inspired him to take up conducting. The third, his senior thesis of April 1939, was a virtual manifesto calling for an organic, vernacular, rhythmically based, distinctly American music, a music that he later championed from the podium and realized in his compositions for the Broadway stage and operatic and concert halls.[2]

### EARLY YEARS: PROPHETIC VOICE

Bernstein as an Old Testament prophet? Bernstein's father, Sam, was born in 1892 in an ultraorthodox Jewish shtetl in Russia. His hopes for a rabbinic career dashed when he was called up for compulsory service in the brutal czarist military, Sam fled to America in 1908, took a job eviscerating fish in New York's Fulton Fish Market, and after a number of years, wound up a highly successful beauty-supply businessman in Lawrence, Massachusetts.[3] Apparently Sam, denied a rabbinical vocation, was nevertheless a rabbi by avocation. His wife, Jenny (née Resnick), born in 1898 in Russia, arrived in America in 1905, and in 1912, at age fourteen, went to work in the Lawrence woolen mills.[4] Sam and Jenny married and set up a conservative Jewish home. Sam, by day a businessman, was at night, according to his son Burton, an "Old Testament figure," who presided over family life with a "commanding, omniscient presence."[5] He was a prophet at the dinner table, around which sat Louis, later renamed Leonard, born on August 25, 1918; Shirley, born in 1923; and Burton, born in 1932. Sam held forth on subjects running from Talmudic meditations and the history of the Jewish people from biblical times to their plight under Nazi power in Europe.[6] In Jewish homes in those days, the talk ran also to the condition of American Jewry and devotion to President Roosevelt, whom many Jews saw as a bulwark against foreign and domestic fascists such as Father Coughlin, whose broadcasts reached across the nation, and other anti-Semites.[7]

Sam's hopes that his firstborn would realize his own thwarted rabbinic plans were dashed when Sam's sister, Clara, gave the family a piano and thereby set Leonard's musical destiny in motion. Leonard not only became inseparable from the piano, but also showed precocity in and joy for musical performance from the start. Apparently Jenny encouraged Leonard's piano work, but not Sam, to whom Leonard's incessant piano playing sounded like percussive poundings and caused the paterfamilias to bellow in rage. The teenage Leonard apparently took his father's anger in stride. Leonard soon turned his musicality to advantage, recruiting

Shirley and other youngsters to take on roles in various musical theatricals that he directed from the piano and that his troupe performed before adult audiences at the lakeside resort where their families took their summer vacations.

Leonard cajoled Sam into paying for piano lessons, and he progressed rapidly from beginner to accomplished musician under the direction of a number of teachers, among them Helen Coates, who served as Bernstein's secretary from the 1940s into the 1970s. Bernstein attended concerts, became increasingly preoccupied with music, and upon graduation from the prestigious Boston Latin School in 1935, was accepted by Harvard as a music major. Sam had hoped that if Leonard were not to become a rabbi, he would at least take his place in the Bernstein business. But music? Music making was a craft held in low esteem by Eastern European Orthodox Jews whose religious tradition had no Bachs, no Telemanns, and indeed no instrumental music. The cantor sings a capella, and save for the blowing of the shofar, or ram's horn, on the high holy day of Yom Kippur, music has no place in the Orthodox synagogue.[8] Whatever place existed for instrumental music in Yiddish culture was for the lowly art of klezmer music, performed at weddings and bar mitzvahs by artists who were expected to eat their meals with the kitchen staff and then depart via the back door. Thus, to Sam, Leonard's choice of career seemed a step backward from the family's climb from its poor immigrant status—a blot on the family escutcheon. Leonard nevertheless got his way, and in September 1935, he entered Harvard Yard and moved from shtetl to cosmopolis.

## BERNSTEIN AT HARVARD: MITROPOULOS

As Bernstein began his fall 1935 freshman semester, news from afar was sobering: Hitler's violation of the Versailles Treaty by rearming Germany was met by barely a whimper from France. Mussolini's fascism had gained the Catholic Church's imprimatur, and fascism also reigned in Austria, Portugal, and Rumania. In America, homegrown fascists, and for that matter, many in the Republican Party, were ready to back General Douglas MacArthur for president.[9]

But if the young music major worried about this grave news, he also found excitement in college. Harvard seemed alive with a new music full of rhythmic volatility, a wide pallet of instrumental color, and a devil-may-care chromaticism that tended toward dissonance and even atonalism. In all these features, this music declared a radical break with nineteenth-century classical and romantic music. Moreover, heady debates arose within the two great camps of the new music: the French-Russian neo-classicists and the German atonalists. The former, of which Eric Satie, Maurice Ravel, and Igor Stravinsky were exemplars, promoted economy, simplicity, clarity, and a sense of irony and the burlesque; the latter, led by Arnold Schoenberg, Alban Berg, and Anton Webern, found in atonality and serialism a way around what they considered the rigidities of tonalism and saw these as the optimal way to give expression to social and political chaos and psychological breakdown. Nevertheless, whatever the battles between these contending groups, all the champions of the new music agreed that the traditions of eighteenth- and nineteenth-century music had little to say about the twentieth-century machine-age metropolis and its cacophonic and kaleidoscopic effects upon the senses. Not that the new guard intended to dishonor older masters. Unlike avant-garde Italian futurist and Russian cubo-futurist poets who disdained the past, these new composers venerated their predecessors. However, they wanted a new music that would express present-day realities. And, especially exciting to these young American musicians was the increasing exploitation of jazz forms by Stravinsky, Ernst Krenek, Kurt Weill, and Darius Milhaud to represent contemporary emotional states—for example, a boulevardier's saunter; a primitive Dionysian savagery; a slatternly, sullen eroticism and seductive sensuality; a shiver of nightmarish terror; a sensation of dark brooding or leering irony, sarcasm, and cynicism; or a whirl of drunken intoxication, dizziness, or delirium. These states were far removed from the sense of security, affirmation, and triumph transmitted to concert-hall listeners by the centered tonality and solid consonances and cadences of eighteenth- and nineteenth-century classical and romantic repertoires.

The new music had important venues at Harvard and in Boston. The American modernist Walter Piston sat on the Harvard music faculty, and across town, the Russian émigré Serge Koussevitzky regularly conducted the Boston Symphony Orchestra in performances of French, Russian, and American modernist works. Although Bernstein would meet Koussevitzky in 1940, with enormous consequences for the young man's career, his first fateful meeting with a great musical mentor was with another champion of modernism, the conductor Dimitri Mitropoulos. In January 1937, Bernstein went to a Mitropoulos concert in Boston and was bewitched by the maestro's expressive conducting style. Through a stroke of luck, Bernstein was asked by a Harvard Greek society to play the piano at an affair honoring Mitropoulos, and he was able to wangle a private meeting with the conductor, at which he apparently impressed the older man. In February 1938, a year later, Bernstein memorialized this encounter with the fictionalized account of their meeting, "The Occult." The essay reaches an apogee of gastronomic-erotic sensuality as the maestro places an oyster from the end of his own fork into the mouth of his swooning young protégé. Meeting the young man in the aftermath of thunderous applause from a concert audience, the maestro exhorts his student to fulfill his destiny, his "mission"—to compose.[10] But something else happened to Bernstein when he watched what Mitropoulos's biographer calls the "choreographic ecstasies," "sheer physicality" and "sexual encounter with conductor and orchestra" of a Mitropoulos performance.[11] Bernstein discovered his other destiny—to conduct.

### DAVID PRALL

From 1935 to 1939, his Harvard years, Bernstein's principal mentor was the aesthetics professor David Prall. Bernstein met Prall in 1936 and was initiated into Prall's circle of graduate students, which included the composer Arthur Berger, the painter Robert Motherwell, and the poet and essayist

Delmore Schwartz. Prall had an enormous influence upon these men, creative artists who felt alienated from Harvard's analytically oriented academic community. Academic life in those years was heavily biased toward the positivistic—toward facts verifiable by the canons of scientific method and toward criticism that revealed causes and analyzed structures. Even professors of aesthetics embraced positivism, dwelling not on the beautiful but on the *concept* of the beautiful and treating works with clinical detachment while devaluing the *experience* of the work. That young artists were left feeling insecure, frustrated, and inhibited is not surprising.

The quality that attracted them to Prall was his attack upon the officially ordained positivistic standards of beauty and study and his contrasting validation of experience and feeling. The field of aesthetics, he argued, was not a rarefied cerebral sanctum reserved for the specialist. Rather, people experience natural objects and humanly constructed works, including works of art, as "aesthetic surfaces." One's grasp of the significance of a work of art is enhanced to the degree that one works at understanding its sensuous qualities (a painting's hues, masses, shapes and forms; a musical work's melodies, motives, rhythms, and mix of timbres) and its spatial-temporal ones (in painting, the spatial relationship between hues on a canvas; in music, pitch relations as ordered by major or minor scales and chromatic patterns). For Prall, knowledge and feeling were not mutually exclusive. Instead, the listener or auditor gleans a kind of knowledge as he or she intuits and senses the "aesthetic surface" of a work of art.[12] Prall thus insisted that form, alone valued by the academic community, and feeling, so long devalued, both have value; they are two ways in which the work comes into being and is experienced. In putting forth this view, Prall essentially dignified feeling and legitimized innovation.

Prall also argued for studying an artwork in context. Years after his time at Harvard, Bernstein acknowledged Prall's additional demand that students study a work from a variety of disciplinary and philosophic viewpoints.[13] He may have also taken to heart Prall's seeming insistence, at least as stated in his 1936 *Aesthetic Analysis,* that tonal music is natural.[14] Prall also advanced the view that the artist has a social vocation to produce artworks that enliven viewers and auditors with the spirit of their age; thus, the artwork joins creator and audience into a social and politically significant community.[15] Bernstein came to champion this view; indeed, it became a foundation of his outlook, finding expression in his composition, his repertoire, his aesthetic and social philosophy, and his political commitments.

## COPLAND AND AMERICAN MODERNISM

One day in 1936, Arthur Berger thought to introduce his bright young colleague to Aaron Copland's 1930 *Piano Variations*. A work of severe austerity, often jarring and discordant, with a somber if not brooding mood, and miles from the lyricism of a Liszt or a Brahms, the *Variations* had become the anthem of the young American modernists.[16] Bernstein was bowled over by the piece and immediately told Prall about it. Prall, who must have sensed from Leonard's euphoric response that the *Piano Variations* was indicative of the new spirit sweeping American music, insisted upon purchasing the sheet music for Bernstein and studying it with him. Bernstein quickly mastered the Copland piece and committed it to memory.

Then one evening in November 1937, Bernstein went to a concert in New York and found himself seated next to Copland, at which point the ever-gregarious Leonard struck up a conversation. Copland was taken by the young man's verve and invited Bernstein to a party at his studio. There, Bernstein bragged to the skeptical Copland and assembled guests, including Virgil Thomson and Paul Bowles, that he knew the *Piano Variations* by heart. Dared by Copland to play the piece, he did so, thereby announcing his arrival on the New York modernist musical scene.

Thus, at nineteen, a sophomore undergraduate, Bernstein was still at home within Sam's old Jewish world but otherwise in Prall's circle at Harvard and in Copland's circles of central figures in the New York art worlds.[17] Moving in Copland's circles not only took Bernstein from Boston to New York but also plunged him directly into the heady brew of modern art. Already, Copland was having an extraordinary influence upon the new American music. Every young American musician knew Copland as a leader and organizer of American composers.

Copland, born in Brooklyn in 1900, advocated a form of American music that fit within a larger endeavor to create a distinctly modernist American culture. The movement was already under way in the first decade of the century when the photographer Alfred Stieglitz exhibited works of Cézanne, Brancusi, and other French modernist painters and sculptors in his New York City gallery, and it received a huge forward jolt from the 1913 Armory Show. In 1915, the critic Van Wyck Brooks argued in *America's Coming of Age* that the time was ripe for Americans to create their own literature, to cast aside the Puritan legacy that had forced the individual to choose between mutually antagonistic cultures—"highbrow" versus "lowbrow," "theoretical" versus "practical."[18] For Brooks, this cultural bifurcation had alienated the inward-thinking individual from the public culture—which was dominated by the values of the businessman, scientist, and engineer—and the latter, in turn, suffered from philistinism because of the devaluation of elevated and heightened expressions of the inner life. No middle ground existed to link the individual to the living, palpitating "organic" life of his or her fellow citizens. Thus, the new moderns needed and wanted a new, unified, "organic" culture, forged from American roots and intent upon forming an American identity. Inspired by such exemplars as Walt Whitman, every "Young American"—member of a reformist upsurge in the mid-nineteenth century—could find his or her authentic voice and place within this new, vibrant American culture.

Whitman had pointed the way to inclusiveness through his vernacular poetics. He celebrated the exuberant individual and the collective to which the individual belonged, a pluralistic, democratic multitude making up a life-affirming, erotically charged democracy. A new, modern "Young America" could now search for what Brooks in 1918 called a "usable past"—experiences and modes of expression long forgotten or submerged under official discourse—to create this new national culture.[19]

In no way did this call seek to create an American provincialism. Over the next decades, the members of these modernist circles—including critics

Lewis Mumford, Waldo Frank and Paul Rosenfeld, Eugene O'Neill, and Harold Clurman—understood this new cultural upsurge to be an exploration of American themes within the various international modernist artistic idioms. Many exciting new works, such as O'Neill's *Hairy Ape* (1922), Elmer Rice's *The Adding Machine* (1923), and Virgil Thomson's and Gertrude Stein's *Four Saints in Three Acts* (1927), used modernist techniques to give expression to powerfully vivid and moving aspects of contemporary life, not least to the alienating and tragic aspects neglected by the business optimism (epitomized in Sinclair Lewis's 1922 ironic novel, *Babbitt*) that dominated American public discourse.

Copland had early on enlisted in this modernist movement. He had gone to Paris in the early 1920s to study with the famed teacher Nadia Boulanger and had returned to compose music integrating the French and Russian modernist and American jazz idioms—best exemplified in his Piano Concerto of 1926. In quick order, members of the Brooks circle saw that they had in Copland an exemplary young American artist. In 1929, Rosenfeld saw in Copland a musician for the new age, for composing music which moved its listener to feel as one with "the stream of metallic, modern American things."[20]

In the mid-1930s, advocates of the new American modernism began joining the Popular Front: the compact of liberals, progressives, socialists, and communists to oppose fascism.[21] By November 1936, Bernstein's second year at Harvard, the American Popular Front was gaining momentum as millions of workers entered the new industrial unions that were forming with the encouragement of the Roosevelt administration. This new climate had first appeared in 1933, when first lady Eleanor Roosevelt and her associates began to document the hardships faced by countless Americans, many of whom had been living lives of quiet desperation for years if not decades before the Crash of 1929 and the ensuing depression. This work indicated that the Roosevelts meant to take action. Secretary of Interior Harold Ickes, one of Bernstein's heroes,[22] set in motion the Public Works Administration, and Roosevelt's associate Harry Hopkins established the Federal Emergency Relief Administration and the Works

Progress Administration, programs that aimed not only to reemploy millions but also to modernize American cities and suburbs. Thomas Hart Benton, commissioned by institutional and corporate sponsors and, by 1934, by the Federal Arts Project, painted murals on the interior walls of public buildings depicting the productivist outlook of labor as noble and dignified. Inspired by the new art, a new politics emerged whose constituents included workers and others principally urban and ethnic. Many of these participants were new voters who were newly naturalized or first-generation Americans, and great numbers of them took to picket lines, becoming politically conscious members of a mass movement and swelling the ranks of the Democratic Party.[23] They in turn inspired progressives such as John Dewey to push the New Deal administration into wholesale restructuring of the relationship between democratic government and the economy, calling for government to take a greater role in regulating the otherwise-unaccountable power of American industry and finance that had resulted in the Great Depression.[24]

The reformist impulse was transforming knowledge and expression across the cultural landscape. Social scientists and investigators within and outside government were collecting data to understand the structure of American life. Others were discovering and seeking to resurrect heretofore-neglected elements of the American cultural past to inject vitality into new culture. For example, Harvard historian Perry Miller was discovering the moral powers and lyricism within seventeenth- and eighteenth-century American Puritan culture. Others were discovering and recording the music of common folk. Martha Graham choreographed a socially critical modern dance that departed from conventional ballet not only in form but also in content, taking up cases of contemporary victimization of the weak by the strong.[25] John Dos Passos's *U.S.A.* trilogy (1930–36) used new forms of layout and typography, incorporated literary forms from James Joyce's *Ulysses,* and used the montage effects developed in film to create a panoramic epic of America that saw crass commercial values insinuating themselves into every political and social corner of American life. The progressive sensibility was apparent in Maxwell Anderson's 1934 Broadway smash-hit play *Winterset,* a verse tragedy dealing with the fictional son of Sacco or Vanzetti. A year later, the Group Theater's production of Clifford Odets's virtual union-organizing manifesto, *Waiting for Lefty,* played to full houses month after month.

Many people in these Broadway audiences were members of the new unions and of new left-wing organizations, such as the International Workers' Order, the Associated Workers Club, the American League against War and Fascism, and the American Music League. Were they interested in the new serious music? Certainly the composer Marc Blitzstein thought so in the spring of 1936, as Roosevelt geared up for the election in November. "A public is storming the gates," he wrote in *Modern Music,* "a great mass of people" about to "enter at last the field of serious music."[26] John Houseman wrote, "Fifty percent of our public came from organized theatre parties, mostly of the Left—prejudiced and semi-educated but young and generous and eager to participate in the excitement which the stage alone seemed to offer to him in those uncertain times. These were the audiences whose members had 'sat in' with the WPA workers earlier in the month."[27] The famous call "Strike!" at the end of Odets's *Waiting for Lefty* sought to inspire audience members to take action at their workplaces.

Copland himself had been moving in a radical-political direction. He argued that even *Piano Variations,* its apparent austerity and high modernist abstraction notwithstanding, sought to express the "tragic reality" not only "at the core of our existence" but also "of our own age and time."[28] His 1935 "Militant" (the first piece in his *Statements*) was a left-wing call to arms. In 1937, he contributed a May Day song to the far-left magazine *New Masses.* By 1938, in an attempt to compose music more accessible to the masses as well as to support the Popular Front, Copland moved into a popular-elegiac phase of his work, beginning with *Billy the Kid,* commissioned by Agnes de Mille, the first work of a line of nostalgia-filled prairie or, as he said, "cowboy," music.[29] (In fact, Copland's turn toward a popular-elegiac body of work had its origins in his 1936 *El salón México.* During a trip to Mexico, Copland had met the composer Carlos Chávez, who sought to integrate local folk themes into a modernist idiom.) Copland was hardly alone in this struggle to create a specifically American idiom. Edward Burlingame Hill, one of Bernstein's Harvard professors and a composer of jazz and concert-hall works, "encouraged his students to investigate the indigenous music of this country—folk music, gospel—as possible source material for truly American concert works."[30] Marc Blitzstein, Charles Ives, and Carl Ruggles were also giving voice to the turmoil and torments in daily American life. Roy Harris had been composing music expressive of the open prairie as well as of "urban *Weltschmerz*," as Copland characterized it.[31] Roger Sessions, despite his universalism, was explicitly calling for a new American opera that would reflect the present "period . . . so sharply defined by clear historical and social forces" and with "dramatic motives . . . sufficiently real and sufficiently important to both composer and public."[32]

In sum, by the late 1930s, the earlier appeal for a national art had metamorphosed into a call to American artists to forge a new, robust, politically expressive culture. Bernstein heeded that call, his career bent upon championing this new, civically responsible modernist American music.

·   ·   ·

This chapter in Leonard Bernstein's apprenticeship took place as much in New York under Copland's tutelage and influence as at Harvard under that of Prall. In the fall of 1938, the first semester of his senior year, Bernstein was still working with Prall but was essentially commuting between Cambridge and New York. In the latter locale, he was a regular member of Copland's circles, socializing with Copland, Thomson, and Bowles, as well as attending get-togethers and parties of the Group Theater, where the talk ran from left-wing aesthetics and ensemble work to left-wing politics.[33] Then some six years old, the theater had been organized by Copland's close friend Harold Clurman and included Stella Adler, Elia Kazan, Clifford Odets, John Garfield, Morris Carnovsky, and others more or less committed to the organization's left-wing utopianism.[34] This effort, according to Waldo Frank in 1932 at the Group Theater's formation, aimed at "creating a new world, . . . [a] new humanity in the moral and spiritual as well as the economic sense."[35] Basic to the Group's aesthetic outlook was Soviet director Konstantine Stanislavski's demand that the actors stop merely emoting and instead incorporate into their inner lives the violations and exploitations endured by their characters. The members of the Group assumed an intimate connection between art and left-wing Popular Front politics. Kazan, for example, had directed Odets's *Waiting for Lefty,* starring Garfield, which had run on Broadway since 1934 and whose clarion call of "Strike!" was a clear push for action. Not all of Copland's highly politicized friends were pleased by his turn to the more populist folk idiom: *El Salón México* brought scorn from Odets but a proud defense by Bernstein.[36] The young man, Bernstein, despite his adoration for the abstract and nearly atonal *Piano Variations,* found himself quite the partisan of the new cross-cultural eclecticism of tonally centered lyricism and rhythms derived from jazz and Cuban, Mexican, and other Latino sources.

What Copland offered Bernstein through music, Prall offered through aesthetics. Prall attended to rhythm, not only seeing it as a series of systematic events in the flow of time but also reveling in its sensuality, as "bodily flexibility and nervous control of muscular movement . . . that we [can] apprehend . . . through our feet as well as our ears."[37] Bernstein, as we might assume from the subject of his senior thesis, must have been especially attracted to Prall's discussion of syncopation as a kind of drama, "a crossing or conflict in rhythm" felt in body as well as in the listening mind.[38] The modernist Prall did not hesitate to comment upon the "rigor and the technical finality of the most absolute jazz."[39] He even gave a philosophical imprimatur to dance and musical movement: "The significance of bodily motion and hence of rhythm is . . . emphatically indicated, for any natural outlook upon the world, by Spinoza."[40] Hence came Prall's Spinozistic aphorism: "To know our own bodies truly and adequately is to know God. To know their rhythms is to feel the pulse of Nature."[41]

Encouraged by Copland and Prall, Bernstein was becoming a modernist with a particularly gifted rhythmic sensibility.

Bernstein's actual debut in the modernist movement came by way of a review he published in the spring of 1938 in the chief journal of the modern movement, *Modern Music.* After attending a Boston Symphony Orchestra performance of a suite from Prokofiev's ballet *Chout,* the brash young man wrote that the work "strains the word 'cleverness' to a snapping-point." He then added, in perhaps the first but certainly an early sign of his preoccupation with properly centered tonality, "One is thankful these days for a concert piece that has a finale one can whistle while leaving the hall." Writes this *chutzpahnik* of Prokofiev's First Piano Concerto, "Truthfully, it is not a good piece." Prokofiev's *Romeo and Juliet?* Bernstein concluded that it contained some wonderful music, but the music was stretched too thin by the work's length. Walter Piston's First Symphony? Whereas Piston (Leonard's professor) "can always be depended upon for the best in workmanship," the Largo "[seemed] unduly long and uninteresting," and "the work lacked emotional appeal."[42]

## SENIOR THESIS

In the spring 1939 semester, Bernstein worked on his senior thesis, "The Absorption of Race Elements into American Music," a summing up of the fundamental themes explored by Copland, Prall, and others in the new American modernist movement and a call for an "organic" music that would express "a new and vital American nationalism" to connect every American to another, regardless of region, race, ethnicity, class, or religion. Bernstein wrote that otherwise-variegated Americans were bound together by their rootedness in the vernacular traditions of New England Protestant psalm and Negro jazz. Although the former had found expression in the religious and folk music of the Anglo-Saxon North American diaspora, the latter had become widely dispersed and was now virtually ubiquitous, thereby forming the basis for a national music. In an earlier, first period, beginning with the Puritan hegemony and lasting into the nineteenth century, the New England Protestant hymn had metamorphosed into popular music and poetry. But Bernstein argued that the ubiquity of Negro music formed the basis for an American music. He noted that a national music starts as "material" and gradually takes on a "spiritual" cast, proceeding from a clearly recognizable folk heritage to an identity that is no longer "folk" but is nevertheless distinctly national. America had needed a long gestation period to attain the first, "material" stage. In the second period, encompassing most of the nineteenth century, American composers wrote music imitative of then-prevalent European romanticism, producing a derivative body of work that led Bernstein to write, "America has never had a classical music."[43] A third period, under way since the end of the nineteenth century, had received its impetus from the Czech composer Antonin Dvorak's call to incorporate Native American themes into serious music. This idea died stillborn, Bernstein argued, because these themes had no relevance to the everyday life of most Americans. Only since the 1920s and 1930s had American music come of age and its jazz rhythms permeated musical culture from Tin Pan Alley to the dance hall and then to the Broadway theater, the concert hall, and the opera house.

The critically important aspect of the form then called "Negro" music was syncopation, formed either melodically by lengthening and shortening notes or rhythmically, by borrowing not only North American Negro rhythms but also Caribbean and Latin Negro sources, especially in the use of rumba rhythms. Bernstein noted that George Gershwin, Copland's predecessor, used these musical forms to create his distinctive American music. But where Gershwin had incorporated syncopation into nineteenth-century romanticism, Copland had incorporated syncopation into a distinctly modernist idiom, as Bernstein illustrated with examples from Copland's Piano Concerto and *Piano Variations*. Contemporary American music, such as that composed by Copland and Sessions, thus contained elements of the original Negro "scale" and rhythms in its driving substructures but was no longer necessarily identifiable as jazz. To be sure, he wrote, the New England strains lived on in the music of, among others, Roy Harris, but the dominant form lay in the syncopation that forms the spiritual, distinctly recognizable form of American music.

### BERNSTEIN AND BLITZSTEIN

While he was writing his thesis, Bernstein found a work of music that appealed to his musical and political passions: Marc Blitzstein's radical *The Cradle Will Rock*, written in 1937.

Blitzstein had found inspiration in Weill and Brecht's biting dadalike, satirical style to create a work that was as much a vernacular music-hall revue as an opera.[44] Like Copland, Blitzstein was a serious musical modernist who had trained under the French neoclassicist Nadia Boulanger. Blitzstein joined the Communist Party, and in 1935, he set out to compose socially critical music for the American working-class audience, which, he was convinced, was coming into self-consciousness. Blitzstein needed to find an authentic voice in which to address and inspire this new industrial urban multiethnic and newly immigrant working-class audience, which would find little in common with traditional American country folk music. Nor did he want to use the traditional Broadway-Hollywood forms. He found a good model in the works of Bertolt Brecht and Kurt Weill. In *The Threepenny Opera* (1928), *Happy End* (1929), and *Mahagonny* (1930), Weill set Brecht's raucous and vulgar urban vernacular librettos within an array of popular musical forms, including so-called kitchen songs, folk songs, dance-hall tunes, marches, and biting and sarcastic cabaret music. In so doing, he attacked the German equivalents of Broadway and Hollywood theatrical conventions—those which produced sweet and pretty entertainments affirming the given political orthodoxy and seeking to evade social reality.

Blitzstein followed Brecht and Weill in making his own idioms with which to skewer corporate elites, showing how they colluded with state and military authorities to protect their interests and how they prostituted the clergy, newspaper editors and reporters, and artists into disseminating ideological smokescreens to hide the harassment, beatings, and even murder of labor organizers. Audience members, awakened to the fact that their victimization was not inevitable but was the result of the unchecked power of political and cultural elites, could now organize themselves into a unified mass movement and take action to transform their world.

Not only was *Cradle* a radical work for its disclosure of the collusion between business, the news media, and the pulpit; its premiere in New York turned out to be a radicalizing event for many of its performers and audience members. Hours before the opening performance, the Federal Theater Project authorities, unnerved by attacks from congressional conservatives, demanded that producer Orson Welles cancel the production.

Welles refused, director John Houseman found another hall, and because the musicians could not play in that hall, Blitzstein performed the orchestral parts from a score reduced from orchestral to piano performance.[45]

In a gesture of identification with Blitzstein, Bernstein decided to put on a production of *Cradle* with himself performing the piano reduction. Then, in an unexpected parallel to the New York premiere, the Cambridge authorities banned *Cradle* as obscene. Bernstein moved the production to the Harvard campus, where the Cambridge edict did not apply.[46] This congruence between Blitzstein's premiere in New York and Bernstein's production in Cambridge was extraordinary.

By the time Bernstein graduated from Harvard, Mitropoulos was heralding him as a budding conductor and Copland viewed him as a musician of prodigious gifts and genius and as a rising presence in American musical life, most certainly as a pianistic interpreter of American modernism.

Thus, in four years, Bernstein had become a cosmopolitan modernist, an intimate of two celebrated musicians, and a propagandist for the new American music. Had he a presentiment in that spring of 1939 that he would take the mantle of creative artist upon his own shoulders?

.   .   .

No doubt the newly minted Harvard graduate and his family greeted this milestone with great joy and happiness. But in the underworld of political denunciation, a much darker monument to Bernstein's Harvard years was forming. Bernstein did not know that his efforts with Blitzstein's *Cradle Will Rock* had almost made him the object of a Cambridge police investigation into "Reds" at Harvard.[47] Nor was he aware that an informant had reported to the FBI that he was the director of the local communist John Reed Society.[48] The denunciation went into a newly created FBI dossier on Bernstein, its entry noting that the informant "stated that [blacked out] and Leonard Bernstein wer [*sic*] the real leaders of the group and that the group sponsors speakers on Russia and Marxism."[49]

# CHAPTER TWO

# The Forties

## Ascent and Blacklist

### ASCENSION

Bernstein graduated from Harvard in June 1939 and spent the summer in New York rooming with Adolph Green, his chum from boyhood summer-camp years. Green and two friends, Betty Comden and Judy Holliday, had formed a musical group called the Revuers and invited Bernstein to spend the summer accompanying them at the piano on club dates as well as recording two of their satirical works, *The Girl with the Two Left Feet* and *Joan Crawford Fan Club*.[1] Bernstein left in the fall for the Curtis Institute in Philadelphia to study piano, but with the prodding of Mitropoulos, he sought out Fritz Reiner, then on the Curtis faculty, and switched to a conducting major. In February 1940, armed with recommendations from Reiner and Copland, Bernstein introduced himself to Serge Koussevitzky, the conductor of the Boston Symphony Orchestra and a champion of American modernism.[2] Koussevitzky, impressed with the talents of the young virtuoso, invited Bernstein to take conducting lessons at the new Tanglewood center opening in the Berkshires that summer.[3] Bernstein soon became an intimate of the Koussevitzky family, and Koussevitzky, quickly finding the young man living up to expectations, entrusted him with conducting, among other works, Copland's *Outdoor Overture* and Stravinsky's *Histoire du soldat*.[4]

Though Bernstein was not yet twenty-one, his path into the classical musical world seemed laid out for him by his mentors Copland, Mitropoulos, and Koussevitzky. Moreover, through his collaboration with Comden and Green, he had unwittingly taken his first step onto another path, the American musical stage.

He was also taking his first steps as a political activist. He returned to Philadelphia in the fall of 1939 and by November, was invited to direct the Philadelphia People's Chorus. He wrote his former piano teacher and now secretary, Helen Coates, that he was seriously committed to the "proletariat" and planned to conduct an "All-Negro Symphony orchestra" to be formed by the National Negro Congress (an affiliate of the Communist Party). Among "further proletarian items," he explained, were his lectures and an intended performance for a "Youth Arts Forum."[5]

Bernstein's musical career burgeoned even as he continued his studies: thus, in January 1940, he made his first classical-arts recording, his friend David Diamond's Prelude and Fugue no. 3 in C-sharp Minor.[6] He graduated from Curtis in the spring of 1941 and headed back to New York, renting an apartment in Carnegie Hall to work on his clarinet concerto while earning a meager living as an arranger and occasional accompanist for ballet classes (where he caught the attention of Agnes De Mille).[7] His apartment was only a few blocks from the jazz-club district on West 52nd Street, a perfect address for the aspiring champion of rhythmic variation and new American music.[8]

But the backdrop of much of his music and his public life was the war in Europe. With the Nazi invasion of the Soviet Union in June 1941, the Russians had become, if not yet official, certainly sentimental, allies of the Americans, standing alone against the complete Nazi conquest of Europe while bearing the full brunt of the Nazi war machine. The Nazi invasion was three pronged: in the north against Leningrad, in the center through Kiev to Moscow, and in the south through Sebastopol and the Caucasus, past Stalingrad to the oil fields at Baku. The Nazis took Kiev in August 1941, and British prime minister Winston Churchill broadcast reports of mass executions of Russians by the Nazis.[9] By September, the invaders had reached the outskirts of Leningrad and placed the city under siege. Sebastopol fell in October. The United States sat out the war until December 7, when the Japanese bombed Pearl Harbor. Congress declared war on Japan on December 8, and on December 11, Germany and Italy declared war on the United States. The Russians and the Americans were now allies against fascism. For people like the Bernsteins, news such as the December 26, 1941, report of Nazi massacres of Jews at Kharkov could only increase their ardor for the Russians.[10]

Support for the Russians enlisted the various machineries of cultural life, including a series of performances of Shostakovich's 7th Symphony, *Leningrad,* itself the offspring of the war. Shostakovich began composing the work while trapped within the besieged city; the authorities smuggled him out to Kuibyshev, east of Moscow, where the completed work premiered on March 5, 1942.[11] The score made its way out of Russia and quickly became a symbol of humanity's heroism against Nazism. Toscanini and the NBC Symphony Orchestra broadcast the Shostakovich 7th on July 19, 1942, and Koussevitzky led the Boston Symphony Orchestra in the work's concert premiere at Tanglewood on August 14, 1942, with Bernstein at the bass drum.[12] Bernstein, who had been rejected for the draft because of his asthma, was doing what he could for the war effort. On October 11, 1942, he was in Boston to play a *Victory Jive* for a Youth for Victory rally—a fact duly recorded by the FBI.[13]

In September, the Nazis began the siege of Stalingrad with horrific devastation of life. By January 1943, however, the Russians had turned the tide, encircling the German forces and trapping them within Stalingrad, and on February 2, Russian officers accepted the surrender of German general von Paulus and the German 6th Army. The Soviet counteroffensive now forced the Germans into retreat from the Caucasus, but again with terrific loss of life. That month, Arturo Toscanini made a symbolic gesture of solidarity between the United States and USSR by adding the *Star-Spangled Banner* and the *Internationale* to Verdi's *Hymn of Nations* for a radio concert by the NBC Symphony Orchestra. Meanwhile, reports such as that by Rabbi Stephen Wise on February 14, 1943, uncovering Nazi atrocities against Jews, and that of July 14, 1943, in which Moscow radio reported the Nazis' murder of six thousand civilians at Krasnodar, began to appear in the press.[14] Support for the Russians by American musicians had become axiomatic: the editors of the Republican-leaning *New York Herald Tribune* did not think twice about publishing Paul Bowles's notices and reviews of "Duke Ellington in Recital for Russian Relief" at Carnegie Hall (January 25, 1943), "All-Soviet Works Heard in Carnegie Hall" (October 25, 1943), or "Philharmonic Gives Another Russian Tribute" at Carnegie Hall (November 29, 1943).[15]

By summer's end, Bernstein's career was ready to take off. In August 1943, the Philharmonic's music director, Arthur Rodzinski, having learned from Koussevitzky, Mitropoulos, and Copland of Bernstein's talents, offered Bernstein the position of assistant conductor. On November 13, 1943, the French soprano Jennie Tourel sang the premiere of Bernstein's song cycle, *I Hate Music,* a set of five songs that, if they hardly showed the talent about to be unveiled within a year, did exhibit Bernstein's wit. But what happened next was miraculous indeed: on November 14, with Rodzinski unavailable, Bernstein was called upon to substitute for the ailing Bruno Walter in a performance by the Philharmonic to be broadcast nationwide on CBS. The program included Schumann's *Manfred Overture,* Miklos Rózsa's *Theme, Variations and Finale,* op. 13, and Richard Strauss's *Don Quixote.* The event—a junior and unseasoned assistant conductor taking over the New York Philharmonic and conducting a stellar broadcast concert—skyrocketed Bernstein to fame. Nine days later, on November 23, the clarinetist David Oppenheim (married to Judy Holliday) recorded Bernstein's *Sonata for Clarinet and Piano* with Bernstein at the piano.[16] Bernstein returned to the podium of the Philharmonic from December 2 to 5, conducting Bloch's *Trois Poèmes Juifs,* and on December 16 and 17, conducting the *Star-Spangled Banner,* Brahms's *Variations on a Theme of Haydn,* Delius's *Paris, A Night Piece,* and Beethoven's Violin Concerto with Albert Spalding.[17] The program offered a full pallet of orchestral work.

As a new celebrity, Bernstein was widening his circles, not only enjoying his friendships with members of the Group Theater, but through the Group actress Stella Adler, meeting, among others, George Gershwin's friend and pianistic interpreter Oscar Levant, the literary critic Irving Howe, and the budding actor Marlon Brando.[18] He was also in demand for war-related morale builders and fund-raising performances. Thus, on December 19, 1943, his greetings were announced to the First Empire State Conference of the New York State American Youth for Democracy—a group the FBI named as "the successor organization to the Young Communist League."[19]

## JEREMIAH

On January 28, 1944, Bernstein conducted the Pittsburgh Symphony in Pittsburgh, with Jennie Tourel singing the solo in the premiere of his Symphony no. 1, *Jeremiah.* He had conceived the work in 1939 when he sketched out the piece that would become the third movement, "Lamentation," but he wrote the first movement, "Prophecy," and the remainder, including a rewritten "Lamentation," in late 1942.[20] Audiences heard a work that, as Paul Bowles wrote after the New York premiere of the symphony in March, "resembles what comes out of Russia today."[21] The first movement opens with searing passages, which give way to a rising sense of juggernaut from the percussion section's unrelenting ostinato that is reminiscent of Prokofiev. The second movement, a scherzo, begins with passages evocative of an Eastern European Jewish dance, closely followed by passages of contestation. The third movement, a setting of the biblical text of Jeremiah's "Lamentations upon the destruction of Jerusalem," bears a family resemblance to the "Field of the Dead" section of Prokofiev's *Alexander Nevsky* but retains reminiscences of the earlier movements of the symphony. By thus keying memory and association, Bernstein's *Jeremiah* provided its audience with a sense of solidarity with suffering Jewish populations and Soviet allies.[22]

## JEROME ROBBINS:
### *FANCY FREE* AND *ON THE TOWN*

Meanwhile, the choreographer and dancer Jerome Robbins had sought out Bernstein to collaborate on a ballet about three sailors on shore leave who hope for the attention, if not the affections, of young women. The ballet, *Fancy Free,* performed by the American Ballet Theater, opened on April 18, 1944. Bernstein's production was electrifying, percussively driven by drums or piano; full of surprises; witty, bright and extraordinarily energetic; yet briefly wistful and reflective. The prelude, a fragment of a Billie Holiday torch song emanating from the saloon's jukebox, is abruptly terminated by four rapid and sharply delivered beats banged out on the rim of a snare drum that signal the entrance of the sailors into the saloon; this call to order is immediately followed by a major rhythmic motif that pushes the work along. The piano does a boogie-woogie in short, nervous impulses that maintain forward momentum; and if that momentum sometimes slows, the effect is that of a coiled spring ready to burst forth again. A second major rhythmic motif is followed by a Latin *guajira.* Touches of Gershwin and Stravinsky provide a sense of communal fun for audience members. This work, written and performed in the midst of a war, epitomized an expansive, brash, all-inclusive American culture. Powerful, right on target, the music swings from serious introspection to raucous extroversion; its American idiom celebrates the pure joy of being alive.

Bernstein made the leap from first-class composer to first-class conductor with the greatest facility. On March 11, he led the Philharmonic in a performance at West Point, conducting Wagner, Beethoven, Johann Strauss Jr., and Tchaikovsky. He was back with Philharmonic at Carnegie Hall in March and April to perform Mozart, Mendelssohn, Tchaikovsky, Copland, and his own Symphony no. 1, *Jeremiah.* His star was in the ascent. The writer Dawn Powell attended a performance of *Fancy Free* on May 18, 1944, and the next morning wrote somewhat ruefully about Bernstein and the politics of "making it" in New York: "Jerome Robbins' 'Fancy

Free' with Oliver Smith sets, Leonard Bernstein music, and Bernstein, the new-wonder boy, conducting. This gay work, spontaneous and arrogant, made me aware as I constantly am of the factor of luck in art—the confidence, super cock-sureness of early success, accidentally being friends with powers-soon-to be, learning early the manner of success. I have always felt that the *manner* of success came first—the inside later, if at all."[23]

Bernstein had indeed combined talent with power, and if he enjoyed the support and patronage of Copland, Koussevitzky, Mitropoulos, and Philharmonic music director Arthur Rodzinski, he did so because these men were attracted by his extraordinary talent. Or "talents," we should say, for this twenty-six-year-old was not only gaining attention by crossing the chasms separating the classical, vernacular, and popular musical worlds; he was a frequent conductor of the New York Philharmonic, the composer of *Jeremiah,* and a figure of importance in the world of modern dance. All in all, he was rapidly becoming a dominant champion of the new music. After Bernstein conducted the Philharmonic in a program that included William Schuman's *American Festival Overture* at Lewisohn Stadium on July 14, 1944, Bowles, in typical modernist fashion, admonished the "spectacular young conductor" whose "particular genius" is modern, "living" music, such as the Schuman piece, to stop wasting his time and his audience's by performing old and tired war horses like the two others on the program, Mendelssohn's Violin Concerto and Sibelius's Symphony no. 1, as if he, Bernstein, were just another "aged conductor."[24]

Bernstein recorded *Fancy Free* for Decca in June 1944 and was already working with Robbins, Comden, and Green on their next collaboration.[25] *On the Town* opened on December 28, 1944, revolutionizing the American musical theater in its combination of modern dance and orchestral score loaded with exuberantly syncopated jazz-swing rhythms, sweet lyricism, shamelessly hilarious paraphrases of Prokofiev and Bizet, and coarse and rude gabber (not least that of a sexually aggressive woman taxicab driver). The first minutes follow a pattern similar to that in the opening of *Fancy Free:* after a lyrical 6 A.M. sunrise wakeup song comes a sudden explosion—in this case, the relentlessly energized "New York! New York!"

We again have three sailors—now named Gabey, Chip, and Ozzie—on twenty-four-hour passes to see the sights and perhaps find female companionship. The rest is a madcap, top-speed tour through midtown Manhattan and Coney Island that culminates at 6 A.M. with the three sailors walking up the gangplank to meet three other sailors coming down, ready to begin their own twenty-four hours of freedom. The curtain falls with the six sailors singing their paean to the city, "New York, New York!"

Wartime New York was filled with servicemen on leave, looking for excitement before going back into combat. Gabey, Chip, and Ozzie are of course only representatives of the mass of young men recruited and drafted from across the country to serve in the armed forces. With the young women they met in New York, they formed swarms of carefree, nervous but patriotic humanity in the heart of the city. Marshall Berman has argued that Robbins and Bernstein's employment of a Japanese dancer, Sono Osato, to play the role of Ivy and of blacks and whites to dance together on stage—"Times Square as a democratic space"—were indicative of the New Deal–wartime progressive outlook.[26] "Taken together," Berman concludes, "*Fancy Free* and *On the Town* may be the deepest and most original art of the Popular Front."[27]

*Fancy Free* and *On the Town* shared their era with Mondrian's *Broadway Boogie Woogie*—a grid enlivened by objects in motion, Manhattan itself. But more than Manhattan, *On the Town* conveyed a wartime spirit of an unconquerable, unified America, a city on a hill, not in the dry Puritan sense but in a lighthearted, free-spirited and good-natured sense; its zany hilarity and boisterous vulgarity is of a piece with the comedic Dada wackiness and exuberant lunacy of the Marx Brothers and Olson and Johnson. *On the Town* had a run of 463 performances.[28]

## BERNSTEIN AND THE POPULAR FRONT

In the meanwhile, reports of horrific atrocities by the Nazis on the eastern front had only increased the urgency to aid the Soviets. Bernstein was increasingly being asked to perform at and sponsor rallies and fund-raisers and sign petitions in support of Russian refugee relief and friendship with the Soviet Union. He performed at a benefit concert in Carnegie Hall on April 13, 1944, just days after the premiere of *Fancy Free*.[29] At a rally the next month, he shared the bill with Paul Robeson, at the apogee of his career, whose songs epitomized Popular Front ideals of racial, ethnic, and religious harmony; the nobility of hardworking, plain-speaking, and uncomplicated workers (Marc Blitzstein's "Purest Kind of a Guy"); and common struggles against fascism.[30]

Besides making music, Bernstein was living an active political life. He answered affirmatively to an appeal by Lily Pons to lend his presence to an exhibit of photos of Nazi atrocities on October 16, 1944.[31] In December 1944, he attended fund-raising dinners in Boston and New York in support of the Joint Anti-Fascist Refugee Committee (JAFRC), which had been set up in 1939 to aid people in flight from the Franco regime and was now licensed by the federal government to help others escaping fascism.[32] He joined the Friends of the Spanish Republic at the invitation of Freda Kirschway, president of the Nation Associates on December 8.[33] On January 5, 1945, he gave his support to a demand for justice for Recy Taylor, a black woman gang-raped by white men who were never indicted. Reports of such support earned their place within Bernstein's FBI dossier.[34] On February 12, he sent $25 in response to an appeal to aid refugees signed by Paul Robeson.[35] The FBI received a report on February 13, 1945, that Bernstein had been nominated for a fund-raising position with the JAFRC.[36] On February 27, 1945, Bernstein lent his support to the Abraham Lincoln Brigade's call, "For America's Sake: Break with Franco Spain."[37] At Dorothy Parker's request, he sponsored a dinner, chaired by Pablo Picasso and with guest of honor Lillian Hellman, at a Spanish Refugee Appeal fund-raiser.[38] And with all of this political activity, Bernstein's conducting career went on apace: in February 1945, he was in the RCA studio recording dance pieces from *On the Town* as well as his *Jeremiah* with Nan Merriman and the St. Louis Symphony Orchestra.[39]

He barely separated his politics from his musical life. In April 1945, Bernstein began thinking about composing an opera based upon Maxwell

Anderson's play *Winterset,* a smash hit on Broadway a decade before and a work heavily inspired by the tragic fates of Sacco and Vanzetti, whom the Left had considered martyrs since their executions in the late 1920s.[40] On April 11, he received an invitation, with Koussevitzky's and Copland's names on the letterhead, to join the Music Committee of the National Council of American-Soviet Friendship.[41] Two days later, he conducted a benefit concert for victims of Stalingrad.[42] He was in Detroit on May 4, 1945, where, according to an FBI informant, he performed at the home of "a member of the Detroit Professional Club of the Communist Political Association" in support of the Detroit Civil Rights Federation.[43] Bernstein signed petitions, printed in the *Daily Worker* in late September 1945, in support of the reelection of Communist Party representative Benjamin Davis, a black man, to the New York City Council.[44] (Some years later, an informant told the FBI that at the time of the Davis campaign, Party officials had told him that Bernstein was an "adherent to communism" and under "communist discipline.")[45] On November 21, 1945, Bernstein attended a dinner convened by the American Committee for Spanish Freedom.[46]

Two months earlier, in August 1945, Bernstein had accepted the La Guardia administration's offer of music directorship of the New York City Center and its New York City Symphony Orchestra. The use of City Center, once the city's largest Masonic lodge, as a cultural center was an extraordinary initiative by Mayor La Guardia. The mayor, a progressive of the first order, had come up with the idea, put into effect in 1943, to bring into the theatrical interior three artistic institutions—the New York City Drama, the New York City Ballet (its choreographer at the time was George Balanchine), and the New York City Symphony Orchestra—and to make ticket prices affordable for the average worker. Bernstein, like the orchestra's first conductor, Leopold Stokowski, happily undertook the job pro bono but was upset to learn that the income from ticket sales was too low to afford the musicians a living wage. In November, at a meeting of the National Council of American-Soviet Friendship, Bernstein made an impassioned plea for funds from the city, demanding that the left-liberal administration remember the great benefits of the Works Progress Administration's sponsorship of the arts and reminding his listeners that the right-wing Congress had attacked President Roosevelt for his efforts to use governmental resources to ensure the accessibility of great art to a populace in need of subsidies.[47] But in his extempore remarks, he claimed that inasmuch as the city made no contribution to the orchestra's upkeep, to call it a "New York" orchestra amounted to "fraud."[48] La Guardia answered the next day, claiming that Bernstein did not understand that subsidies had not been part of the agreement that launched the venture, added that he was "very fond of Mr. Bernstein" and expected him to come to understand that "he was unfortunate in his choice of words."[49] With some egg on his face but his point made, Bernstein went on to conduct a heady mix, ranging from Mitropoulos's arrangement of Beethoven's String Quartet no. 14 to the premiere performance of Mark Blitzstein's *Airborne Symphony* on April 1, 1946.

On April 16, 1946, Bernstein was back in Detroit, where "Detroit Informant" (whose name is blacked out in the FBI dossier), reporting on "technical surveillance" of the American Youth for Democracy Headquarters, "advised that Phil Schatz, executive secretary of the organization in Detroit, had arranged for an interracial reception for Leonard Bernstein following the latter's direction of the Detroit Symphonic Orchestra."[50] Five days later, the FBI received information from "Detroit Informant" (name blacked out) that Bernstein was "guest of honor" at a Young Americans for Democracy "musicale."[51]

At the end of April 1946, as Bernstein left for Paris, en route to Prague to conduct the Czech Philharmonic, he might have learned that the House Un-American Activities Committee (HUAC) was investigating the Joint Anti-Fascist Refugee Committee and demanding that its trustees turn over the names of supporters and donors.[52] On May 2, 1946, he participated in a Russian Relief concert at Carnegie Hall.[53] In Prague a week later, he basked in the festive climate in this recently liberated city, denying Hearst newspaper stories that Czechs were living under a "Red Terror."[54] He returned to New York later that month to make his debut with the NBC Symphony Orchestra performing Blitzstein's *Airborne Symphony*.[55] Reports came to the FBI on July 24, 1946, that Bernstein was working with the National Council of American-Soviet Friendship to arrange a concert tour for two Russian violinists.[56] He was soon off to London but returned on August 6 to lead the performance of the American premiere of Benjamin Britten's *Peter Grimes* at Tanglewood. On October 5, the peripatetic Bernstein performed a concert at Carnegie Hall for the American-Soviet alliance.[57] On October 17, he added his name to those of Louis Adamic, Canada Lee, and Howard Fast as sponsors of the Citizens Committee for Decent Department Store Wages.[58]

Bernstein began the New York Symphony Orchestra's 1946–47 season on September 24 with a performance of Shostakovich's Symphony no. 7. The *New York Times* made note of a group of delegates from the Ukrainian Society for Cultural Relations with Foreign Countries, which was present at the invitation of the "American Soviet Music Society, which is headed by Dr. Serge Koussevitzky with Mr. Bernstein as vice president."[59]

When not studying scores and conducting, Bernstein was at work with Robbins on a new ballet, *Facsimile*. If the two men's earlier productions had been euphorically driven, the new one went in the opposite direction: it was an angst-ridden story in a bleak surreal "open and desolate" setting: a lone woman meets two men, is almost physically torn apart by their desires for her, but ends up alone again.[60] *Facsimile* premiered on October 24, 1946, with the Ballet Theatre in New York. Bernstein's agenda shows him scheduled for a "Soviet Music Meeting at 300 West End Avenue" on November 7.[61]

People were denouncing Bernstein behind his back. On December 19, 1946, someone claiming to be a member of Local 802 of the Federation of Musicians Union informed the FBI that Leonard Bernstein was either a Communist or a member of the Communist faction of the union.[62] On December 20, 1946, a report to the FBI stated that Bernstein was a cochairman of the Salute to Young America rally at Manhattan Center, New York City.[63]

Throughout the war years, in a position consonant with Roosevelt's, Bernstein had actively supported the Left's mobilization against Franco.[64] He was soon to learn that the world was changing. In September 1945, one month after the end of the war, the JAFRC organized a rally in Madison Square Garden to reveal the close connections between the Franco regime and the Vatican. In a speech transmitted by radio, the British Socialist Harold Laski claimed that the Roman Catholic Church had been opposed to freedom throughout its history. The actor Frank Fay denounced Laski and the actors who had been at the Garden, thereby igniting a campaign on the Catholic right against irreligious and secular liberalism in general and organizations opposed to Franco, such as the JAFRC, in particular. Bernstein was conducting in San Francisco in February 1946 and was about to perform and deliver a speech at a JAFRC dinner when he received a telegram from Arthur Judson, head of Columbia Concerts, Bernstein's management firm, and virtual czar of New York Philharmonic hiring policies. Judson ordered him to decline the invitation on grounds of a contractual stipulation forbidding his presence at "'quasi-public appearances.'" Bernstein was furious and suspected that Judson was demanding that he fall into line with the resurgent Right.[65] The affair reeked of fascism, he thought, but he acceded to the all-powerful Judson's demand that he not perform, although he did attend the dinner.[66]

Bernstein was not about to concede his political life to the Right. An FBI dossier entry of February 28, 1946, listed him as a sponsor of a "Win the Peace" Conference to be held in Washington.[67] Bernstein signed a petition of the Citizens United to Abolish the Wood-Rankin Committee [HUAC] that appeared in the *New York Times* of March 14, 1946.[68] The *Daily Worker* of March 16, 1946, carried a Bernstein endorsement for a fund-raiser for the American Committee for Yugoslav Relief.[69] The *Daily Worker* of March 17, 1946, reported Bernstein's membership on the National Board of the National Citizens Relief Committee to Aid Strikers' Families.[70] He remained loyal to the Spanish Left: on March 18, 1946, he was a guest of honor at a dinner for the Spanish Refugee Appeal at the Waldorf-Astoria.[71] An FBI report claimed that on March 24, 1946, Bernstein performed and spoke at a function of the American Youth for Democracy.[72]

Bernstein was participating in the formation of the new Progressive Party, which sought to restore the wartime U.S.-Soviet alliance, or at least to put a brake on the accelerating Cold War. Thus, on March 25, 1946, according to an FBI "Buffalo Confidential Informant," he attended a reception held by the Progressive Citizens of America in Detroit, and, in the informant's words, "addressed the group speaking for about thirty minutes on the conditions of the world today and the United States in particular. Bernstein expressed a desire that all progressive groups merge into one, stating that the one group should be the Progressive Citizens of America."[73]

During this period, Bernstein continued to conduct the New York City Symphony, programming the fall 1946 season with standards of the European repertoire as well as works by Americans such as William Schuman, Alex North, and Samuel Barber. He did not stop his political activities. For example, he joined Dashiell Hammett, Rockwell Kent, and Billie Holiday on December 5 at an American Youth for Democracy dinner to greet Jose Giral, a member of the Spanish Republican government in exile.[74]

Bernstein's Judson-inspired JAFRC crisis was only one symptom of the Left's marginalization that was emerging during 1946 and became most manifest over its reaction to the Truman administration's atomic-weapons policy. To many in the progressive camp, such as Einstein, humanity's interests demanded that atomic science and technology come under international control rather than remain a nightmarish weapon in the hands of irresponsible politicians and generals. The Truman administration was aghast at the idea of giving others access to those weapons. When Henry A. Wallace, secretary of commerce and New Dealer par excellence, openly campaigned for a peace treaty with the Soviet Union and for virtual recognition of Soviet hegemony in Eastern Europe in exchange for open trade, Truman fired him on September 20, 1946, and thereby virtually ended the influence of the left wing within the administration.

During the summer of 1946, those in the political right wing had been seeking to break the remaining elements of the New Deal by claiming that liberal policies were communistic. This rightward move continued.

In California, Richard M. Nixon had campaigned for his congressional seat by smearing his opponent, Helen Gahagan Douglas, as communist tainted. On October 20, 1946, HUAC began hearings on communist influence in the motion-picture industry. The climate induced by the hysteria of the Red Scare worked: in November, the Republican Party retook the House of Representatives for the first time in decades.

In January 1947, Eleanor Roosevelt, Harold Ickes, and other New Dealers who were upset about the communist presence in Progressive Citizens of America had formed the Americans for Democratic Action. This action must have been met with some consternation by Bernstein, whose position had remained consistently with the Progressives over the preceding year, and who, on February 14, 1947, took out membership in the Progressive Citizens of America.[75] Indeed, Bernstein spoke at a Progressive Citizens of America meeting on March 25, 1947, just days after the administration announced, on March 12, the Truman Doctrine to mount military opposition to communist revolutions, and on March 21, inaugurated the Loyalty-Security Program to investigate federal civil servants.[76] With these actions, Truman was virtually mobilizing the full array of U.S. military, police, and investigative forces for an anticommunist crusade.

The March 31, 1947, indictments of the JAFRC board for failing to turn over its membership lists to HUAC had to be unsettling to the organization's sponsors and members. But if Bernstein worried about becoming a target of these proceedings, his concern did not stop him from taking a stand in two causes célèbres in the summer and fall of 1947—the confrontations between Hanns Eisler and the Hollywood Ten with HUAC—that might well have moved his name closer to the danger zone.

Bernstein's involvement in the Hanns Eisler case seems to have originated on or before December 12, 1946, when an FBI garbage surveillant recovered "a letter written by [name blacked out] to Louise, wife of Hanns, with copy to Clifford Odets, suggesting that Odets introduce Eisler to Bernstein in order that the latter would perform Eisler's music."[77] Odets had gone to Hollywood and had struck up a friendship with Eisler, who had fled Nazi Europe and settled in the Hollywood film colony.[78] Eisler

(1895–1962), a composer of symphonic works, film scores, songs, and opera and the author of numerous articles on music and politics as well as a text of considerable reputation, *Composing for the Films*,[79] became caught up in the HUAC investigations as a result of the hearings of his brother, Gerhart, and his sister, Ella, known as Ruth Fischer. Gerhart and Fischer were members of the German Communist Party but, according to Fischer, had a falling-out when Gerhart became a GPU (secret police) operator. Fischer testified that Gerhart had come to America ostensibly in flight from Hitler but in reality under orders of the Comintern to take control of the U.S. Communist Party. Called to testify before HUAC, Gerhart Eisler refused to be sworn in and was soon deported to East Germany. Fischer ended her testimony by informing HUAC that her other brother, Hanns, had been in touch with Gerhart and that he was "a composer of films and he is a Communist in the philosophic sense."[80] Her statement was good enough reason for HUAC to subpoena Hanns Eisler for a hearing on September 24, 1947. Committee members questioned Eisler about his supposed membership in the late 1920s and early 1930s in the German Communist Party and in later years in the International Music Bureau, which he claimed was an organization of composers and performers of antifascist music for workers. Eisler's response to his characterization by HUAC inquisitor Robert Stripling as "the Karl Marx of communism in the music field" was sardonic if not contemptuous: "I would be flattered."[81] As the hearing was coming to an end, Eisler lit into Congressman Rankin's characterization of some of Brecht's poems as "filth," at which point the Justice Department gave him the choice of leaving the United States for good on his own or facing deportation.

American and overseas artistic and intellectual circles rallied on Eisler's behalf. Harold Clurman wrote Aaron Copland on October 25, 1947, that Bernstein was ready to "sign every protest—public and private" and expected that Copland's signature would induce other musicians to sign.[82] Bernstein had Eisler to his home, added his name to those of Albert Einstein and Thomas Mann in asking Attorney General Tom Clark to stop the deportation, and performed in a concert to support Eisler.[83]

As the Eisler case moved through the legal machinery, Bernstein embroiled himself in the struggles of the Hollywood Ten, the screenwriters opposed to testifying before HUAC. The committee had issued subpoenas to some forty-one Hollywood creative artists, of whom nineteen refused to testify, claiming that their freedom of expression was under unjust assault by HUAC. Members of the film colony, led by Humphrey Bogart, organized the Committee for the First Amendment (CFA) to defend civil liberties and to handle strategy and publicity. On the eve of the hearings scheduled for October 27, 1947, the CFA delegation flew into Washington, joined by members of the CFA Broadway contingent, including John Garfield and Bernstein, to lobby Congress to get rid of HUAC as well as to lend moral support to their beleaguered colleagues.[84] According to Bogart's biographers, the CFA members were quite buoyant, for they had the support of the studio heads, whose spokesman, Eric Johnston, was to set the tone at the HUAC hearings by protesting attempts to censure Hollywood. A three-part debacle ensued. First, the Hollywood stars, fully expecting their press conference to take the limelight, were stunned when HUAC chair J. Parnell Thomas's "bombshell" announcement of a Soviet-Hollywood connection stole the headlines. They were further rocked when Thomas called writer John Howard Lawson, instead of Johnston, to testify. Thomas got into a shouting match with Lawson, and court officers removed him from the chamber.[85] Eric Johnston delivered the third and perhaps most profound shock of all to the CFA: instead of announcing his support for CFA principles, Johnston told HUAC that he welcomed its investigations into communism in Hollywood.

The CFA contingents left Washington thoroughly stunned and demoralized. Shortly thereafter, Lawson and the other members of the so-called Hollywood Ten were indicted for contempt of Congress, and in December, the studio heads fired them. For any of the ten to gain future employment, he or she would have to be acquitted of the contempt charge or win exoneration from the committee by forswearing Communist ties in testimony and otherwise satisfying the committee that he or she was no subversive. The studio heads made clear to the unions and agencies that they were not to recommend for employment anyone under suspicion. The blacklist was now Hollywood policy.[86]

If the Hollywood CFA members were devastated, those in New York were in a fighting mood. On December 1, the Arts, Sciences and Professional Council of the Progressive Citizens of America, Bernstein included, wrote an open letter to the Hollywood studio heads expressing outrage about their capitulation to the HUAC inquisition and their participation in censorship and blacklisting across all fields of expression.[87] And, in an act of bravura that openly challenged the rightward-turning authorities, Bernstein scheduled performances of Blitzstein's *The Cradle Will Rock* to begin at the City Center on November 24, 1947.

Bernstein's decision to stage the revival took its impetus from this resurgence of Progressive politics. Throughout 1947, the Progressives, still enamored of the American wartime alliance with the Soviet Union, had become increasingly appalled not only by Truman's belligerent foreign policy but also by his domestic loyalty-security probes that seemed to match the virulence of the HUAC witch-hunters. A third-party run at the presidency was not out of the question, but certainly many Progressives were lobbying furiously to put the old Roosevelt program back on the congressional agenda. Earlier in 1947, on May 16, the Progressive Citizens of America had set up a National Youth Lobby, and Bernstein had added his name to the list of sponsors to promote "federal aid to education, the eighteen-year-old vote, increased veterans subsistence pay, on-the-job training programs, FEPC, health and housing legislation," . . . and to "oppose compulsory peace-time military training."[88]

In the fall of 1947, progressives, despite the demoralizing Eisler and Hollywood Ten affairs, were hoping to mobilize a resurgence of the New Deal political movement, and Bernstein's revival of *The Cradle Will Rock* took place within this confrontational context. Virgil Thomson understood Bernstein's strategy. Writing in the *New York Herald Tribune* directly after Bernstein's premiere performance on November 24, Thomson wrote, "In a year when the Left in general, and the labor movement in particular, is under attack, it is important that the Left should put its best foot forward. . . . If the standard Broadway musical plugs what Thurmond Arnold called 'the folk-lore of capitalism' [that is, affirms the political-economic system], this play with (or in) music recites with passion and piety the mythology of the labor movement. . . . Its power is due in large part to the . . . morality it expounds. That morality is a prophetic and confident faith in trade unionism as a dignifying force."[89]

Bernstein's decision to revive this radical work was a strike back at the inquisitors—HUAC, the Loyalty-Security Board, the blacklisters responsible for the immiserization of Eisler and the Hollywood Ten. But it was also a call for the progressive audience that had supported Roosevelt in the great New Deal days to revive itself, to find inspiration and lend support to a powerful civil rights plank. Bernstein did some campaigning for the cause, writing an article that appeared in the *New York Times* on Sunday, November 2, 1947, about the National Negro Congress's campaign to overcome discrimination against blacks in the music industry.

The Progressive ideological revival was gaining momentum. And when, a month later, December 29, 1947, Wallace announced his candidacy for the presidency, that Progressive revival became a campaign.

## THE GREAT AMERICAN OPERA

Two weeks later, on January 14, 1948, amid the rise of a national Wallace-Progressive movement, Bernstein announced his desire to write "one real, moving American opera that any American can understand (and one that is, notwithstanding, a serious musical work)."[90] In an interview in *Harper's* in February, he added, "I am the logical man to write the Great American Opera."[91] Bernstein biographer Humphrey Burton has noted that Bernstein's remark alluded to his performances of *Cradle;* Bernstein added that *Cradle* was "a forerunner of American opera" but held that he could write a better opera than any of Blitzstein's.[92] But my argument goes well beyond Burton's. These *Cradle* performances, the euphoria of the Progressive revival, Wallace's decision to run for the presidency in January 1948, and Bernstein's compositional impulse ran concurrently. In other words, Bernstein's American operatic ambition was conjoined with his Progressive political aspiration.

# 1948

In February, when Bernstein noted in *Harper's Magazine* that he was the logical person to write the great American opera, the Wallace campaign was calling for plans for full employment; implementation of President Franklin Roosevelt's Economic Bill of Rights to guarantee every American nutrition, housing, medical care, education, and work; repeal of Taft-Hartley antilabor legislation; and termination of congressional and executive-branch investigations into political beliefs. In the international arena, Wallace opposed rearming Germany and otherwise sought to reverse Truman's aggressive foreign policy and to continue the wartime Soviet-American alliance using diplomacy and negotiation in concert with the United Nations.[93] These positions seemed to be winning over a goodly portion of the electorate. On February 19, 1948, James A. Hagerty of the *New York Times* wrote an article under the headline "Big Aid to Wallace Is Seen in Victory of Bronx Protégé." Progressive Leo Isacson's victory over the Democratic, Republican, and Liberal party candidates in the congressional race in his Bronx district, wrote Hagerty, had, among "many repercussions" the "realization that Henry A. Wallace . . . would poll a much larger vote then had been expected by any except his most ardent supporters." Not only might Truman lose New York state, but also chances for Progressive Party candidates elsewhere might be rising.[94] Bernstein must have been among these euphoric Progressives; indeed, an FBI informant spotted him addressing a rally of the American Labor Party (the Progressive Party's branch in New York state). Wallace seemed to be making particular gains among Jews, many of whom were upset by Truman's failure to support recognition of a new Jewish state in Palestine—and most significantly, among working-class voters.[95] He made clear that he opposed Truman's policies of forgiving Nazis and of seeking to integrate a rearmed

West Germany into the European defense system, a position with which Bernstein was in full agreement.[96]

By February 24, 1948, surveys were indicating growing support for Wallace and for Progressive Party congressional candidates in California and much of the industrial Midwest. Most salient for anyone hoping for a revived New Deal coalition were surveys revealing support for Wallace among industrial workers in Missouri and Pennsylvania.[97] These reports must have given Progressives a positive jolt after the traumas of the previous two years.

Bernstein conducted a Hanns Eisler concert in New York on February 28, 1948.[98] On March 8, he resigned from his position as music director of the New York City Symphony in protest against budget cuts.[99] On March 17, 1948, he cosponsored a JAFRC reception honoring Madame Irene Joliet-Curie.[100] The next month, according to a newspaper report cited by the FBI, Bernstein signed a protest against American attempts to manipulate elections in Italy.[101]

Meanwhile, Bernstein was apparently embroiled in yet another conflict, a struggle within the left-wing civil rights movement. On February 2, 1948, he reputedly helped Paul Robeson fend off an attack upon the left-wing leadership of the Council on African Affairs, listed by the attorney general as a Communist front group. The attack was led by Max Yergen, who had been since 1937 Robeson's close associate in the council's leadership. Yergen had turned vociferously anti-Communist and broken ties with Robeson, W. E. B. DuBois, and others in this so-called Communist faction—in which he included Bernstein. He maintained that this group was attempting to take over the council and thereby promote black votes for the Wallace Progressives.[102] Yergen's attempt to take control of the council received only a minority vote.[103]

Later in February, Bernstein left for a tour of Europe and Israel on the *Queen Mary* and wrote a fictional dialogue expressing his disappointment that his cabinmate was not Henry Wallace or Jean-Paul Sartre but one Léon Trirème, to whom he describes his political dream of universal cosmopolitanism, of a world where all "symptoms of nationalism" disappear, a world without "passports," "what Wendell Wilkie called One World, what the church calls Universal Brotherhood under God, what Communists call the International, what industrialists call Free Trade, what democrats call Full Equality, what Yogis call being part of the All."[104] Bernstein refused to accept Cold War logic. On March 19, he had sent a postcard from Budapest to the Marcuse family in Detroit jesting about the iron curtain, with the inscription "Love from behind that Cellophane Curtain" (this after the Communist coup d'état in Czechoslovakia).[105] On May 3, he was in Paris courtesy of a State Department–sponsored concert tour of Europe and wrote Helen Coates that the people he was meeting were terrified of a "war-plan . . . being instigated and manufactured in America."[106] On May 5, he wrote from Munich that while Jews sat in misery in displaced-persons camps, fascistic Germans were just waiting to start a new war, this time with their American allies, against the Soviet Union.[107] He reported to his sister, Shirley, the same day, "The de-Nazification process has been a farce. (In fact, the chief de-Nazi officer at lunch today laughingly referred to it as a Re-Nazification. It's a joke, son.)" The rightward turn of American Cold War politics was evident: though ex-Nazis were getting away without punishment, Bernstein wrote, he was "suspect" among American officials because he was a "Wallace man."[108]

On April 26, 1948, according to an FBI memorandum, he had signed on to a protest against the repressive Mundt-Nixon Communist Control bill.[109] He arrived back in New York and on May 29, signed a statement by musicians claiming that only one of the three national candidates was "in the Roosevelt tradition": "[Wallace is for] Peace, Full Employment, Repeal of the Taft-Hartley Law, [for] Equal Opportunities and Civil Rights, 15 Million New homes, Global Reconstruction through the United Nations, National Health Program and a National Cultural Program" [and against] "War, Universal Military Training, [the] Truman Doctrine, Inflation and Depression, all forms of Discrimination and Thought-Control."[110]

By the end of that summer, the Wallace support was in free fall as voters, worried about Dewey's projected victory, started to turn to Truman as the lesser evil. Bernstein had by this time put aside the idea of composing his American opera and had instead begun work on a symphony, his second, based on W. H. Auden's *Age of Anxiety*. He was in Israel on election day, where news arrived of the Truman and Democratic congressional victories in Congress and the ignominious defeat of the Progressives, who received about 4.5 percent of the vote in the Northeast but only about 2.37 percent of the national total. The coalition the Progressives had hoped to fashion had gone to the Democrats. Wallace did best among working-class Jewish voters in districts like Isacson's in the Bronx that contained sizable numbers of blacks and Hispanics. But Truman's decision to recognize Israel ensured him most of the Jewish vote, and his decision to integrate the military, along with black leaders' outspoken antipathy for Paul Robeson and the Progressives, helped him win the bulk of black voters.[111]

A more crucial reason for the failure of the Wallace constituency to grow into a massive voting bloc was the issue of communism. Early on, the Americans for Democratic Action and the Democrats had pounded away at Progressives for their acceptance of communists within their ranks. This theme caught on among Irish Catholic voters, who followed the church hierarchy and especially Cardinal Spellman in support of Franco and HUAC. Polish Catholics, upset with the Soviets, had also moved to the right.[112] Another factor that helped Catholic and non-Catholic blue-collar workers forgo the Progressives and remain in the Democratic fold was their new, or anticipated, economic condition. Fundamental to the outlook of postwar Truman liberalism was a turning away from the driving forces of progressive New Dealism. The latter had been energized by the idea that the government could ensure a more egalitarian distribution of incomes, upgrade social services and offer universal medical care, and regulate the economy to ensure high employment. But Truman liberals deemphasized many of the progressives' goals and emphasized instead a model best exemplified by steel- and autoworkers unions' obtaining higher wages based on increased productivity in return for leaving the running of industry to managers. In this way, higher-waged workers joined others in the new consumerism that, fed by a combination of pent-up demand and reaction to the Depression and war, had become the regnant outlook of many Americans who no longer were interested in class politics. Bernstein's hopes for finding a progressive public to be inspired by his American opera had been dissolving over the summer and died on election day, November 2, 1948.

## AGE OF ANXIETY

Defeated Progressives still hoped to preserve a popular front internationalist spirit against the chill of cold war. Koussevitzky, Copland, Bernstein, Arthur Miller, and Norman Mailer were among the sponsors of the three-day Scientific and Cultural Conference of World Peace that took place at the Waldorf-Astoria Hotel in New York from March 25 to 27 in 1949, with Dimitri Shostakovich a member of the Soviet delegation. In the meantime, unbeknownst to Bernstein, his name had arisen in high governmental circles. The people around Truman thought Bernstein might prove an embarrassment were the president to appear with Israel's president, Chaim Weizmann, at a function at the Waldorf-Astoria in which Bernstein was to perform.[113] On March 2, 1949, White House aide David Niles asked the FBI to provide documentation of Bernstein's politics. On March 15, 1949, an FBI agent reported that Niles "was greatly disturbed by the fact that Bernstein was undoubtedly mixed up in a lot of Communist and Liberal Movements [*sic*]." The White House had already received a "'stinging' letter of protest . . . from the publication 'Counterattack' and was fearful that other complications would arise if Bernstein were permitted to appear on the program." Truman was in a difficult position. In the end, however, he was able to avoid appearing with Bernstein by canceling a number of engagements, including the one with Weizmann, claiming an overloaded agenda.[114]

Bernstein probably had no idea of these discussions between the Truman inner circle and the FBI about his activities. If he had, he might have been even more upset than he was when he got news on March 15 of his rejection by the trustees of the Boston Symphony as successor to Koussevitzky as music director, a plan Koussevitzky had been promoting since

1947. This rejection was a second blow: in February 1947, he lost out to Erich Leinsdorf to head the Rochester Symphony Orchestra.[115] According to Bernstein biographer Humphrey Burton, Koussevitzky made his last plea to the trustees on March 10, five days before they would make their decision to reject Bernstein and the other leading candidate, Mitropoulos, and to hire Charles Munch instead.[116]

The Waldorf conference got under way later in March. A high point was Aaron Copland's address of March 27 at the Fine Arts Panel, "Effect of the Cold War on the Artist in the United States," in which he deplored the climate of rancor between the United States and the USSR that he claimed was distorting international artistic life.[117] His speech fell on deaf ears. *Life* magazine, in those days the mass-media evangelist of American optimism and power, laughed off the conference as a "comic opera" and ran the equivalent of a photographic rogues' gallery of some fifty "hard working fellow travelers to soft-headed do-gooders," in which Bernstein's photo was sandwiched between those of Copland and Episcopal bishop Edward L. Parsons.[118]

Bernstein's emotions must have been mixed on April 8, 1949, only four days after the publication date of that issue of *Life,* as he sat at the piano during the premiere performance of his Symphony no. 2, *The Age of Anxiety,* the corner of his eye fixed on the podium where his mentor, Serge Koussevitzky, was leading the Boston Symphony Orchestra. W. H. Auden wrote the poem on which the work was based between 1944 and 1946 and won the Pulitzer Prize for it in 1948. The poem deals with three men and a woman who meet in a bar in wartime New York, briefly commune, and then part. Auden exposed characteristic postwar themes of anonymity, estrangement, and rootlessness, and he spoke of loss of faith or the effort to hold on to a faith that offers little solace, a faith uttered with a world-weary, compassionate irony. Bernstein had met Auden, and given his own intellectual and religious preoccupations with loss of faith, not to mention his angst, he must have felt that this narrative would support a symphonic work. His adaptation of the Auden piece was, and remains, a monument to the period's restlessness, an extended tone poem of a New Yorker's sensibilities and felt experience within an ethos of metropolitan blues and Kierkegaardian *angst*. Bernstein departed from Auden by concluding the work with a long orchestral passage of optimism and resolution that depicts faith intact—or at least his hope of some kind of reconciliation between man and cosmos. In doing so, he announced a philosophic theme that would characterize virtually all his work in the future.

## DESCENT: BLACKLIST

Reconciliation, however, was not in Bernstein's own immediate future. For virtually the entire decade of the 1940s, Bernstein's career had been in the ascendant. Music director of the New York City Symphony Orchestra, frequent guest conductor at the New York Philharmonic and other orchestras across the nation and across Europe, and if twice rejected for music directorships, nevertheless regular conductor of the Boston Symphony Orchestra at Tanglewood, possessor of a recording contract from RCA,[119] composer of two ballets danced on the stage of American Ballet Theater and of a hit musical that had made him quite well-to-do, his climb seemed limitless. He had become famous as much for his virtuosity as his glamour.[120]

By 1950, however, his career seemed in precipitous descent. On February 26, 1950, he was identified as a subversive in the witch-hunting periodical *Counterattack*.[121] He may have been "The Boy Wonder Hopelessly Fated for Success" according to the March 1950 issue of *Look*, but he was a dangerous Red according to *Red Channels*, published in June 1950.[122] Any such listing was the inevitable prelude to blacklisting by the radio, television and film industry. And indeed, in short order, Bernstein was placed "off-limits" by CBS.[123] Seven years before, CBS had carried the fabled Philharmonic broadcast that had catapulted him into fame. Now he was cast out by CBS—in short, blacklisted.

Now in June 1950, just as the Korean War began and the hysteria of the Red Scare was accelerating, Bernstein was being dealt a devastating blow with the publication in *Red Channels* of his supposed communist affiliations based largely on a HUAC compilation using FBI data.[124] Bernstein was now banned from official State Department functions overseas and was otherwise to be treated as a loyalty and security risk.[125]

More trouble lay ahead; whether he knew it or not, Bernstein was starting a career as a subject of presidential and FBI investigation. In the years that followed, he probably remained ignorant of much that was going on behind his back, but he caught enough glimpses to make his life a long "Age of Anxiety" indeed.

# CHAPTER THREE

# American Biedermeier

## *1951–1959*

### HIATUS FROM CONDUCTING

In the days surrounding New Year's Day, 1951, Bernstein was on board a ship from Cherbourg to the United States to conduct the New York Philharmonic in February and to share conducting duties with Koussevitzky during the Israel Philharmonic's American tour, which would last through March. He was in some turmoil: he had been in a long-term relationship with the Chilean-born actress Felicia Montealegre Cohn—the two had become engaged in 1947, but Bernstein had soon broken it off—but she was to meet him when the ship docked on January 2.[1] He also committed to running an arts festival in 1952 at Brandeis University, for which he was to prepare the program and conduct the premiere performance of his so-far-unfinished opera, *Trouble in Tahiti*. And, of course, he was living under threat of further acts of governmental and corporate repression. All of these matters were on his mind as he sailed to New York.

Also on board were Robert Rossen, the left-wing playwright and Hollywood film director, and Vincent Hallinan, a lawyer who was prominent in the Progressive Party.[2] While in conversation on the ship, they met up with another group that included the Hollywood producer Boris Morros. According to Morros (as reported to the FBI by either

Morros himself or an unidentified person), Bernstein had let on that a "well-to-do Jewish man," upset that a left-winger like Bernstein was leading the Israel Philharmonic, wanted Bernstein to sign a loyalty oath. Rossen expressed his disgust for this idea (according to the informant), saying "that the United States 'stinks' and is going to Hitlerism and reaction," and "we have to do something before it is too late," and "everyone is scared to death." Although the FBI document is not clear about the sequence of events, it repeats Morros's report that Bernstein "made the statement that *Life Magazine,* in a recent issue, made a list of the fifty most prominent 'Reds' and said that he, BERNSTEIN, was very proud of the fact that he was on the list." The report also said that Morros "was talking about a picture he proposed making." When "Bernstein asked him why he did not hire him," Morros responded that he "could not hire a Red." At this point, Morros and his group turned their backs on Bernstein.[3] Insult aside, Bernstein now knew that the blacklist was extending from overseas American embassies and consulates to CBS radio and then to Hollywood. Would it stop there? As he alighted upon American shores, the young conductor must have been worried.

The following day, January 3, Dimitri Mitropoulos, the new conductor of the Philharmonic, reported to the board the names of the guest conductors for the 1951–52 season. Bernstein's was not among them.[4] Assuming the decision was Bernstein's, and that he had made it months before, what led him to it? The simplest hypothesis is that he needed a composing sabbatical to finish *Trouble in Tahiti.* Nor was this the first time he had sought a conducting sabbatical: just over a year before, he had asked Koussevitzky for release from summer 1950 Tanglewood duties, needing time to compose and overcome physical and emotional ailments, but he was refused—in fact rebuked—by his mentor for even suggesting a leave of absence.[5] Seen in this light, he was taking the sabbatical to make up for the one he had missed the summer before. But the events that followed suggest an alternative hypothesis. In the days after his arrival in New York, he apparently felt some urgency in reaching yet a new sabbatical decision, one well beyond that announced to the Philharmonic board on January 3.

On January 15, he informed Koussevitzky in no uncertain terms that he was not coming to Tanglewood in the summer and, in fact, was taking a sabbatical not only from the Philharmonic but from all other consulting engagements, certainly for one and perhaps as many as two years.[6] That this extended sabbatical plan was a sudden inspiration is evidenced not only by this January 15 letter to Koussevitzky but by Helen Coates's response to an inquiry from Nelly Walter of Bernstein's agency, Columbia Artists Management. On January 22, 1951, Walter had inquired about Bernstein's availability to conduct in Europe and must have been quite surprised to hear the following from Coates so late in the day: "Evidently, the word has not been passed on to you that Mr. Bernstein has made a definite decision to take a year's rest from conducting, beginning this coming April, 1951. He plans to rest and compose, and will not be available for any conducting until the fall of 1952."[7]

Bernstein made his decision public on February 15, when the *New York Times* reported that he would end his current tour in Mexico City, remain there for a few months, and spend up to a year and a half composing. Later that day, he was off to Carnegie Hall to conduct the New York Philharmonic in performances of Prokofiev and Stravinsky. Over the next week and a half, he performed music of Rachmaninoff, Copland, Franck, Milhaud, and most significantly, on February 22, the world premiere of Charles Ives's Symphony no. 2.[8] He fulfilled two more recording dates in March and left New York for Mexico City, having written to Copland that he was "giving up conducting for at least two years."[9]

All seemed quite normal on the surface, a matter of Bernstein's setting priorities. But the question remains, What led him to the January 3 and the extended January 15 sabbatical plans? As he had explained to Koussevitzky when he petitioned for the sabbatical for the 1950 summer, as Helen Coates intimated to Nelly Walter on January 22, and as he explained in a letter to Koussevitzky on May 30, he had wanted a sabbatical not only to compose but for his physical and mental health.[10]

What disturbances, if not torments, were causing him to take flight from the podium? Threats to his career cannot be discounted. He was blacklisted by the State Department and by CBS and was living with threats of new intimidation and repression by the growing ranks of the witch hunters. Certainly, the possibility of further damage to his career loomed large given what he had just learned from Morros and company aboard ship. His American conducting career, not to mention his chances of getting an orchestra of his own, would be dashed were the blacklist to extend to the concert hall. Given this darkening repressive atmosphere, he might well have pursued the sabbatical plans not only to give him time to pour his energies into *Trouble in Tahiti* and prepare for the Brandeis festival but also to provide him with a safe way to remove his name from the Philharmonic board's scrutiny of proposed guest conductors, thereby preempting a board decision to reject him and make him persona non grata. Removing himself from the Philharmonic board's deliberations by taking refuge in the comparative safety of the composing studio and the Brandeis campus would deliver him from the nightmare of a new, crippling blacklisting.

It is, of course, possible that the Philharmonic board had no intention of blacklisting Bernstein. Indeed, was a Philharmonic blacklist possible? Bernstein had been under contract with the Philharmonic for the 1943–44 and 1944–45 seasons. From 1945 to 1948, he was conductor of the New York City Symphony. He was a guest conductor of the Philharmonic in 1949–50, and had accepted an invitation in early 1950 to conduct during the 1950–51 season.[11] CBS blacklisted him in 1950, and once he fulfilled his long-scheduled appearance with the Philharmonic in February 1951, he remained away, only to return in 1956, after his removal from the CBS blacklist.[12]

Keeping in mind the need to avoid the *post hoc ergo propter hoc* fallacy,[13] one must nonetheless note that CBS and the Philharmonic had closely related interests and that Bernstein's hiatus from the Philharmonic virtually coincided the period of the CBS blacklist. William S. Paley, chairman of the board of CBS and an aggressive blacklister—his Clearance Office was manned by ex-FBI agents—sat on the Philharmonic board (he served from 1937 to 1957).[14] (Paley was also founder and board member of Columbia Artists Management, the head of which was the politically conservative Arthur Judson.[15] Judson was comanager of the Philharmonic and executive secretary and member of the board of directors and executive committee of the Philharmonic Society until his resignation in August 1956.)

More direct evidence of the close association of CBS and the Philharmonic appears in the following examples: In December 1950, CBS let the Philharmonic board know that certain sponsors were unhappy by the scheduling of a "prize winning but unknown violinist" to perform during broadcast time.[16] On the Philharmonic board's agenda for the 1950–51 season were concerns about CBS radio memberships, sponsorships of CBS Sunday broadcasts, CBS Young Peoples concerts, and diminishing subscriptions and other income sources. Connections with Columbia Records were evident, for example, when, on November 19, 1953, the board took up a request that Bruno Walter reapportion his time so that he could record more and perform less.[17] In that meeting, CBS Radio asked the Philharmonic board not to publicize the departure of Willys Motors as sponsor of the Philharmonic broadcasts lest the announcement derail negotiations with potential sponsors.[18] In sum, ties between the CBS and Philharmonic boards were quite close. If nothing in the New York Philharmonic's archives verifies the hypothesis that Bernstein's absence from the podium from 1951 to 1956 was due to the CBS ban (not to mention the State Department ban), the congruence of corporate interests invites such speculation.

One more element of this congruence of interest between CBS and the Philharmonic board is pertinent. In early April 1951, the FBI initiated the process of placing Bernstein's name on the so-called Security Index mandated by the 1950 Internal Security (McCarran) Act; the list named those who were to be picked up and incarcerated in detention camps in the event of a national emergency.[19] "The subject [Bernstein] is White, Male, Native Born, and, of the three possible categories, 'Communist,' 'Socialist Worker,' or 'Independent Socialist League,' the first, 'Communist.'" He was to be incarcerated in the areas reserved for "prominent persons."[20] This behind-the-scenes maneuvering, we can safely assume, was unknown to Bernstein. It was, however, more than likely known to the ex-FBI agents in charge of clearing names for the Philharmonic's partner, CBS.

At just that moment, Bernstein took up residence in Cuernavaca, Mexico, a town of lush beauty. There, he met frequently with his good friend the famed correspondent Martha Gellhorn, as well as a number of blacklisted writers and directors who had exiled themselves from the United States. He seethed at the news from the States of the sycophantic pageantry mounted by the city of New York, the media, and the Congress to honor General Douglas MacArthur, recently fired for insubordination by Truman after McArthur almost forced the Chinese into war with U.S. forces in Korea. But Bernstein was not so much bothered by MacArthur as by those participating in the "farce of informing in Washington" (ongoing since March with HUAC's investigation of supposed communist infiltration in Hollywood).[21]

But he had more personal reasons to feel this anxiety. Back in the spring of 1950, television impresario and *New York Daily News* Broadway gossip columnist Ed Sullivan had told Jerome Robbins that unless Robbins revealed the names of people who had attended a party at his apartment for the Soviet Friendship League, Sullivan would (in modern parlance) "out" Robbins and tell all about his homosexual affairs.[22] For the homoerotic left-winger Bernstein, who was in and out of New York in the spring and might very well have been at the party, it was possibly believed he was in double jeopardy. On March 24, 1951, just before he left New York for Cuernavaca, Bernstein would have quickly learned that Sullivan was calling for a HUAC investigation of Robbins, suggesting that "Robbins can give the Committee backstage glimpses of the musical shows which have been jammed with performers sympathetic to the Commie cause." And if this news were not enough to get Bernstein to focus on his potential vulnerability, Sullivan remarked, "You can be equally sure Robbins knows and can name Communists who are prominent as conductors and arrangers in concert music."[23] The article quickly made the rounds in New York, and we can be sure that it made the rounds within the communities of the blacklisted in the United States, Mexico, and Europe.[24]

The terror ran unabated: on May 16, in a rather distracted state, Bernstein wrote his sister, Shirley, that Robert Rossen had just visited him in Cuernavaca and was distraught about his blacklisting; Rossen had decided to return to the States to appear before HUAC. Rossen was miserable, not knowing where to turn or where to take his family to start life again. Bernstein told Shirley that he was afraid he might suffer Rossen's fate: "He feels finished in the States. It's a mess, and I am very sorry for him. It can also happen to all of us, so we had better start preparing our blazing orations now." Meanwhile, he had been listening to Albert Maltz and other blacklisted Hollywood writers in exile and was sickened by Maltz's stories of prison life in West Virginia. Bernstein had no kind words for another of the Hollywood Ten, Edward Dimitryk, who had served time in prison for contempt and remained blacklisted, but who on April 25 reappeared before the committee and now gave names. Bernstein was most worried for John Garfield: "He will wind up in a great perjury mess if he doesn't watch out. It may already be too late. Actually, I suppose there is nothing to be done when your life and career are attacked but strike back with the truth and go honestly to jail if you have to. This dandling [*sic*] about to save a career can neither save the career nor make for self-respect." Bernstein concluded, "I hope I'm as brave as I sound from this distance when it catches up to me."[25] The letter offers clear evidence of Bernstein's cast of mind in this period. He clearly thought that he was most vulnerable to more blacklisting and, worse, to a subpoena to testify before HUAC.

Bernstein thus had more than enough reason to empathize with John Garfield, whose life had become wretched indeed. The two had been friends for years, meeting in the circles around the Group Theater since the late 1930s and in Hollywood at Gene Kelly and Betsy Blair's open houses in New York and Hollywood after the war.[26] In the early 1950s, even a tangential association with the Group Theater was enough to taint a person: HUAC member California Republican Donald Jackson made the claim that the Group Theater "for all its artistry was shot through with the philosophy of communism."[27] He made this statement on April 23 at Garfield's appearance before the committee, just three weeks before Bernstein wrote to Shirley. Garfield had been asked whether his political beliefs followed the Communist Party line and about his ties to the Joint Anti-Fascist Refugee Committee, the National Council of American-Soviet Friendship and the Progressive Party—all of which groups Bernstein had been supporting. If, by the end of Garfield's testimony, nothing on the surface pointed to his coming martyrdom, HUAC was nevertheless turning him into an object of disgust. Word was out that the committee, having rejected Garfield's statement that he knew nothing of his associates' supposed communist ties, had decided to seek his indictment for perjury. Witnesses before HUAC who were in the New York theatrical or Hollywood movie industries were now having to testify about their associations with Garfield, and an affirmative answer was tantamount to contamination and blacklisting. Elia Kazan noted that Garfield, after his appearance before HUAC, began to disintegrate.[28]

Garfield's martyrdom, and potentially Rossen's, was on Bernstein's mind as he wrote to Shirley on May 16, and he told her that he was expecting to be subpoenaed and hoped he had the strength of character to refuse to name names even if he would face a prison sentence as a result. He was afraid but hoped that he had the courage to do the right thing in the event that he were called to testify, "when it catches up with me."[29]

On June 4, 1951, Koussevitzky died, and Bernstein took over guidance of the musical life of the Berkshire Festival, leading the orchestra and teaching conducting.[30] On the political front, however, matters were going from bad to worse: Robert Rossen appeared before HUAC on June 25, 1951 and was asked about his relationship with Garfield. Rossen avoided direct answers, saying only that his and Garfield's relationship was strictly business. Rossen was interrogated about his theater life before the war and before his move to Hollywood, and about his connections with, among others, the Joint Anti-Fascist Refugee Committee. He declined to respond when asked whether he knew a number of other people and remained on the blacklist.[31] On June 26, 1951, HUAC questioners pointedly asked J. Edward Bromberg, another alumnus of the Group Theater who had left for Hollywood, about Garfield's alleged membership in the Communist Party. Bromberg refused to answer. Nor did he reply to demands that he reveal his own political history.[32]

In September 1951, Bernstein, no doubt worried about his citation in *Red Channels,* asked his attorney whether his sponsorship of the Joint Anti-Fascist Refugee Committee, which was on the attorney general's list of subversive groups, left him exposed to subpoena. He was told via Helen Coates on September 19, 1951 not to worry inasmuch as sponsors have no policy or administrative powers.[33]

Bernstein's crisis was somewhat mitigated by other matters. On September 9, Felicia and Bernstein married and took their honeymoon in Cuernavaca, where Bernstein continued to work on *Trouble in Tahiti.* In mid-December, he declined an unofficial offer from the Pittsburgh Symphony Orchestra for a one-year position as full-time director for the 1952–53 season. The position was hardly what he was hoping for. He allowed that though he did not know if he would accept an offer from the Boston Symphony orchestra, which might arise were Charles Munch too ill to continue, he would certainly accept an offer from the Rome Symphony Orchestra.[34] In short, he was betwixt and between, at loose ends. Later that month came news that Bromberg, under blacklist, had died in London of a heart attack on December 19.

Bernstein was back in Boston in late February and early March 1952 to conduct the Boston Symphony Orchestra for the ailing Charles Munch. On March 8, Bernstein confided to his friend François Valéry, vice president of the UNESCO Council (and son of the poet Paul Valéry), that he was quite excited about a possible offer of the musical directorship of the Rome Orchestra. He implied that he had no chance of getting the New York Philharmonic and that if he couldn't have New York, Rome was the next best option—and he and Felicia were prepared to move overseas to take on the assignment.[35]

He may have been Professor Bernstein of Brandeis, but he was in fact floundering. Helen Coates, in a note she penned on a March 13, 1952, letter from Nelly Walter of Columbia Artists Management, which she probably meant to send to Walker in reply, said that Bernstein "for the moment does not know what he will be doing."[36] And all the while he was living with the threat of subpoena.

Bernstein must have breathed a sigh of relief after Judy Holliday's March 16 appearance before HUAC. Holliday was asked to provide information about Betty Comden and Adolf Green's associations, and their appearances on behalf of Spanish Civil War refugees, but none of the committee members mentioned Bernstein's name, most likely because he had left the Revuers before those performances.[37] But then came the first of the real shockers to the left-wing theatrical, musical, and Hollywood worlds. On April 10, Elia Kazan appeared before HUAC and named names. A month later, on May 19 and May 20, Clifford Odets, who had been close to Hanns Eisler and John Garfield, appeared before HUAC and saved his Hollywood career by naming names of people he had known to be members of the Communist Party. Odets, however, did not betray Garfield. Asked if he knew that Garfield had been a Communist, Odets replied, "No sir; I never knew."[38] Testifying the next day, May 21, Lillian Hellman delivered her famous line to HUAC: "I cannot and will not cut my conscience to fit this year's fashions."[39] Hellman's stand—she declined to answer questions about her own or others' politics—provided but brief respite from the full effects of victimization, character assassination, and betrayals that resulted from the HUAC investigations, for the same day, John Garfield suffered a fatal heart attack. He was only thirty-nine years old.

## AMERICAN BIEDERMEIER:
### THE PROGRESSIVES MARGINALIZED

American progressives like Bernstein were now on the margins, if not isolated from the mainstream of American liberalism. The progressives' plight was less because of the McCarthyites than because of their abandonment if not betrayal by centrist liberals who either expressed only lukewarm opposition to McCarthyism or joined it. Arthur Schlesinger Jr., in

*The Vital Center,* the 1949 book that served as the ideological manifesto of Truman liberalism, had castigated progressives as intellectually and ideologically naive fellow travelers who failed to understand the nature of Stalinism and whose analyses had not been tempered by the responsibilities of power.[40] Although Schlesinger was contemptuous of HUAC, he did support Truman's use of the Loyalty-Security Program to purge people suspected of supporting Soviet interests.[41] Schlesinger believed that Truman would ensure constitutionally acceptable "procedural safeguards" against improper dismissals—such a procedural regime would "prevent witch hunting"—but would also "resolutely reject the curious progressive doctrine that prosecution of Communists or fellow travelers in any circumstances is a violation of civil liberties."[42]

The centrist Cold War liberal assault on the progressive left only intensified the following year when senators Hubert Humphrey (D-MN), Paul Douglas (D-IL), and Herbert Lehman (D-NY) voted affirmatively for the 1950 Internal Security Act, which provided for detention of supposed subversives. In 1952, a number of leading liberal American intellectuals agreed with the editors of *Partisan Review* that the once-radical critic now felt quite at home within American business and cultural life. They suggested that American democracy was providing the bulwark against the "Russian totalitarianism [that] threatens world domination" and that even if writers were confronted by an anti-intellectual mass culture, they would "no longer accept alienation as the artist's fate in America; on the contrary, they want very much to be a part of American life." They had "ceased to think of themselves as rebels and exiles."[43] Others—including the literary critic Newton Arvin (who had argued in 1936 that "native American thought . . . moves on toward Marxist socialism as toward its culmination"), the social critic James Burnham (who was making his move from Trotskyist to the far right), and writer Allan Dowling—echoed the editorial statement.[44] The literary critic Leslie Fiedler wrote of the "American belief in innocence and achievement" and the nation's "uncompromising optimism."[45] The writer Mark Schorer offered a curious response, arguing that "we have had almost no dissent worth taking seriously since the

1920's." He noted that despite the openness of American political democracy, "the United States has seldom experienced a more restrictive political atmosphere than at the present time," but he placed the blame on "moralistic clichés and the political falsehoods that they propagate" and made no mention of propagators such as Senator McCarthy or the members of HUAC.[46] To Lionel Trilling, the once radical but now reformed intellectual could learn from writers such as Thoreau and Melville and opt "for satire, for humor, for irony, for despair, for tragedy, for the personal vision affirming itself against the institutional"—in short, could choose from a palette of styles to write about his or her sense of alienation.[47]

For these writers, the moral collapse, harassments, betrayals, and destructions of friendships, careers, and lives going on in the interrogation chambers of HUAC and in the McCarthy and Internal Security Committees, might just as well have been happening on some other planet.

Not all liberals and former progressives accepted the official mythology. The social theorist and theologian Reinhold Niebuhr was less sanguine than most, warning readers that much as America had been pushed into the role of hegemon to protect the free world against the Soviets, the greater foes were internal to the nation: "the spirits of hysteria, hatred, mistrust, and pride."[48] Norman Mailer and Philip Rahv were mindful of the havoc being wreaked upon artists and writers by Cold War forces. Mailer noted that the contemporary critic had no clear enemy to face because the economy was under control ("society has been rationalized"): the old economic nemeses were weakened, so "the expert encroaches upon the artist," the contemporary intellectual has moved his or her sights from "without"—from the external forces whose examination was the province of the left radical—to "within"—to individuals' inner life. To inquire into the workings of the society was now "dismissed as mere mechanical leftism."[49] But Mailer saw real problems external to the individual that ought not to be ignored: "No one of the intellectuals who find themselves now in the American grain ever discuss—at least in print—the needs of modern war. One does not ever say that total war and the total war economy predicate a total regimentation of thought." The artist rushing from the political left had a convenient cover:

"Rather, it is suggested that the society is too difficult to understand and history too difficult to predict. . . . It has become fashionable to sneer at economics and emphasize the 'human dilemma' as it was fashionable to do the reverse in the thirties. Economics is now for experts and the crisis of world capitalism is considered dull enough to be on par with the proletarian novel. One never hears about the disappearance of the world market, nor is it polite to suggest that the prosperity of America depends upon the production of means of destruction, and it is not only the Soviet Union which is driven toward war as an answer to its insoluble problems."[50]

Mailer's statement was, by the standards of the 1950s, rather subversive. Rahv, a Trotskyist who had not forsaken his outlook and who had served for years as an editor of *Partisan Review,* noted that many intellectuals had come to see the realities of the Soviet system and were "chastened." They had developed a greater sense of identity with American culture inasmuch as it had outgrown its older narrow business worship, artistic provincialism, and immaturity. Intellectuals were now fully employable in the universities and in government. But, he argued, some had allied themselves with uncritical anti-Stalinism, so much so that they could "put up with the vicious antics of a political bum like Senator McCarthy."[51] Rahv pointed out that communism was an external danger and to assume equivalent danger from domestic communism was to fall into "the shadow-world of political sectarianism and sheer obsession."[52]

Mailer's and Rahv's were voices in the wilderness: the depoliticization of literature was merely indicative of a general depoliticization of America life. The forces behind the Red Scare had considerably narrowed the formerly expansive political discourse of the 1930s and 1940s. Moreover, the purge of left-wing New Dealers had only added to the foreshortening of debate. The political system was now a centrist polyarchy: a system run by entrenched and bureaucratized elites and careerists in various institutional fields, labor, industry, politics, agriculture, entertainment, and communications—all in competition for markets or funds but mutually countervailing as well. A mighty consensus was being forged by the eradication of dissident voices from the print and electronic media, whether by advertisers' coercion or media executives' preemptive blacklisting. In many respects, then, the American social and political order of the 1950s bore great similarities to the European order imposed in 1815 by the Congress of Vienna: politics would be left to the authorities, while the new middle classes would enjoy uncontroversial public entertainments and the purchase of commodities that would enhance family and household life and personal beauty. Order was maintained by an official censorship, secret police, and a judiciary ready to sentence malefactors to long prison sentences. The newer system had its own kind of censorship and secret police; its own forms of excommunication, ostracism, and banishment; and its own methods of promoting self-repression and self-censorship. Historians dubbed the post-1814 system the Biedermeier system. The newer one was an American Biedermeier.

### REPRESSION

In the spring of 1952, Bernstein was at Brandeis setting up the festival he was organizing for June; preparing to conduct Weill's *Threepenny Opera,* with Blitzstein's translation of Brecht's libretto; and planning the premiere of his own *Trouble in Tahiti.* At this time, he was also toying with writing an opera about the life of Evita Peron, a project that would provide him the opportunity to create a political work—safely taking place in Argentina—while supporting his penchant for Latin rhythms.[53]

*Trouble in Tahiti* had its premiere in June 1952. The work tackled material that was then modishly daring but not dangerous; like its predecessor *Age of Anxiety,* the work was far from the more radical genre, such as an adaptation of *Winterset* that Bernstein had thought to compose before the HUAC-Truman-McCarthy-blacklist machinery came on the scene. Bernstein, true to his formal project, crossed high and low art with radio jingles, vernacular speech, and elevated lyricism to elaborate upon the strains on middle-class professional families who had moved to the new paradise, suburbia. Sam, the protagonist of *Trouble in Tahiti,* is commuting to work in the city and consumed by his career, and he has no time for his wife, Dinah, or their child.[54] His marriage is falling apart.

Like *Age of Anxiety,* this work assumed that the fault lines in modern life were aspects of an irremediable "human condition,"—this time not urban alienation but suburban alienation, This premise was daring indeed, but not, of course, worthy of FBI or HUAC attention. Nevertheless, Bernstein's progressivism sneaked in: first, in his criticism of the processes of commodification, the outpouring of household consumer goods that nevertheless proved no antidote to familial strains; and second, in his bleak view of American imperialism. This latter comes in a moment when Dinah, having just seen a film, *Trouble in Tahiti,* fantasizes about romance and "island magic," at which point the scene segues into a cavort between white American sailors and brown native girls—a spectacle at once audience pleasing and showstopping, in *South Pacific* fashion, but also embodying a critique of American exploitation of native populations overseas.[55] However, the supposed criticism expressed in this song and dance sequence would have gone over the heads of anyone not predisposed to a critique of American practices abroad. In no way did *Trouble in Tahiti* suggest a meaningful exposure of the roots and practices of American power. The message that everyone caught was the sobering idea that the move to "garden city" is at best only a temporary palliative, one that does not remove the underlying problems of contemporary life.

Meanwhile, the right-wing assault upon American artists was accelerating: Copland's *Lincoln Portrait* was dropped from Eisenhower's inaugural in January 1953 because of Copland's political history.[56] On February 19, the new secretary of state, John Foster Dulles, issued an order to remove from the International Information Administration libraries and Voice of America broadcasts works of any communist or fellow traveler. These works would include recordings of Bernstein's music, along with those of Copland, Gershwin, Sessions, Thomson, and Harris.[57] (The ban was secretly removed in that year as the Eisenhower administration began to join into the cultural Cold War, as we will see shortly.)

For at least a moment, the blacklist and the witch hunt seemed a long way from Broadway: Bernstein's *Wonderful Town* opened in February 26, 1953. A collaboration with Betty Comden and Adolph Green (who adapted the play from Ruth McKenney's book *My Sister Eileen* and the play adaptation by Joseph Fields and Jerome Chodorov), the show was an immediate hit.[58] The light-hearted, cheerful, optimistic, and good-natured work depicts the travails of two sisters from Ohio who have arrived in New York's Greenwich Village to seek careers and adventure. Plunged into the cacophony of the city and the rapid pace of business life, the sisters are at first overwhelmed by the crazy Village types they meet, wondering, "Why, oh why, did we ever leave Ohio?" In short order, however, the younger sister, Eileen, is happily pursued by myriad admirers, including a bunch of New York cops, and finds her true love; the older sister, Ruth, played by Rosalind Russell, sheds her nervous constraint to join in the zaniness and, against seemingly impossible odds, lands her man.

The work had a Broadway run of some 559 performances. Actually, it should have run for 560. When Ed Sullivan thundered his outrage in the *New York Daily News* that the left-wing newspaper *The National Guardian* had purchased a block of tickets for April 8, 1953, the producer, George Abbot, simply canceled the performance.[59]

This incident, indicative of the depths to which Sullivan and the blacklisting industry could sink, did not touch Bernstein, whose political travails remained largely unpublicized. To the Broadway public and the publicity machinery, Bernstein was simply the charming wunderkind; in fact, he was escaping opprobrium by the skin of his teeth.

On May 5, Jerome Robbins appeared before HUAC and began his testimony with a roll call of his Broadway works. The HUAC counsel, Frank S. Tavenner, then asked Robbins, "What was your first ballet?" Robbins answered that it was *Fancy Free,* first performed on April 18, 1944. Tavenner asked Robbins if HUAC's information that he had been a member of the Communist Party "at one time" was correct, a question Robbins was sure to decline to answer on Fifth Amendment grounds.

But came the surprise answer "Yes; it is." Robbins had thus signaled his willingness to inform on others: by his admission of membership, he closed off the possibility of invoking the constitutional protection against self-incrimination to avoid answering questions about others. Still the conversation did not fasten upon the names of others, at least not yet. Tavenner did ask about Robbins's activities within the Communist Party, in the course of which Robbins mentioned that he had been a member of a party "theatrical transient group." He told the committee that a party official had once asked "in what way did dialectical materialism help me do *Fancy Free*." Robbins told the committee, "I had created *Fancy Free* before I had become a member of the political association [the Communist Political Association, as it was known in the war years], and I found the question ridiculous and outrageous, both." Tavenner's and Robbins's conversation then moved to *On the Town:* "The idea was mine," Robbins began. "The purpose of it was to show how an American material and American spirit and American warmth and our dancing, our folk dancing, which is a part of jitterbugging, part of jazz, could be used as an art form. . . . It's always been identified everywhere it's played as a particularly American piece, indigenous to America, and that its theme has great heart and warmth, as far as representing our culture is concerned."[60] Robbins then named those of his associates who he thought were communists.

Bernstein could only be thankful that he had not been a member of the party, for Robbins would have had no hesitation in serving up his name. Two days later, May 7, Robert Rossen returned to the committee to recant his earlier testimony and to name names, even carefully spelling them out.[61]

These were the days not only of the Red Scare but of the "Lavender Scare," when McCarthyite forces sought to expose and ferret out gays in government and other areas of influence where they might be loyalty and security risks.[62] David Diamond was called to testify, and as he wrote, "called Aaron" (Copland) in a "panic" and asked, "What do I do?" "'David,' he said, 'take it easy. Just do what the legal advisors tell you.' I said, 'I'm not going to inform on anybody.' Aaron said, 'Well, naturally, I hope not.' I said, 'What, however, if I'm asked a question directly about you, about Lenny?' He said, 'You say what you feel you have to say.'"[63] More than likely, Diamond was referring to his fear that he would be questioned about his homosexuality. Diamond was never asked about Bernstein's homosexuality; nevertheless his prehearing torture was quite evident.

For Copland, Rossen, Bernstein, and their many friends and associates, these days were a time of terror.[64] The progressive Left was deserted by its old labor constituency, demonized as a bastion of fifth columnists, and under attack not only from the political right wing but from the new "anticommunist liberals," who, in setting up the Americans for Democratic Action and recruiting Eleanor Roosevelt, had fashioned themselves as inheritors of the New Deal. The group was isolated, marginalized, and now disintegrating.

On May 26, Copland was called to testify before McCarthy's committee but gave his questioners nothing to whet their appetites.[65] On June 2, 1953, Group Theater alumnus Lee J. Cobb, who had played Willy Loman in the original cast of Miller's 1949 *Death of a Salesman,* was called, and like Kazan and Odets before him, informed on his former associates.[66]

Bernstein might well have reflected upon his introduction to the Group Theater via Copland, his place within Stella Adler's salon. A long time had passed since Waldo Frank had declared that a new form of social life was developing in that hothouse! And now, Kazan, Odets, and Cobb had turned on their Group Theater allies, Robbins had turned on his, and Garfield and Bromberg were dead of heart attacks.

## AFFIDAVIT

Now came Bernstein's time, but not in the venue he had expected. He was not subpoenaed to appear before HUAC or Senate committees but was instead drawn into living hell in July 1953 by the U.S. State Department's refusal to renew his passport.[67] He was in trouble: besides carrying the stigma of refusal, he might be forced down the same road as Paul Robeson, blacklisted in the United States and unable to return to Europe where his career had flourished. Bernstein hired an attorney skilled in obtaining clearances, James McInerny, once a top investigator at the Justice Department and, as Bernstein later wrote his brother Burton, "an old

Commie-chaser" who had lightened the otherwise "ghastly and humiliating experience."[68]

But Bernstein did not reveal to his brother the precise nature of this
"ghastly and humiliating experience"—namely, that he was forced to
undergo a humiliating confession of political sin and to sign an affidavit
stating that he was not a communist and had never followed the communist line, and that if he had supported or associated with certain organizations held suspect, he had done so only "casually," as a naïf ignorant of
their deeper purposes. He swore that he had never gone to any meetings
of these organizations and did not know the names of their officials. He
confessed that his associations with anti-Franco Spanish political forces
had been at best "nominal," his work for the Joint Anti-Fascist Refugee
Committee had amounted to attending a dinner, and his association with
Paul Robeson had amounted to a meeting when both were "backstage
during a concert." He swore that his participation at the Waldorf conference in April 1949 with, among others, Copland and Shostakovich had
nothing to do with the "propaganda efforts" promoted by the conference
leadership, that he learned of his failures from the April 4, 1949 *Life* article
(cited above), and that he had purged and thus reformed himself. This
process of normalization called for more expiation: he declared allegiance
to a politically orthodox religion—in his case, Judaism.[69] He testified that
he was "active in Jewish philanthropy and the promotion of Israel as an
independent state free from Soviet domination." Indeed, as a Jew he was
"necessarily . . . a foe of communism." He testified that he had done much
service for charity. He was chagrined to learn that he might have been "a
source of possible embarrassment to the government of the United States."
He avowed that he had voted only for Democrats and Republicans. His
musical criticism had always been opposed to the Soviets. He realized that
he had made things difficult for himself back in 1949, when, after *Red
Channels* and *Life* had published their accounts of his politics, he should
have immediately "made a public disavowal" of his unpatriotic organizational associations. He said that he did so now, and he reaffirmed his loyalty to the United States.[70]

The affidavit apparently assuaged the authorities, for on August 12, he received his passport for travel to Italy to conduct at La Scala in December 1953. He conducted *Medea* with Maria Callas to universal applause and approbation. But he was on a long leash and potentially marked as a self-debasing coward: the affidavit was his passport to freedom, but at the same time it was a mark on him—if not as an informer upon others, as an informer upon himself. He had betrayed his principles and beliefs, his history, his friends: all were degraded. Signing the affidavit was hardly the "blazing oration" to the Inquisitors that he told Shirley he wanted to deliver when he wrote her on May 16, 1951. And now the affidavit was to be circulated to the archconservatives he so deplored! Bernstein had been asked to compose music for the film *On the Waterfront* and to obtain clearance from Columbia Pictures, his theatrical attorney, L. Arnold Weissberger, was prepared to present Bernstein's affidavit to the American Legion—a necessary step to be removed from the blacklist.[71]

Bernstein had in the meanwhile been waiting to find out whether he would receive an extension of his passport. He received a letter of April 9, 1954, from his attorney in the passport case, James McInerney, reporting contact with Passport Office officials, including the office's director, Ruth Shipley, and adding that he had heard rumors that a certain unnamed federal agency was involving itself with Bernstein's case.[72] (Was this agency the FBI, and was McInerney's comment perhaps Bernstein's first inkling that he was under surveillance?) The same day, Bernstein's longtime attorney, Murray C. Bernays, applied for clearance for Bernstein, assuring Francis J. MacNamara, editor of *Counterattack* and a top official of the Veterans of Foreign Wars, that Bernstein had never been a subversive and was in fact a loyal American.[73] On May 14, McInerney reported that State Department passport investigations officer Ashley Nicolas lacked confidence in Bernstein, given his political record, and that Bernstein's application would be treated like that of any other blacklisted Hollywood artist. McInerney suggested that Bernstein write him a letter that would convince Nicolas that Bernstein had honored his country with his last trip abroad. Bernstein complied with this request. In his response to McInerney on May 20, 1954, Bernstein indicated that he had done well by his country in his performances in Brazil and Italy; proof positive was the fact that he had impressed American diplomats and especially the ambassador to the Vatican, Clare Boothe Luce.[74]

Bernstein's gestures of contrition seemed to have worked: Columbia Pictures now approved him to compose the music for *On the Waterfront*, which would become the film's urban blues soundtrack. Ironically, the film was written by Budd Schulberg, directed by Elia Kazan, and starring Lee J. Cobb—all informers before HUAC now hoping the film could justify informing on associates.

### REHABILITATION: TRIUMPHANT RETURN TO THE NEW YORK PHILHARMONIC

According to Mark Goodson, the CBS producer, "The first major company to break the blacklist was Ford Motor Company with a broadcast of a Leonard Bernstein concert. They were strong enough and conservative enough that nobody could accuse them of anything."[75] Woodson meant the Ford Foundation, not the Ford Motor Company. When Robert Saudek of the Ford Foundation invited Bernstein to appear on the CBS program *Omnibus* on November 14, 1954, CBS did not complain, and in effect, the airing of the program removed Bernstein from the blacklist.

Actually, the groundwork for Bernstein's rehabilitation had been laid two years before in the premiere *Omnibus* program, for which Saudek had hired a blacklisted set designer cited by *Red Channels*. As Saudek explained, unless an individual was proven to be a communist, the Ford Foundation would hire any person of merit, even if that person had been cited by *Red Channels*.[76] CBS had gone along with Saudek's initiative because the Ford Foundation guaranteed the network that it would make up any income lost if a sponsor were to pull out of a program because of the presence of a blacklisted person. For their part, sponsors such as Willys Jeep and Aluminium Corporation found the benefits of association with the prestigious Ford Foundation high enough to risk the anger of *Red Channels* and other blacklist supporters.[77] In short, Bernstein's reinstatement on CBS was due to the Ford Foundation's liberality and its guarantee to protect CBS's finances.

The following year, Bernstein, now removed from the CBS blacklist, was invited to perform as a guest conductor with the New York Philharmonic for the 1956–57 season, thus ending the hiatus that had begun at the end of the 1950–51 season. From then on, his ascension was meteoric: he was appointed coprincipal conductor (with Mitropoulos) for the 1957–58 season, and then music director starting in the 1958–59 season. He also received a lucrative, long-term contract to record with Columbia Records.[78] How he was able to return to the Philharmonic needs some discussion.

To begin with, the Philharmonic needed Bernstein. For some years, the orchestra had been slipping into deep financial crisis. By 1955, many critics and board members had concluded that the Philharmonic's decline of fortune was largely the fault of the music director, Dimitri Mitropoulos, a sometimes-brilliant interpreter of works but a supposedly poor disciplinarian whose choice of programs was not drawing audiences.[79] Particularly devastating to Mitropoulos was an essay by *New York Times* critic Harold Taubman on April 29, 1955, taking Mitropoulos to task for failing to maintain discipline and allowing the orchestra to slip into mediocrity.[80] He belittled Mitropoulos's interpretive skills, arguing that whereas the conductor might be a master of the new music—"Strauss, Mahler, Schoenberg . . . Berg," he was not up to the "proportion, delicacy [and] occasional repose" requisite for the performance of "classical and early romantic music." Taubman didn't say so, but the Philharmonic board understood his message quite clearly: a new music director was needed, one who would maintain the highest standards, fill seats in the concert hall, and attract music lovers to the CBS radio and television networks.

The new music director would need to meet certain criteria. Back in April 1952, Arthur Judson had written the board of directors that the Philharmonic needed to attract younger people and therefore had to schedule more performances of new American music as well as modern works and even "semi-classics."[81] None of the heirs apparent to the fading

Mitropoulos—including Bruno Walter, George Szell, and Toscanini's protégé, Guido Cantelli—met the specifications for music director (and Cantelli died in an airplane crash in 1956).[82] The ideal candidate would be a proven master of the one hundred plus master instrumentalists; have American music in his veins and yet be in touch with the standard European classical and romantic repertoire; and have the star glamour that would prompt people in the rising middle classes in the New York City area (where a large percentage were Jewish) to purchase concert tickets.[83] Ultimately, the search led in only one direction: (the now exonerated and rehabilitated) Leonard Bernstein.[84]

But also at stake were the roles of the Philharmonic within New York's international cultural, commercial, and financial positions and in the politics of the Cold War. In 1926, when Toscanini had taken over the New York Philharmonic, New York had already achieved status as a global financial capital, but Americans were nagged by a sense that Europe, though politically and economically tired and aging, maintained cultural preeminence.[85] Toscanini was going to help Americans catch up to the Europeans. By the end of the Second World War and the start of the Cold War, New York's cultural institutions were claiming hegemony, especially in painting, thanks to the domination of the international art world by the New York school of abstract expressionists and the financial and curatorial power of the Museum of Modern Art. Toscanini may have dominated the New York musical world, but by the early 1950s, he was old and would soon retire. New York clearly needed a new conductor with stature approaching that of Toscanini.

Meanwhile, other issues began to give more context to the search for a successor to Toscanini. Members of the Eisenhower administration, arm in arm with the Ford Foundation and other private foundations, were about to export American art to demonstrate to prominent European and Latin American left-wing intellectuals who dominated informed opinion that Americans, not the Soviets, had the verve and moxie to break molds and create afresh in the modern world.[86] Toward this end, the newly inaugurated Eisenhower was about to set in motion the cultural

Cold War with the formation of the United States Information Agency (USIA). Nevertheless, this step, taken in June 1953, as with others taken by the Eisenhower administration, had to be done with great care to avoid arousing the hostility of the congressional inquisitorial forces, many of them isolationist and xenophobic. To placate those forces, Eisenhower had canceled the performance of Copland's *Lincoln Portrait* for the presidential inauguration and Secretary of State Dulles had banned the music of Bernstein, Gershwin, and Copland, among others, from overseas libraries and broadcasts in February. McCarthy, however, was not to be placated and sent his associates Roy Cohn and G. David Schine to Europe to ferret out supposedly radical and communist materials from those overseas libraries. Although its State Department predecessor and the USIA did remove numerous works from its shelves, the Eisenhower administration apparently took some countermeasures, quietly relaxing the ban on Bernstein and the other composers that had been in place since the Truman administration.[87]

In this context of the buildup of the Eisenhower cultural Cold War policy, Nicholas Nabokov, a composer and leading light in the Congress for Cultural Freedom (secretly funded by the Central Intelligence Agency) and head of its creation, the Congrès pour la Liberté de la Culture, invited Bernstein on July 21, 1953, to take part in the international conference Music in the XXth Century in Rome the following April.[88] Organized by the European Center of Culture, which was nominally an independent organization but was secretly funded by foundation money under CIA direction, the conference would bring together musicians and critics to discuss the new music—twelve-tone, pure atonalism, electronic. The discussion there would make plain the contrast between the freedom of musical expression in the West and the narrow orthodoxies imposed upon musicians in the Soviet bloc. To many, including Copland, who was invited and accepted, Nabokov was simply a liberal humanist interested in promoting artistic progress: the CIA connection would emerge only later.[89]

That Bernstein could be removed from the USIA blacklist and invited to Nabokov's conference yet be denied his passport reveals the contradictions and cross-purposes within the Eisenhower administration. The Passport Office was a perfect case of what political scientists called an iron triangle: a symbiotic relationship of an executive branch agency, powerful congressional policy and appropriations committees, and interest groups with stakes in the agency's actions. Executive-branch agencies in such a triangle are more loyal to their congressional and interest-group allies than to the department and organizational hierarchy of which they are nominally and formally a part. The State Department's Passport Office was in such a triangle, sharing political outlook with the archconservative McCarran Senate Internal Security Committee and the vigilante groups that enforced the blacklist. Contending with those agencies and vigilante groups were those organizations, such as the CIA and the Fund for the Republic, involved in the so-called cultural Cold War. The struggles between these groups came to at least a temporary resolution. The vigilante groups that were on the government's list to receive Bernstein's noncommunist affidavit gave him their imprimatur and ensured his rehabilitation, permitting him to compose for Warner Brothers. Saudek's invitation to Bernstein to appear on the CBS–Fund for the Republic television program *Omnibus* virtually completed his rehabilitation.

Thus cleared, Bernstein was ready for affirmative action by the Philharmonic board. He was completely at home with the standard classical and romantic repertoire as well as the sharp and ebullient rhythms of modernists such as Stravinsky and Copland. He was a master of New World idioms. He was glamorous, not only in his own right but in the culture of Cold War 1950s, as a solid family man—husband to Felicia and father of Jamie, born in 1952, and Alexander, just born on July 7, 1955—thereby preempting suspicions that he was a gay man. He was not only cerebral, but he could propagandize for classical music on television, bringing his charisma to this medium of extreme importance to improve the financial fortunes of the hard-pressed Philharmonic. His presence at the podium would increase audience attendance at Carnegie Hall, the newly planned hall at the venue that would be called Lincoln Center, and could have only a salutary effect on audiences attending State Department–sponsored tours of the Philharmonic abroad.[90] In short, whereas Toscanini had decades before legitimated New York's coming of age, Bernstein would now personify New York's ascension to capital of Western culture.

On October 24, 1955, Bernstein went to the United Nations to conduct the Philharmonic in celebration of United Nations Day.[91] On November 18, he received a telegram from Bruno Zirato, the Philharmonic's managing director, informing him that Mitropoulos wanted him to be "engaged as guest conductor" for the 1956–57 season.[92] Bernstein was back at the Philharmonic. Within a year, he would be appointed co-conductor, sharing top duties with Mitropoulos.

This story of Bernstein's rehabilitation from the blacklist had a coda. In March 1956, he was notified that he was about to be investigated by the House Committee on Appropriations chaired by Representative John Rooney, a Democrat from Brooklyn. The issue was Bernstein's appearances with the Symphony of the Air, the new name the network chose for the old NBC Symphony Orchestra after Toscanini retired. CBS had engaged the orchestra for Bernstein's first *Omnibus* program on November 14, 1954. The next year, the orchestra was to tour Asia under the sponsorship of the State Department, and another such trip was scheduled for the Near East in 1956. Bernstein had conducted the orchestra for a number of concerts in Carnegie Hall in 1955, but he was not scheduled to perform with the orchestra on its upcoming trip. Suddenly, Rooney announced that the trip was to be postponed until the matter of a supposed but unnamed communist within the orchestra could be cleared up. Despite assurances that Bernstein was not scheduled to go abroad with the orchestra, Rooney sought to interrogate Bernstein about his politics and those of his associates.[93]

Bernstein was clearly frightened. He had survived years of blacklisting, had escaped HUAC's inquisitors and the publication of his degrading anticommunist affidavit, but now, with *Candide* about to open in December, his career once again faced catastrophe. According to the former managing director of the Symphony of the Air, Jerome Toobin, Bernstein "literally clutched his throat when he talked, and shook his head from side to side, and groaned, 'My God, what a time for this. Oh, what are we going to do, it's so—so, stupid, for Christ sake.' And he wrung his hands, and chain smoked, and thrashed around."

After more of this demonstration of angst, Toobin asked Bernstein to recount the facts of his political past, but

> Bernstein didn't remember half the organizations he was supposed to have joined and had never heard of the other half. He admitted in a calmer moment, with giggles, that in his extreme youth he would join anything if they would put his name in print—Committee for Greek, Polynesian, Eskimo, or Transylvanian Freedom. He remembered letterheads, he told us, that read: "Agranapos, Avanopoulos, Bajoulopoulos, Bernstein, Cachamapoulos . . ." No idea what the outfit really did, but he was a joiner if his name got into print. And he was twenty-two, twenty-three. During the war, when everybody joined everything. This was the grist for Rooney's mill. So Bernstein alternated between angry contempt and hysteria.[94]

Bernstein was in a panic about matters he had thought buried and forgotten and that he was now desperate to disown. Granted that he had signed any number of petitions and subscriptions for funds years before and granted that, as the evidence shows, he had deliberated about many a call for support and passionately advanced his progressive position in correspondence and in speeches in those heady pre-repressive years, the casual addition of his name to a suggested cause seemed the thing to do; the matter was largely unproblematic.

In any event, Bernstein never had to appear before the Rooney committee because, according to his biographer Humphrey Burton, Bernstein's friend Senator John F. Kennedy intervened on Bernstein's behalf and persuaded Rooney to call off the investigation.[95] Bernstein was off the hook, ready to make his ascent to the podium of the New York Philharmonic.

Nevertheless, the FBI not only maintained Bernstein's dossier but also for years hoped to find evidence of his membership in the Communist Party to have him indicted for perjury—all to no avail.[96] Not only were the blacklisters a vulgar lot to people such as Robert Saudek; they were an acute embarrassment to the cultural Cold War liberal who had to explain them away. In short, the Bernstein case pitted the cultural Cold War, CIA, and State Department forces against the blacklist, FBI, HUAC, and McCarthyite forces. The former won, and the FBI and congressional investigators found themselves increasingly marginalized.[97]

.   .   .

By 1956, his blacklist days apparently over, Bernstein teamed with Lillian Hellman to adapt Voltaire's *Candide* to the musical theater, an idea she had first broached to him in 1950. Hellman by and large followed Voltaire's narrative, but she added material to give the work a radical tint—for example, depicting a cash nexus between Pangloss and his young female consorts, giving new weight to the Inquisition scene and darkening Candide's mood at the conclusion of the work. Bernstein's score was among his finest achievements, giving musical expression to the Voltairian satires and *burlesqueries* as well as to moments more reflective and sentimental. Hellman etched each of the characters sharply, depicting Candide's development from simple oaf to introspective sufferer, Cunegonda's vapidity, Pangloss's Leibnizian simple-minded optimism, and the old lady's ribaldry.

Hellman, having survived her moment before HUAC, was out to use the Lisbon earthquake and Inquisition scene to lampoon the Red Scare witch hunt. Pangloss informs Candide that the Inquisitors are "a group of wise men who settle public problems with justice for all," but justice is purely summary.[98] Candide is arrested for carrying "earthquake germs," brought to the Inquisition, and pronounced guilty.[99] The prosecutor intervenes, insists that the Inquisition "observe certain legal, civil, and moral law as written into the code of Western Liberalism," and then turns to Candide to inform him that it will be "death by hanging."[100] Pangloss is condemned for being "a foreigner," "a bore," and "a German scientist."[101]

Hellman's lines were spoken; Bernstein did not set them to music. Nevertheless, Bernstein went out on a limb by agreeing to let the show open with this satirical mockery of the witch-hunt committees. The scene was probably as much as could be staged in those repressive days.

*Candide* was essentially an operetta—by Bernstein's definition, a theatrical work set in an "exotic" place with nonvernacular speech and lyrics—and thus was a great departure from Bernstein's American program.[102] All in all, its great verve, dynamism and brilliance, finely wrought characterizations, and comedic ambience did not fit the interests of the Broadway public of 1956, and the show closed after only seventy-three performances.[103]

On December 13, 1956, twelve days before *Candide* opened, Bernstein had made his return as guest conductor to the Philharmonic for the first time since February 1951. His concerts through January 6, 1957, were devoid of American music: he conducted performances of Beethoven, Cherubini, Handel, Hindemuth, Mozart, Ravel, and Tchaikovsky. In his second stint, from January 20 to January 30, American music made its appearance in his program with Roy Harris's Symphony no. 3, but otherwise his repertoire remained European: Beethoven, Prokofiev, Stravinsky, and Vivaldi. But on January 27, 1957, he led a performance for broadcast on CBS that included, along with the Harris work, his "Suite" from *Candide*.

Bernstein's contract with Columbia Records was reaching its first fruit with recordings of Handel on December 31, 1956; Prokofiev with Isaac Stern on January 21; and the Beethoven Concerto no. 2 scheduled for studio performance with Gould in April.[104] He was back in business, his conducting career in the ascension, as if the years of repression had never happened.

## TRIUMPH

Already the machinery to recreate Bernstein as mythic culture hero had begun its work. Here was a democratic celebrity wonderfully fit for the image of the romantic maestro-hero-sufferer—Lenny, the commoner, whose most mundane activities would become newsworthy for the charisma-creating media. And who better to create the new image of culture hero than the press that had nearly destroyed his reputation just a few years before? On January 7, 1957, in the midst of his Philharmonic run, *Life* ran a story of Bernstein relaxing at home after a day's work at the podium, offering the headline, "Busy Time for a Young Maestro." Bernstein's canonization came a few weeks later, on February 4, when *Time* ran a story entitled "Wunderkind," mentioning his family life and his career but nothing about his blacklist and passport woes. Apotheosis was assured by his image on *Time*'s cover, not photographed but painted, for if a photo is a fugitive image, a painting suggests membership in an enduring pantheon of larger-than-life transcendent beings.

Even before his work on *Candide,* Bernstein had collaborated with Robbins, Arthur Laurents, and Stephen Sondheim to compose a musical based on Shakespeare's *Romeo and Juliet. West Side Story* opened on August 20, 1957, in Washington and on September 26 at the Winter Garden on Broadway.

Bernstein had long sought to create a new American musical theater, announcing plans for such a venture as far back as 1948 with his proposal for an American opera. In his lecture "You, the Public," which he delivered at Brandeis University on May 13, 1952, he had argued that the public, any public, has a general sensibility that develops within its historical and cultural matrix. The American public's sensibilities would grow out of its theatrical traditions. From the more important works of the American musical stage—he named *Oklahoma!, Finian's Rainbow, Pal Joey,* and *On the Town*—a new form of opera would emerge. He alluded to his own new work at the time, *Trouble in Tahiti,* suggesting that it was a harbinger of the new genre, a smaller work that did not make demands on Americans who, after all, did not live in "a contemplative society." Americans would not necessarily shy away from "difficult composers" provided that the works, such as *Wozzeck* or *Survivor from Warsaw,* were theatrical, or, like Alex North's score for the film adaptation of *A Streetcar Named Desire,* accompanied or provided incidental music for dance or film.[105]

He advanced this theme of correlative development of the intellectual and aesthetic sensibilities of his audiences and the search for new forms of musical-theatrical expression in his essay of November 1954, "What Ever Happened to That Great American Symphony?" He maintained that this sanctified form was dying if not dead but predicted that something new would rise in its place.[106] In the third of his *Omnibus* essays, "American Musical Comedy," broadcast on October 7, 1956, Bernstein called for work that would fuse the American vernacular art forms, such as ballet and modern dance, speech and recitative, with "extended musical sequences, counterpoint, [and] orchestration."[107] The emergent musical theater would occupy a new place along the spectrum from revue to musical comedy, operetta, and grand opera, combining elements of each yet no longer adhering to any one of these models.[108]

*West Side Story* seemed to fit this bill. Bernstein was out to put his Latin and jazz rhythmic sensibility and his lyrical imagination to work to create a very urban American score. The blues flavor that he had developed in his score for *On the Waterfront* signaled tragic foreboding in this later work, providing background to balance the comedic scenes. The alternation of street-gang vernacular and idiom combining wisecracking and physical mayhem; the Puerto Rican young women singing of the great contradictions in American society; the euphoria and then desperation of the star-crossed and doomed lovers: all of these elements combined with Robbins's large-movement choreography to raise the level of American theater.

In this regard, Bernstein's projects—the *Omnibus* programs, Young People's Concerts, public lectures, *West Side Story*—disparate as they were, were nevertheless of a piece: in all these cases, he took his audiences seriously, encouraging them to broaden their sensibilities. In his inaugural Young People's Concert, "What Does Music Mean?" of January 18, 1958, Bernstein talked to the children but not down to them, appealing to their budding precocity, drawing out their interests, demonstrating by gesture and intonation that music was something important that they ought to consider seriously. No doubt some of the children were unable to concentrate on the music, but their presence with their eager parents and with other children could only tell them that they were participating in something important. And then they took in the aural and visual spectacle in front of them, hearing Bernstein address them and then hearing the Philharmonic players respond to his gestures, their instruments flooding Carnegie Hall with brilliant orchestral sound. By offering these experiences, Bernstein meant to raise their intellectual and aesthetic faculties.

Bernstein was going to use his return to the Philharmonic to fulfill the charge he had received from the board, which echoed a charge he had given himself years before: to give public expression to his American contemporaries. He chose, however, to inaugurate his position as co-director on January 2, 1958, with a celebration of his November 14, 1943, program, scheduling Robert Schumann's *Manfred Overture* and Richard Strauss's *Don Quixote* in addition to Ravel's *La Valse* and the U.S. premiere of Shostakovich's Piano Concerto no. 2 with himself at the piano. On January 9, however, he honored his old friend David Diamond with a performance of the Symphony no. 4.

He continued to champion American music the following season. On October 2, 1958, his first as sole musical director of the New York Philharmonic, he programmed, in addition to Beethoven's Symphony no. 7, two American works: Charles Ives's Symphony no. 2 and William Schuman's *American Festival Overture*. In later performances that month, he programmed works by John Becker, George Chadwick, Arthur Foote, Henry Gilbert, Edward McDowell, Wallingford Riegger, and Carl Ruggles. (Bernstein's placement of Riegger on the program may have been particularly delicious to him: Riegger had recently been under attack by the House Un-American Activities Committee).[109]

On May 8, 1959, the now solidly established Bernstein was among the celebrities invited to appear at a televised party for former President Truman's seventy-fifth birthday.[110] On May 14, Bernstein officially greeted President Eisenhower at the corner of 64th Street and Broadway to break ground for Lincoln Center, to signal New York's ascension to the world's culture capital and to accentuate the United States' pronounced role as international cultural benefactor.

In August, Bernstein, now a veritable cultural ambassador for the president's Special Fund for Cultural Exchange, conducted the Philharmonic on a long tour of Europe and in a number of performances in Moscow, Leningrad, and Kiev. His ten days in the Soviet Union were enormously successful, with audiences adulating the American maestro and the Philharmonic musicians. These days had great significance for Bernstein, not least because his father, Sam, reunited with a brother not seen for decades. Bernstein bearded the Soviet cultural officialdom by seeking out and meeting Boris Pasternak, the poet and author of *Dr. Zhivago,* now in near ostracism for embarrassing the Soviet authorities by receiving the Nobel Prize (which he gave back). Bernstein also created another flap. He had expected to scandalize the authorities by programming the émigré Stravinsky and the modernist Ives; but when he broke orthodoxy by discussing the music at the rostrum before beginning the performance, his effrontery was too much for the minister of culture, whose audible protests at Bernstein's mention of Stravinsky and Ives could be heard through Bernstein's address. Most critical reviews were glowing, but Bernstein was irritated by a review that criticized his repeat of Ives's *Unanswered Question* (a very short work of rather purposefully ambiguous tonality). As he told the National Press Club in Washington on October 13, 1959, he responded with a "boiling mad statement about it to the press." But Bernstein was no simple anti-Soviet Cold Warrior: standing at the Press Club lectern, he launched into a criticism of the American press, telling his audience of an incident that he called "a real shocker." During the Russian tour, Bernstein had assented to a request by the minister of culture to perform outdoors or in a sports stadium seating one hundred thousand people. Unfortunately, the bitterly cold temperatures forced the authorities to move the concert indoors, to a much smaller hall. The American press (Bernstein did not mention a particular publication) gave this report a distorted, anti-Soviet twist, making no mention of the freezing weather and claiming instead that Soviet officials, supposedly upset with "the crowd appeal inherent in the dynamic conductor's podium acrobatics . . . refused Bernstein's plea to play one or more concerts for the massed thousands who could be accommodated in either the 10,000 [*sic*] Sports Palace or one of the city's parks." Bernstein told his audience that he was "filled with shame" by this report in the American press and asked his audience to remember their "almost sacred" responsibility to the truth.[111]

Bernstein thus came out of the McCarthyite decade scarred but triumphant. His left-wing politics, forged in the days of New Deal progressivism and the alliance with the Russians against the Nazis, had plunged him into years of fear, if not terror. He had seen his friends and associates called before the McCarthy and House Un-American Activities Committees, the ethos of which required betrayals, humiliations, degradation, and recriminations. Some of the witnesses he had known had died. He himself had been forced to sign his confessional affidavit so that he could retrieve his passport and continue to conduct. He had thus betrayed his past and his most cherished political values. He had distanced himself from a man he admired, Paul Robeson. And the document had circulated within the networks of the people he most despised, the far right-wing vigilante groups whose imprimatur guaranteed his removal from the blacklist.

If Bernstein's FBI dossier and *Red Channels* record did not differ much from those of many artists in the period,[112] Bernstein's case was unique in the speed of his rehabilitation: in the course of a few years, while McCarthyism was still raging, he not only came off the ban but did so spectacularly, taking over the New York Philharmonic, appearing on CBS, obtaining a new, long-term contract with Columbia Records, going on tour with the Philharmonic, and in so many other ways achieving extraordinary success—with the terrible experience of blacklisting, the passport affidavit, and other humiliations kept secret from the public or forgotten altogether.

The affidavit seems to have opened the door to his removal from the blacklist, but his ultimate rehabilitation resulted from a confluence of efforts by foundation heads, educational reformers interested in upgrading domestic American cultural life, and federal government officials seeking to export a vision of America as a liberal-democratic civilization to bring intellectuals and artists to their side in Cold War struggles for cultural hegemony. Concert-hall enthusiasts, publicists, civil libertarians, establishment liberals, and national security managers needed Bernstein at the podium in New York, on national television, and as American cultural ambassador abroad. And as much as he was the Philharmonic's musical director, he was also a vernacular hero: where New Yorkers had held Toscanini in awe, Bernstein was "our Lenny." Any scar tissue that remained from his years of terror was hidden from public view, and maybe from himself, at least for the moment.

# CHAPTER FOUR

# The Long Sixties

## *1960–1973*

At the top of Bernstein's January 1960 agenda was the Philharmonic's celebration of the Gustav Mahler centennial.[1] Although he was to share the Mahler symphonic cycle over the next seasons with Barbirolli, Mitropoulos, Solti, Steinberg, and Walter, he had signed a contract with Columbia Records to record the nine Mahler symphonies, the first such endeavor. His apotheosis continued apace: Columbia Records was about to unveil its "New Bernstein Look" in June, and *West Side Story* was scheduled to open for another run in April.[2] He was on top of the world.

Bernstein had other exciting news: his friend John F. Kennedy was preparing to enter the race for the Democratic nomination for the presidency. Democratic victories in the 1958 congressional elections had raised the possibility of a left-liberal if not progressive revival, and in anticipation of further victory, a number of congressional Democrats were welcoming the prospect of shifting moneys from military arms procurement to programs that would alleviate poverty, bolster education, and support the arts. The success of this agenda depended on the outcome of the 1960 presidential race, but one great stumbling block to a Democratic victory was the decision by Adlai Stevenson to seek a third nomination for the presidency. Stevenson, the intellectual's hope in 1952 and 1956, remained the sentimental favorite in 1960, but every indication was that he would lose for a third time, leaving the nation in the hands of the Republican nominee, Richard Nixon. The liberal Democratic senator Hubert Humphrey seemed therefore a better choice for the nomination. But Kennedy, the otherwise insignificant junior senator from Massachusetts, had begun to catch fire, impressing listeners with a level of intelligence and rhetorical gift that raised political discourse above the banality of the Eisenhower age. And when Kennedy, having achieved the nomination, telephoned Martin Luther King's wife, Coretta, to give his support to King, then imprisoned and awaiting trial for resisting racist laws, the revival seemed even more real.[3]

Kennedy was suddenly the man of the hour, not least for Norman Mailer, whose widely discussed *Esquire* essay, "Superman Comes to the Supermarket," seemed to capture the hopeful mood of many on the Left. Kennedy, wrote Mailer, would revive the American people's historic adventurousness and verve, which had long been submerged by the "excessive hysteria of the Red wave."[4] Kennedy's invitation to Robert Frost to read his poetry at the inaugural ceremony was impressive; more so was Kennedy's inaugural speech, which called on Americans to serve an overarching public interest and identified poverty, illiteracy, racism, and war as social ills needing remedy. His ascendance to the presidency seemed a resurrection of the idealism lost when FDR died in April 1944—underscored when Kennedy asked the chronicler of the New Deal, Arthur Schlesinger Jr., to chronicle the New Frontier. John Kenneth Galbraith and other old New Dealers rushed to Washington as if coming out from the cold. In short order, the Kennedys were recognizing writers and artists as national treasures and inviting them to White House functions. Kennedy's vitality, combined with his knack for delivering self-deprecatory comments with enormous wit and self-confidence, made him extraordinarily popular with many intellectuals and artists: he recognized them, listened to them, and thus lifted them from their Eisenhower-age impotence into his own realm of charm, glamour, and power.

Bernstein, who had been invited by master of ceremonies Frank Sinatra to perform a fanfare of his own at the Kennedy Inaugural Eve ball on

January 19, 1961, was certainly lifted into that auratic realm. Of course, he was one of New York's great celebrities. (I remember the adulation of the audience celebrating Bernstein at "A Valentine's Day for Lenny" on February 13.) But he was now in for bigger things. Bernstein's intimacy with the Kennedys was televised for all to see at the inaugural of Lincoln Center and the first performance at Philharmonic (later to be renamed Avery Fisher) Hall on September 23. The festivities were in form similar to those of the 1959 ground-breaking ceremonies. Bernstein began them by leading the Philharmonic in the *Star-Spangled Banner.* John D. Rockefeller III thanked those from the arts, education, philanthropy, business, labor, and government who had contributed to the venture, and Bernstein and the Philharmonic performed Copland's *Connotations for Orchestra,* the "Gloria" from Beethoven's *Missa Solemnis,* and the second movement of the Mahler 8th Symphony. Then came the pressing of flesh—not, as in 1958, Bernstein's shake of the president's hand, but this time kisses: one for Felicia and one for Jacqueline Kennedy. His kiss on the first lady's cheek scandalized many but signaled that Bernstein was more than just another courtier in Camelot. Confirmation of his insider status came on November 16, when Jacqueline Kennedy not only invited him and Felicia to attend a performance by Pablo Casals at a reception for José Luis Alberto Muñoz Marín, the governor of Puerto Rico, but also asked them to return the next day and stay for dinner. The Bernsteins received a similar invitation from the Kennedys in January 1962 to attend a White House reception for Igor Stravinsky.[5]

These were heady days indeed: the American moral climate was changing. The Hollywood and radio and television blacklist era had just come to an end.[6] A new latitudinarianism was spreading across the arts: the return of Dada and surrealism and the emergence of pop art; the music of Boulez, Stockhausen, and John Cage; the hilarious cynicism of Joseph Heller's absurdist *Catch 22;* the immediate popularity of the first of the James Bond films, *Dr. No* (1962), which parodied the panoply of secret agents and deployable weapons of mass destruction. All these media found ready audiences desperate to break from the rigidities of the 1950s.

Many were joining what Stanley Kaufmann coined the Film Generation: the mass coterie of filmmakers and their audiences who were interested in experimental techniques that sought to explore existential and ethical questions and thus in artworks that no longer served the stupefactions of culture-industrial entertainment.[7] Kennedy's victory thus seemed to usher in waves of cultural expression that would work their way through moral and political life as well.

## KADDISH

Bernstein was finding in this liberating moment the inspiration to compose a work of larger political significance. During the summer of 1961, he began work on a symphonic setting of the Kaddish, the Hebrew and Aramaic chant that glorifies God and conventionally memorializes the dead.[8] On the surface, the work is fundamentally religious, concerned with faith lost and faith rediscovered. In Bernstein's hands, however, the prayer and the texts that he wrote for the work took on a radically different significance, expressing themes of anger with a God who has allowed his creatures to unleash genocidal and nuclear murder, but also a theme of reconciliation; in turn, the work demystified God, calling instead to the collective human spirit now energized through a Kennedy-led rebirth of American progressive liberalism.

The work has been less well-received than most of Bernstein's output, with critics thinking it superficial or worse and calling it an embarrassing display of Bernstein's indulging his ego with an overly theatrical, stentorian-voiced, and gushingly sentimental oedipal moment between Lenny and Sam/God. In truth, Bernstein devoted a lot of time to working out the themes and the social theory behind them; when the work is understood within its period—the coincidence of a religious-humanistic revival led by Pope John XXIII with a new embrace of secular humanism—it takes on a much different meaning.

More than likely, Bernstein was relying upon his father's immersion in the mystical Jewish tradition, drawing on the idea that not only are God's plans to be completed by humankind, but God and man are in intersubjective dialogue—in the I-Thou relationship described by the Jewish mystic Martin Buber, the fullest expression of God on earth. Behind Buber's thought was the radical suggestion by the nineteenth-century German philosopher Ludwig Feuerbach that human beings, living in mutual alienation and distrust and thus unendingly frustrated in their craving for mutual love, mercy, and justice, reify these latter traits into the predicates or qualities of a God to whom they now pray to deliver these gifts to them. But once men and women come to understand that "God" is only a name for this missing collective, humanity itself, they will find the means to create a society of love, mercy, and justice. In short, theology is transformed into political sociology. This is the fundamental idea that underlies Bernstein's *Kaddish*.

The work begins with a speaker invoking God tenderly as a father rejected and despised by his own children. Lest one think this Kaddish is for God, however, the Speaker quickly announces that the Kaddish is for herself (as in the original text; the 1977 revised text permits *herself* or *himself*) because death could come at any moment.[9] In the next section, *Kaddish* I (Invocation), the chorus sings the text of the Hebrew Kaddish in a syncopated chant above highly percussive music; this discordant and hair-raising episode reaches cacophony only to be stopped in its tracks with a burst of the Speaker's "Amen," yelled at top volume, and a call to God to bring order to this chaos. The second movement, "Din-Torah" would normally be God's judgment, but in Bernstein's version, God is judged.[10] With the chorus humming behind him, the Speaker, who is humankind's inner voice, addresses God with "a certain respectful fury" and accuses him of allowing men to run wild, armed "with new-found fire, avid for death"—an allusion to the World War II firebombing of cities and the unleashing of the atomic bomb on Hiroshima. God needs to be held accountable. The Speaker cries to a God who has betrayed humankind, "You with your manna, your pillar of fire! . . . Your covenant!" With sneering irony, the Speaker indicts him as "a tin God!" Calming suddenly, the Speaker apologizes to God for having hurt him.

He would even hold the old man against his own strong body and "rock [him] into sleep."

*Kaddish* II, sung by soprano and boys' choir, is followed by the Speaker lulling God to sleep, there to dream. The third movement, Scherzo, begins with the Speaker virtually telling God a bedtime fantasy. Imagine, dear God, your heaven as promised, an idyllic place where "Lambs frisk. Wheat ripples. Sunbeams dance." But, admonishes the Speaker, your heaven does not exist; it does not reflect reality, its rage and its pain. In an interesting turn, the Speaker tells his creation, God, of a promise, a covenant with humankind ("My promise, my covenant!")—that humankind come to believe in itself and thus restore that long-dormant collective sensibility. Thus, humankind, not God, is the subject of this Kaddish: "*magnified . . . and sanctified . . . be the great name of man.*" And as the Speaker asks man/God to "Believe! Believe!" Bernstein paraphrases Copland, bringing in a reminder of the opening theme in *Appalachian Spring,* that quintessential late–New Deal work that Martha Graham had set to dance in 1944, a work of a progressive egalitarianism itself long dormant but now, in 1962, able to awaken and come alive. The chorus sings the Kaddish prayer, but again, humankind is the hallowed force. The Speaker pleads with God— that is (through a Feuerbachian transformation), with humankind—to believe in himself/yourself, and "you shall see the Kingdom of Heaven / On Earth, just as you planned." The music continues with playful varia- tions on the Copland-like theme, with the Kaddish sung by the boys' choir. Over music that is somber yet serene, the Speaker announces the return to the present reality. "The dawn is chilly; but the dawn *has* come" for a new reconciliation between God and man. The Copland reference returns, its passages a leitmotif for renewal of the populist-progressive dream. The work that had begun with atonality arrives at a tonal conclusion, in which soprano, boys' choir, and chorus sing the Kaddish, thus reinforcing the idea that the present social context and structure can be transformed, reformed, and revolutionized into a new trajectory.

*Kaddish* was a theatrical work billed as a symphony, a product of Bern- stein's search for a form that would cross through symphonic, operatic, and Broadway genres to express social and political ideas fit for the coming age. That Bernstein was in search of a method by which to compose socially provocative theatrical work was apparent when, in September 1962, he teamed up with Betty Comden and Adolph Green to work up a "Brechtian/Pirandello" dramaturgy for a musical adaptation of Thornton Wilder's *The Skin of Our Teeth*. Wilder had satirized middle-class foibles, trivialities, and shallow emptiness by zeroing in on the lives of the Antrobus family—husband, wife, daughter, son, and maid—who survive the Ice Age, the Flood, and the Napoleonic Wars in their comfortable suburban New Jersey home. All seems perfectly apolitical American Biedermeier, at least until the last scene, when the son, who has grown into a sullen menace, is ready to attack his father, if not the whole of humanity. Mr. Antrobus now comes to see the shallowness in his own life as the contributing factor to his son's murderous inclinations (writ large, loss of faith, contributing to war and genocide). Bernstein had hoped to use the Brechtian dramaturgical device in which the actors step out of their personae and draw the audience into questioning whether the play, or for that matter the human race, can go on.[11] Unfortunately, his collaboration with Comden and Green fell apart.

On October 11, the international spirit of reconciliation that had been on the rise since the turn of the 1960s received a great boost when Pope John XXIII opened the Second Vatican Council with an ecumenical program meant to unite Catholics, Protestant and Orthodox Christians, Jews, and others of non-Christian faiths while recognizing their differences.[12] That new spirit was consonant with a developing thaw in the relations between the superpowers, but in late October, with the onset of the Cuban missile crisis, thaw turned into freeze. The weeklong sense of apocalyptic gloom that ended with an agreement between Kennedy and Khrushchev only made all parties eager for even greater reconciliation and rapprochement. This spirit seemed to survive the sudden death of John XXIII on June 3 and that most traumatic of events, Kennedy's assassination on November 22. Jacqueline Kennedy asked Bernstein to perform at the funeral ceremony, and he chose Mahler's Second

Symphony, *Resurrection*. He now dedicated his *Kaddish* Symphony to Kennedy's memory.

Whether by a program of reform or by a revolution in style, John XXIII and John Kennedy had contributed to the opening of private and public spaces that had been closed down by their various predecessors since the late 1940s. This new generation's confidence in its ability to open its cultural and ethical sensibilities only grew throughout 1964. The economy was at full employment, and with passage of the Civil Rights Act, the 24th Amendment declaring the poll tax unconstitutional, and the omnibus War on Poverty, the nation seemed committed to its grand egalitarian ideals. Coupled with the commitment to thaw out U.S.-Soviet relations, these actions seemed proof positive that Kennedy's successor, Lyndon Johnson, was fulfilling progressive hopes for a New Frontier and a Great Society.

Certainly, Bernstein and other members of his generation believed that their days on the sidelines of American politics were over. Lincoln Center had become a collective temple of artistic reconciliation where the once-blacklisted Bernstein was now honored—with Rudolf Bing, head of the Metropolitan Opera; and George Balanchine, head of the New York City Ballet—as one of the triumvirate resident powers, and Arthur Miller, like Bernstein dubbed a "communist dupe" by *Life* magazine in 1949 (see chapter 3), now had pride of place at the Vivian Beaumont Theater.[13]

Bernstein basked in his celebrity status: he had taken a sabbatical from conducting the 1964–65 season and at its end, had composed a report in verse form informing readers of the *New York Times* of his activities away from the podium.[14] Most important of these extracurricular endeavors was his new composition, *Chichester Psalms,* a work that captured that moment of national prosperity and international reconciliation. Sung in Hebrew, the work is a hymn to ageless humanity's yearning for peace of mind and peace among nations. The first of three parts begins with a *maestoso ma energico,* majestic and energetic, syncopated, percussively driven introduction music that does "arouse the dawn" (Psalm 108) and then, with chorus, leaps in "joyful noise" (Psalm 100). Part II consists of Bernstein's ethereal setting to Psalm 23:1–6 that is interrupted by an *allegro feroce* outburst for

the setting of "Why do the nations rage?" (Psalm 2:1–4) before returning to quiet with a setting for "Thou preparest a table before me," the
remainder of Psalm 23. Part III begins with a searing prelude to the setting for Psalm 131, a reflective moment for a soul—be it an individual's
or a nation's—that has emerged from torment into calm. This section
opens with a men's chorus, which is then joined by a women's chorus
before strings take over the conversation, the music ever rising until the
concluding words from Psalm 133:1, "Behold how good / And how pleas-
ant it is, / for brethren to dwell / Together in unity." A universal "Amen,"
sung in hushed tones and followed by the orchestra, with music dying
away, brings the work to conclusion.

## ETHICS AND POLITICS: TAKING A STAND

In 1965, the forty-seven-year-old Bernstein was thoroughly established,
his pariah years long forgotten: the only controversy he now generated
concerned his extrovert podium manner, reviled by those who expected
conductors to avoid exhibitionism, beloved by those excited by his irre-
pressible urge to communicate with the orchestra and the audience. And
yet, like many other long-quiet progressives and liberals, Bernstein soon
reentered the political arena, joining the civil rights and antiwar movements and taking on increasingly dissident positions on the nature and
exercise of American power.

The way back was not easy: many of Bernstein's generation were still
traumatized by the betrayals, degradations, and humiliations wrought by
the congressional inquisitions of the 1950s. Livelihoods and careers had
been endangered if not ruined; some of the people targeted during the
period had fled into exile, some were imprisoned, and some had died
prematurely. If so many had retreated from political life, however, they
were now led back in by the younger generation, born in the 1930s or early
1940s. This new generation was minting new expressive forms to expose
and demolish the repressive aesthetic and moral shibboleths and pieties
that had dominated the Biedermeier years of their youth. Their mode of

radicalism was irony, whether through the Beatles' or pop artists' mockery of convention or through absurdism and nihilism, such as Samuel Beckett's work, the mounting of "happenings," or the purposive artificiality of the "camp" sensibility. Joining them were theologians in the "God is dead" movement. Together, these radicals formed a new front, a swarming public whose combined work was to subvert authority in field after field and thereby provide the older progressive generation with the confidence to recover their long-suppressed voice. Bernstein was of an older generation, largely unsympathetic with the new one's artistic interests and the ongoing reexamination of aesthetic values. But precisely as the old values were broken by this new generation, so was crumbling the edifice of American Biedermeier morality that had dominated the first postwar decades.

Replacing the moralizing of the 1950s was an emphasis on conscience and choice, an ethical dimension opposed to single-minded conformity to ritual and dogma. How should one act within extreme conditions? Under what conditions might one properly invoke a "higher law" to justify disobedience to law? What are the psychological and cultural sources of the authoritarian personality and the willingness to commit genocide?

Required reading in those days included the works of Kierkegaard, Nietzsche, Freud, Sartre, and Camus. Exemplary figures included the French Resistance leader Jean Moulin, who died rather than give information to his Nazi torturers, and the German Lutheran pastor Dietrich Bonhoeffer, who not only refused to take an "inner migration" from the events about him but joined a plot against Hitler, for which he was hanged.[15] This age gave top priority to ethical convictions and action and set standards for confronting immoral if not hideous governmental power. Such questions of morality were the burning issues for the generation that had come of age in the postwar years, and these questions took on more urgency from the mid-1950s on as King and the civil rights movement set out to produce crises of conscience within the American public.

The capture of the Nazi Adolph Eichmann by the Israelis in 1961 and his trial the following year incited these moral passions. Bernstein had been particularly interested in Hannah Arendt's discussions of the

Dimitri Mitropoulos, "To Mr. Leonard Bernstein very sympathetically and with all
my wishes for his artistic future. Boston, 23.1.1937." Photographer unknown. Courtesy
of the Leonard Bernstein Collection, Library of Congress.

David Prall, Bernstein's aesthetics professor and mentor. Photographer unknown.
Courtesy of the Leonard Bernstein Collection, Library of Congress.

Aaron Copland, Leonard Bernstein, and Serge Koussevitzky, Tanglewood, 1941.
Photograph by Ruth Orkin. Courtesy of Hulton Archive and Getty Images.

Bernstein with, left to right, Sam Barlow, Paul Robeson, and Muriel Smith, at a benefit for the Anti-Fascist Refugee Committee, May 1944, Boston Opera House. Photographer unknown. Courtesy of the Leonard Bernstein Collection, Library of Congress.

TWENTY CENTS

FEBRUARY 4, 1957

# TIME

## THE WEEKLY NEWSMAGAZINE

CONDUCTOR
LEONARD
BERNSTEIN

Henry Koerner

$6.00 A YEAR

(REG. U.S. PAT. OFF.)

VOL. LXIX NO. 5

Apotheosis: Bernstein on the cover of *Time,* February 4, 1957. Courtesy of Time-Life Pictures and Getty Images.

Crowd for the ground-breaking celebration for Symphony Hall, Lincoln Center, May 14, 1959. Photograph by Al Fenn. Courtesy of Time-Life Pictures and Getty Images.

Bernstein addressing the National Press Club luncheon of October 13, 1959. Unknown photographer. Courtesy of the Leonard Bernstein Collection, Library of Congress.

On top of the world: Leonard Bernstein, George Balanchine, and Rudolf Bing at Lincoln Center, 1966. Photographer: Michael Rougier. Courtesy of Time-Life Pictures and Getty Images.

Bernstein addressing the March 14–15, 1969, Moratorium March. Courtesy of Michael Ochs Archives and Getty Images.

Bernstein leading the New York Philharmonic and the Westminster Symphonic Choir with mezzo-soprano Christa Ludwig and soprano Barbara Hendricks in a performance of Mahler's 2nd Symphony, Avery Fisher Hall, 1987. Courtesy of Westminster Choir College of Rider University.

Eichmann case.[16] Arendt concluded that Eichmann, the Nazi administrator in charge of rounding up and transporting European Jews to the death camps, was no alienated mass man as regnant sociological and psychoanalytic theories (including the one she fostered in *Origins of Totalitarianism* in 1950) suggested. The evil he had committed was rooted in his decision to suspend his faculties of ethical and critical judgment. Eichmann, she argued, was not an example of an incarnate evil; he was a prime example of the banality of evil.

In 1964, the debates on moral action, complicity, and guilt occasioned by Arendt's *Eichmann in Jerusalem* deepened as the result of two works, one by Arthur Miller, *Incident at Vichy,* and another, in the form of a *théâtre verité* by Rolf Hochhuth, *The Deputy*. Miller's play is about a person who substitutes for another about to be victimized by the Nazis. Hochhuth's play sought to expose fully the pope's collapse as moral agent by his refusal to denounce the Nazi transportation of Jews to the death camps, not only across Europe but also from Rome itself.[17] *The Deputy* unleashed a great debate about the role of the church both as universal moral agent and as institution under duress; both Hochhuth's and Miller's dramas raised the great ethical and existential questions about how an individual should respond to tyranny and brutality.

## BERNSTEIN AND THE SELMA MARCH

These issues and debates took place against the backdrop of the civil rights movement in the deep American south. In the wake of the murders of activists James Earl Chaney, Andrew Goodman, and Michael Schwerner of the Student Nonviolent Coordinating Committee in Mississippi on June 21, 1964, during the so-called Freedom Summer, Martin Luther King and other leaders of the Southern Christian Leadership Conference decided to push for a march from Selma to Montgomery, Alabama's capital, presided over by Governor George Wallace, in early 1965. King charged Harry Belafonte with organizing a group of celebrities and notables to give support to the marchers, and Belafonte invited Bernstein, who agreed to attend.[18]

Bernstein's appearance was not simply a form of "radical chic," as journalist Tom Wolfe later suggested in coining the mean-spirited term in a later context, for his presence on the stage put him in danger of a sniper attack. Indeed, King and the march organizers had been under threat of brutality, assassination, and police murder: only a few weeks before, on February 14, 1965, a state trooper in Marion, Alabama, had shot a young black man, Jimmie Lee Jackson, who was protecting his mother during a police melee directed against blacks attempting to register to vote. Jackson died a few days later. On March 7, which would soon be dubbed "Bloody Sunday," Alabama state troopers teargassed and clubbed a line of marchers, an event that was broadcast across the nation, with ABC breaking into a showing of *Judgment at Nuremberg* to offer a living example of state terrorism. Not only was King living under death threats, but the FBI was maintaining an aggressive passivity about attempts upon his life.[19] In fact, the FBI was even attempting to instigate King's demise. In January 1965, Coretta King had discovered a note sent to her husband, written as if it were from a black person, suggesting that he could avoid publication of surreptitiously recorded audiotapes exposing his sexual transgressions and damaging the civil rights movement if he were to commit suicide.[20] (King and his associates, who could expect only hostility from J. Edgar Hoover, kept the matter to themselves.) On March 9, a gang of whites beat to death the Rev. James J. Reeb, a white minister from Boston, in Selma; and on March 16, Montgomery officers viciously attacked black demonstrators. King and the planners of the march to the Alabama state capitol may have gained some optimism from Johnson's speech of the evening before, March 15, in which the president, in perhaps his finest hour, echoed King's "Letter from Birmingham Jail," but the threat of violence nevertheless remained.

The fifty-four-mile march began on March 21, with a federal judge taking cognizance of police brutality, the president ordering a federalized unit of the Alabama National Guard to protect the marchers, and world news media paying close attention. Bernstein flew to Montgomery on March 24 to participate in the salute to the wet, foot-sore, exhausted, and wearied marchers as they arrived at the City of St. Jude Hospital on the outskirts of Montgomery. "I just wanted to come down to be with you," Bernstein told them.[21] The next morning, March 25, he was one of twenty-five thousand marchers who walked the last miles to the state capitol. What happiness the marchers may have felt at that moment would be marred with the news that another marcher, a civil rights worker from Detroit, Viola Gregg Liuzzo, had been shot to death by Klansmen on the road back to Selma.

## RESISTANCE TO THE WAR IN VIETNAM

The previous evening, March 24, 1965, while Bernstein and others had been celebrating the arrival of the marchers into Birmingham, students and faculty members at the University of Michigan held a teach-in, the first of its kind, to question the American intervention in the war in Vietnam. This war had always been an ominous irritant for left-wing Kennedy enthusiasts, but Johnson's escalations of American military efforts were raising anxiety within those ranks. Johnson, like Eisenhower and Kennedy before him, had always discussed the American effort in Vietnam as a defensive fight against ever-voracious international communism. If Vietnam were to fall into the hands of the communists, the victory would encourage the communist great powers—the USSR and China—to subvert and weaken anticommunist resolve in surrounding countries—Cambodia, India, Pakistan, Thailand, Burma—and cause them to fall one after another like dominoes.[22] But as the war grew into a major conflict, critics began to question the government's justifications for the war. They discovered that the Vietnamese communist forces were not pawns of the Soviets or the Chinese but were autonomous, if not fiercely independent fighters. Eisenhower, they learned, had sabotaged cross-Vietnamese elections to preempt the inevitable victory of the communist leader Ho Chi Minh, and had then created the Republic of South Vietnam out of whole cloth, populating its government with conservative functionaries and donating economic and military aid, including some 685 advisors to train and even command South Vietnamese military troops to fight against the communist guerrilla forces that were terrorizing Saigon-installed administrators in hamlets across the region. In short, the war was being waged by an administration obsessed with a fantasy of a monolithic communist power.

Shortly after Kennedy's inauguration, the new secretary of defense, Robert McNamara, had come back from a short visit to Vietnam and dismissed the gravity of the conflict, which reporters were calling "McNamara's War," defending it as a venture fully within the charter of established American foreign policy. Kennedy was adding some 400 members of Special Forces to the number of advisors and, by April 1961, was justifying buildups of combat forces; the total was some 17,000 by November 22, 1963.

The apparent lull in the war making in the months after Kennedy's assassination suddenly ended on April 4, 1964. According to President Johnson's reports to Congress, North Vietnamese forces had attacked the U.S. destroyers *Maddox* and *Turner Joy* on that date while the ships were patrolling peacefully within the international waters of the Gulf of Tonkin. The attack was apparently the second such event, the first having come two days before. Johnson asked for the powers to wage war to defend American forces, and Congress obliged via the Gulf of Tonkin Resolution on August 7, 1964.

From April through the period leading into the November election, Johnson seemed a tower of restraint against the demands for massive bombing by Barry Goldwater, the Republican opponent in the 1964 presidential election. Indeed, the Democrats answered Goldwater's demand for U.S. Air Force bombing campaigns with the now-famous television ad showing a little girl in a field of flowers while a voice-over intones a nuclear countdown—the inevitable consequence, the ad implied, of putting Goldwater in the White House. A sane individual would vote for LBJ. Johnson won by a landslide.

Thus was the shock for those who trusted Johnson when, on March 2, 1965, less than two months after his inauguration, they learned that he was ordering the U.S. Air Force to begin its sustained "Operation Rolling Thunder" bombardment of North Vietnam in response to an attack on American servicemen at an airbase at Pleiku. On Monday, March 8, with the media filled with news about the March 7 "Bloody Sunday" at Selma, U.S. Marines landed at Da Nang. The conflict that had been McNamara's War had suddenly become a real war; the dissentient discussion at that teach-in at the Michigan campus was only one sign of large-scale growing sentiment that Johnson had misled the American people and that he had apparently been making plans to enlarge the war even while asking voters to support him in the face of Goldwater's belligerence.

Was Johnson lying? Had dissenting senators Wayne Morse (D-OR) and Ernest Gruening (D-AK) perhaps been correct in questioning the supposed innocence of the U.S. destroyers, and had the ships been part of joint U.S. and South Vietnamese covert operations against North Vietnamese installations? Had the supposed attack upon American vessels in the Gulf of Tonkin on April 4, 1964, perhaps never happened? Only Morse and Gruening had voted against the Tonkin Gulf Resolution, even though a number of other senators had misgivings or doubts. Perhaps the whole premise of American policy, including the presence of over 183,000 troops, was mistaken or, worse, the result of duplicity?[23]

Johnson further alienated liberal and left-wing intellectuals when, in April 1965, he intervened on behalf of far right-wing interests in the Dominican Republic, marking a clear departure from Kennedy's policies. Kennedy, bent upon developing liberal democratic regimes as a defense against the spread of Castro-like movements across the Caribbean to Central and South America, had supported the presidency of Dominican liberal democrat Juan Bosch after the end of the tyrannical Trujillo regime. Kennedy had aided Bosch in putting down an attempt at a coup d'état by forces of the old Trujillo regime but had to watch with dismay when another attempt succeeded in September 1963. Johnson's new policy maker for South America, Thomas C. Mann, departed from Kennedy's policy by announcing that the United States would support right-wing military overthrows of any democratically elected government that had even tangential ties to a communist movement.

On April 25, a coup d'état organized by young Dominican military officers who were upset with the economic collapse and bent upon the restoration of Bosch seemed to be within moments of victory. But three days later, Johnson ordered a two-stage invasion by U.S. Marines: first, a small force to provide security for Americans in the Dominican Republic, and second, the landing of some twenty thousand, which the administration billed as an intervention to ward off a communist takeover. However, as became clear later, American officials knew that communist involvement was tiny and marginal to the revolt and that the allegation of endangerment to Americans had been engineered by the American embassy in Santo Domingo with the connivance of officials in Washington to justify their support for the military-oligarchic junta. The military intervention of April 28 succeeded in putting down the reform movement, but many in the United States—not least Senator William Fulbright (D-AR), head of the Committee on Foreign Policy—quickly understood that anticommunism was a smokescreen to hide a heavy-handed imperialism, another manifestation of the American policy already evident in the war in Vietnam.[24]

Among the artists and intellectuals of Bernstein's generation, the lines that had hardened between various left-sectarian and liberal movements during the earlier Cold War years were dissolving as their members coalesced around opposition to Johnson's policies in Vietnam and the Dominican Republic. Johnson had invited numbers of them (Bernstein was not included) to the White House for a cultural festival on June 3, but to the president's dismay, the poet Robert Lowell publicly explained that he was turning down Johnson's invitation to protest America's "becoming an explosive and suddenly chauvinistic nation [that] may be drifting on our way to the last clear ruin."[25] Many accepted the invitation but nevertheless signed a statement in support of Lowell's position. In short order, petitions from numerous professional and critical societies, signed by hundreds, began to appear in the nation's major newspapers and periodicals.

### RADICALIZATION

From 1965 through 1967, dissent grew within Congress as others joined Senator Fulbright in discussing the administration's tendency to publicize supposed dangers to legitimize support for regimes friendly to American business and military interests. The question about the administration's veracity was a radical one inasmuch as it pointed to the deep structures of corporate and political power—the dominance of the military-industrial complex that promoted American military adventures and thereby called into question the real power of American liberal-democratic institutions. Many people found themselves in agreement with Fulbright and sympathetic to the younger generation's radical outlook.

Artists who had approached the political arena only obliquely or metaphorically now expressed their anger in politically open voice. The folksong revival, the new pop music, and street theater were now converted into art at the barricades erected against the Johnson and McNamara war. The repressed returned now in fuller consciousness: "Starting in about '66," wrote Nora Sayre, "the theater began to echo the political and social themes of the period. . . . So many plays were nagging at America, reflecting or rejecting what we lived with."[26] The producer Joseph Papp found the freedom and the necessity to move from exclusively Shakespearean productions to contemporary, politically charged theater in 1967.[27] As the number of Americans killed in Vietnam rose from under 2,000 in the period between 1961 and 1965 to over 6,000 in 1966 and over 11,000 in 1967, artists who had eschewed the political, such as Mary McCarthy and Denise Levertov, were compelled to express their alarm and disgust with the war.[28]

Police brutality only increased the radicalization of Americans across the country. On October 17, 1967, Madison police truncheoned students protesting Dow Chemical recruiters at the University of Wisconsin.[29] The leadership of the antiwar movement organized a massive march on the Pentagon that took place on October 21 and was met with tear-gas attacks by soldiers in the afternoon and truncheons swung by U.S. marshals during the night. Norman Mailer had relocated his radicalism to the fringes of existentialist and near-Beat apocalyptic poetics and hip style but continued to write left-wing political essays. His 1965 *An American Dream* hinted darkly of the confluence of unaccountable financial and political power.[30]

But the scenes of marshals bloodying the bodies of young people at the Pentagon pushed him into a new political voice and a new genre of reportage, which found expression in his "On the Steps of the Pentagon," published in *Harper's* in 1967 and in book form the following year as *Armies of the Night*.[31] Mailer's protagonist was his own shaky, near-drunk persona committing comedic pratfalls during the evening before the march on the Pentagon; his report of the day's events (amid the festive army of the day) enhanced the power of his report of what happened later, when U.S. marshals brutally beat passively resisting young people (the army of the night). The shock of this vicious violence in the nation's capital, with U.S. marshals moving in on unarmed young American women and men, moved many, as Noam Chomsky wrote, "from dissent to resistance."[32]

## BERNSTEIN'S MAHLER: THE CATASTROPHIC VISION

Along with the so many others, Bernstein was becoming increasingly politicized in the early to middle 1960s, not only in his public life and outlook but in his case in his musical analysis. Indeed, we can trace Bernstein's evolution during the 1960s in his discussions of Mahler between 1962 and 1968. In 1962, with Kennedy in office, Bernstein couched his understanding of Mahler's work in purely aesthetic terms. Thus, in a talk at a New York Philharmonic preview on January 28, 1962, he saw the new interest in Mahler as a rejection of the "old arguments" that Mahler's music was overlong and bombastic. Now, he argued, one could appreciate in his music the many elements of twentieth-century modernism. Quoting musician and historian Howard Shanet, Bernstein noted the key features of Mahler's music: "wide melodic leaps; themes made up of short-motifs; chamber-music subtleties; kaleidoscopic orchestration; inner emotionality; and morbid preoccupation with death and tragic matters." He then added to this list Mahler's "linear writing—style of such economy, transparency, and reliance upon horizontal writing, or counterpoint, that he fed directly into the new music of our times, that we call neo-classic."

Bernstein then pointed out some interesting "dualities"—"conductor vs. composer; sophisticated vs. naïve; German vs. Bohemian; Christian vs. born Jewish; tragic figure vs. happy child; Western traditionalist vs. Oriental (Chinese); operatic nature vs. symphonic composer; huge orchestra vs. chamber music"—all cast largely within the apolitical critical categories of nineteenth-century historiography.[33]

By July 7, 1966, Bernstein had reentered the political arena, having taken part in the Montgomery end of the Selma march, and now displaced the formal aesthetic approach of 1962 to give priority to political and social crises of fin de siècle Vienna in his understanding of Mahler's music.[34] Thus, in comments at a Columbia Records sales convention about the cultural significance of Mahler's 7th Symphony, he said, "The biggest problem has always been the finale, which critics have traditionally considered unworkable. It combines mighty chorale-music with other music of such tawdriness that it would seem to belong only to Viennese operetta or café-bands. But once we realize that this movement is Mahler's document on the end of the great European tradition, the breakup of the safe, bourgeois 19th century, then the piece suddenly makes marvelous sense, and becomes both ironic and exciting, and ultimately heartbreaking."[35]

By April 1967, with massive bloodshed in Vietnam, Bernstein's Mahler was more than witness: he was now prophet of the twentieth-century catastrophes, albeit something of a Cassandra, because Mahler's earlier listeners thought they were hearing "endless, brutal, maniacal marches—but failed to see the imperial insignia, the Swastika (make your own list) on the uniforms of the marchers."[36] Bernstein's listeners would not make that mistake, if he had his way:

> It is only after fifty, sixty, seventy years of world holocausts, of the simultaneous advance of democracy with our increasing inability to stop making war, of the simultaneous magnifications of national pieties with the intensification of our active resistance to social equality—only after we have experienced all this through the smoking ovens of Auschwitz, the frantically bombed jungles of Vietnam, through Hungary, Suez, the Bay of Pigs, the farce-trial of Sinyavsky and Daniel, the refueling of the Nazi

machine, the murder in Dallas, the arrogance of South Africa, the Hiss-Chambers travesty, the Trotskyite purges, Black Power, Red Guards, the Arab encirclement of Israel, the plague of McCarthyism, the Tweedledum armaments race—only after all this can we finally listen to Mahler's music and understand that it foretold all.[37]

Bernstein thus projected onto Mahler his own evolution from the apolitical aesthetics of the 1950s and early 1960s to the radicalizing politics of the later 1960s. Bernstein had entered the political arena at Selma in 1965; he was now increasingly politically engaged, appealing to his audiences to come to moral and ethical grips with the flow of demonic events.

### SUMMER OF LOVE

In the summer of 1967, Bernstein and his family were in Italy in a rented villa in Ansedonia, a few miles from Rome, enjoying a breathtaking view of the Mediterranean. John Gruen, who had chronicled much of the downtown New York City art world, arrived in town to spend time in lengthy interviews with Bernstein and with a colleague to photograph Bernstein with Felicia and their three children, Jamie, Alexander, and Nina. Bernstein's announcement that he would leave the Philharmonic at the end of the 1968–69 season and the reasons for his departure provided initial themes in their dialogue. He had taken the job in 1956, he told Gruen, because he had been at "loose ends," spreading himself too thin with performing and composing, and needed an anchor to his life.[38] He said nothing to Gruen about his years on the blacklist; nor did he mention his passport travails or the politics that led to his appearance on *Omnibus*—all that was down the memory chute, or at least appeared to be when Bernstein vetted Gruen's text.[39] Bernstein let on that his long stint at the Philharmonic—not only the preparation but the administrative details—had come at the cost of his composing; he had raised the level of orchestra members' morale and performance, but unlike his mentor Koussevitzky, who "proudly brought forth one Copland symphony after another, Roy Harris, Bill Schuman, Prokofiev, Stravinsky!" Bernstein had no "cause to champion—a movement, a group of composers, a school."[40] Now a darker, brooding Bernstein came to the surface. He had been reading Marguerite Yourcenar's *The Memoirs of Hadrian* and was taken by the argument that introspection will not reveal a centered inner self.[41] The conversation moved to the state of the nation, with Bernstein arguing that America had no moral center: "these times, which are so dreamlike—one can't fathom them or take them seriously. . . . America is in the throes of a civil war this morning, and here we are, thousands of miles away reading about it, and shaking our heads, and saying, 'Anyone for water-skiing?' in the next breath: It's so unreal." Against this backdrop, he said, conducting the Philharmonic had little significance. "The world is on the verge of collapse"; indeed, "it's worse than ever, because of the multiplying nuclear arsenals and the total unpredictability of statesmen who are hardly statesman-like. Perhaps, even worse, because of their very *pre*dictability. The farcical, cynical way everything is being handled. The massive lie that is constantly being told. How can one feel that one is part of anything real? I can't."[42]

Bernstein and Gruen got into a long conversation—prompted by a question from Gruen about the state of music—in which Bernstein ruminated about the failure of contemporary art, not least his own, to confront the crises facing humankind.[43] Bernstein's response to Gruen's question was rather melancholic: our civilization's modes of expression—that is, the arts, and for that matter, philosophic understanding—are in serious decline, unable to keep up with scientific and technological advances, especially because these advances are controlled by "military greed." A profound pessimism is casting a pall over everyday life as well as over thought about the future; for example, Bernstein's children had laconically reported to him their expectations of death in an atomic catastrophe. Bernstein did find some succor in music and in friends and associates, but by and large, he believed that people are motivated by desire for gain. Hope may be kept alive by that "divine spark" in each person, but that idea has been turned into a cliché by authorities fundamentally concerned with power. Artists should be expressing something about the present crises of "Vietnam, the Negroes, human rights, civil rights," but instead they were producing "works of despair." Contemporary music is "fragmented, . . . atomized." Artworks are no longer "noble." In a characteristically classical vein that he would reiterate in the coming years as a retort to postmodernism, he said, "Ever since 1945 the face of art has become cool, hip, put-on, campy. Everything except hopeful, noble." The classical linkage between heightened aesthetic and ethical values had been broken, lost. "Those things were sort of relegated to Soviet tractor-art, which you and I have laughed at along with the rest of Western Society. The last noble strains we heard were Shostakovich's Fifth and Seventh Symphonies."[44] Why didn't Bernstein write an opera? Gruen asked him a few minutes later, it will "help people be transported." The conversation thus arrived at a place central to Bernstein's frustrated ambition: the issue that had been plaguing him and would do so to the end of his life (and to which we will return in chapter 7). He brooded aloud, answering Gruen in a manner that suggested that the issue of art's loss of significance had been on his mind a long time. Bernstein found the idea rather strange that "man is so constituted that he has to suffer in this vale of tears and then comes to like his suffering through works of art." That "divine spark of intelligence" in man seeks insight from art into how to improve that human condition, but the whole business is a fraud in which he, Bernstein, would not become complicit: "you wish me to become a party to this whole conspiracy, or game, by providing yet more works of art by which people can experience their suffering and be granted a catharsis thereby"—that is, before going back into that same vale of tears.[45] Gruen persisted, suggesting that Bernstein speak publicly to his audiences, to which Bernstein responded, "If I had any really deep convictions at this moment I think I *would* speak. But I've gotten to the point where I feel I know nothing. I know absolutely nothing." What was the causal agency that had silenced Bernstein, that had supposedly rendered art ineffectual in making sense of the world, offering nothing more than palliatives to its sufferers? What had caused the present crisis? The structure and distribution of economic power and resources: "What the present crisis really boils down to is not only a crisis of faith. It is more basic. It's the greatest in a series of crises. It's a crisis of world revolution. . . . based on the right to eat." Bernstein was now pointing a finger: "And we of the West, who insist on the right to eat at other people's expense, seem to be doing everything we know to prevent this revolution from taking place. Instead of aiding it and making it happen in a positive way, lending our money and power, we are using our money and power to prevent its happening." Now he offered a more concentrated indictment: "The United States as a nation, as an entity, seems to be totally dedicated to that task, under the title of 'Preserving Our Way of Life.' There is still time for that 'divine spark of intelligence' to function in another way, not as an enemy of revolution. After all, we were created in revolution. We made it up. We're so proud of it! Why is it we are always supporting the wrong side?"[46] Bernstein had put the question of American involvement in Vietnam to Kennedy, who told him he wished we could extricate ourselves from that situation.

Bernstein said, "He said he would do *anything* not to be in Southeast Asia. He said it was a thing he had inherited from the previous Administration, that he was stuck with it. I said there must be something he could do about it. He said he didn't know what. This coming from him—of all political men that I have ever met certainly the most moving and compassionate and lovable, and the one to whom most of us turned in trust and hope. Of course, it's very easy to say now, 'If he had lived . . . ' "[47]

Suddenly, however, Bernstein turned to a different image of Kennedy: "But I think the signs, when you look at them coldly, in a harsh, clear light, point to his having followed the same pattern being followed now, because he did actually order increased troops and escalation. He was stuck with it. I don't know what he could have done. That night, when we talked, he had had no answers. He was in a kind of despair himself."[48]

A bit later, Gruen asked, "Did he wish to change the course of events?" Bernstein replied, "Yes. He desperately wanted peace. But then the complexities set in. Face-saving. Power politics. Being accused of being an appeaser. Soft on communism. Attacked by the Congress and by the majority of the country. It's horrible. It's as though he were a slave, instead of a leader."[49]

If a man in power was in fact a prisoner of power, then what about us lesser mortals? If Kennedy was trapped, so too was Bernstein. The artists of old, such as Bach, were wonderfully centered: they wrote for God. The contemporary artist feels out of control, out of synch with the course of the world. "At the moment I am weak in the conviction that to compose is of any importance to me or to anybody else."[50] In short, the whole mood of cynicism and postmodernist irony left Bernstein cold. The crisis threatening Enlightenment certainties had only deepened in the present climate.

## CAMPAIGNING FOR GENE MCCARTHY

On November 7, just two and a half weeks after the Pentagon march, Senator Eugene McCarthy, Democrat from Minnesota, announced that he would run on an antiwar platform against Johnson in the upcoming Democratic presidential primaries. Bernstein quickly showed his support for McCarthy's campaign by appearing on January 21, 1968, in the "Broadway for Peace" program at Philharmonic Hall to raise funds for the Congressional Peace Campaign Committee. At this performance, Barbra Streisand sang a song that Bernstein, Comden, and Green had written for the occasion, "So Pretty."[51]

The cleavage between the dissidents and radicals on one side and the administration on the other had only deepened when, on January 7, 1968, the Johnson administration indicted Dr. Benjamin Spock, the famed pediatrician whose book was the child-rearing bible for most American parents, and four others for conspiring to help young men illegally avoid the military draft. But if Johnson seemed mean-spirited in going after the beloved Spock, he seemed impotent when the North Vietnamese unleashed their Tet offensive on January 30, 1968. The offensive came close to routing the Americans when the North Vietnamese breached the wall around the U.S. Embassy in Saigon. U.S. forces prevailed, but with the incident, General Westmoreland's claims of imminent victory over the communists lost all credibility. This near debacle could not but help McCarthy, who on March 12, won 42 percent of the vote in the New Hampshire primary.

Though McCarthy lost, his showing in the primary was really a victory over the incumbent Johnson, whose vulnerability encouraged Robert Kennedy to enter the race on March 16 and compete with McCarthy as an antiwar candidate. On March 31, the eve of the Wisconsin primary, a demoralized Johnson withdrew from the race and declared a halt in the bombing of North Vietnam.

Then came the hammer blow: on April 4 in Memphis, Martin Luther King was assassinated. The resulting gloom in Bernstein's circles may have lifted a little with news from Czechoslovakia on April 18 of the great governmental and institutional reforms of the so-called Prague Spring and the subsequent explosion of artistic expression and likely spreading sense of élan in May in Vienna, where Bernstein was conducting. News from the United States was mixed: upbeat from New York, with good reviews after the April 29 opening of the musical *Hair,* but gloom from Boston, with the Boston Five of the Spock trial sentenced to two-year terms.

Momentous events seemed to follow one another without cease. Just before the King assassination, on April 1, the Roman Catholic priest Philip Berrigan and the other members of the Baltimore Five had been found guilty of spilling blood on draft records and sentenced to six years in prison. On May 17, Philip, who was out on bail, his brother Daniel, and a number of other left-wing Catholics, broke into the Catonsville, Maryland, draft-board headquarters to burn draft files and then awaited the arrival of police to arrest them. These events would have serious ramifications in Bernstein's life, as we shall see.

On May 28, McCarthy beat Kennedy in the Oregon primary. On June 4, Kennedy won the California primary, but within moments of his victory speech, he was shot dead. Five days later, Bernstein received a call from a grieving Jacqueline Kennedy. He quickly mobilized the Philharmonic to perform Mahler's Adagietto from the Symphony no. 5 at Kennedy's funeral service in St. Patrick's Cathedral.

Eugene McCarthy was now the lone standard-bearer for the antiwar movement. On June 26, Bernstein delivered an address at a dinner for McCarthy at the Waldorf-Astoria, seeing in McCarthy a new manifestation of the great mythic revolution that was manifest in 1776 and was now playing out in the struggle for livelihoods in Vietnam, the campaign for China's admission into the United Nations, the fight for Czech independence, the efforts to improve the lives of the poor, and actions to promote academic freedom and open-mindedness.[52] On August 15, just ten days before the Democratic Convention in Chicago, Bernstein was at a McCarthy rally in New York's Madison Square Garden, arguing that the choice must not be between the "empty-headedness" of Nixon and the Democratic Humphrey, else this "ugly war will inevitably go on," but must offer the option of a McCarthy victory to "restore some rational humanism" to this "psychotic, power-obsessed world." At one point, Bernstein got carried away, arguing that if Humphrey won the nomination, left-wingers should vote for Nixon. If Nixon were to become president, Bernstein argued, he would force the contradictions to sharpen and the issues to clarify, thereby triggering a "short violent clash"—civil war. To vote for the weak ambiguities of Humphrey would lead to endless "genocide" in Asia.[53]

Felicia and Leonard were both committed to working on behalf of McCarthy: she continued this work at home while Leonard, accompanied by his children Jamie and Alexander, left with the Philharmonic on a tour of Europe and Israel that began in Ghent, Belgium, on August 24. The trip came at a time of terrible news, for just three days before, the Soviets had just invaded Czechoslovakia to destroy the "Prague Spring" and dash any hopes that communism would gain a human face. At home, the Chicago Democratic convention was about to inaugurate Hubert Humphrey as the Democratic candidate. Bernstein was in despair. According to Evelyn Ames, who had joined her husband, the Philharmonic's president, Amyas Ames, on this tour, Bernstein, in a postconcert supper conversation, spoke of "our great country—or rather our country which could be so great—and for the time being isn't."[54] On September 1, they learned of McCarthy's defeat in Chicago and were shocked by photos of the ensuing police riot.[55] Bernstein returned to New York in October to appear with Leopold Stokowski on behalf of the candidacy of Paul O'Dwyer, who had a long history of taking on radical causes, for the U.S. Senate position in

New York.[56] O'Dwyer won the nomination but lost to the incumbent, liberal Republican Jacob Javits.

For most of 1968, Bernstein had been collaborating with Robbins in a musical-theatrical adaptation of Brecht's ironic work of class struggle and injustice, *The Exception and the Rule*. In the play, a merchant kills a servant who was about to ask the merchant if he'd like some water. Brought to trial, the merchant is acquitted on grounds that, inasmuch as normal merchant-servant relations are deeply conflictive and thus potentially murderous, the merchant could not be blamed for thinking the worst upon being approached by the servant; therefore, his reflexive act was an unfortunate but innocent act of self-defense. In their adaptation, Robbins and Bernstein wanted to update the work by including racial and ethnic conflict. However, the collaboration, involving Stephen Sondheim and Arthur Laurents, fell apart and the work died.[57]

The collapse of the Brecht collaboration was only the latest of several disappointments for Bernstein and no doubt fed into his decision to shift the center of his musical life away from New York, away from America. His performances with the New York Philharmonic in the spring of 1969 were his last as music director, although the Philharmonic could not quite let go of "our Lenny," naming him laureate conductor.

Bernstein's last performance, on May 17, was Mahler's Third Symphony. He then left for Vienna and remained in Europe, beginning work on his *Mass*. He also strengthened his association with the Vienna State Opera and the Vienna Philharmonic, which had begun in 1966. He had recorded Mahler's *Das Lied von der Erde* with Dietrich Fischer Dieskau, James King, and the Vienna Philharmonic in April of that year and was now remaining in Europe for months on end.[58]

Bernstein had still to work his way out of a rather embarrassing problem. In October 1969, two black musicians who had tried out for but failed to obtain positions in the Philharmonic complained to the New York City Commission on Human Rights that Bernstein and the Philharmonic administration had rejected them on grounds of race. The commission's investigation concluded that their rejection was legitimately about musical skill, and Bernstein was thus exonerated of a charge of racism.[59] He was still the political man: on October 13, at a ceremony at the Hotel Pierre to receive an honorary degree from Brandeis University, Bernstein attacked the Nixon administration for sending massive resources to the military-industrial complex while starving the poor, undermining the public's medical and health needs, and failing to take steps to protect the environment from the poisons constantly entering the atmosphere. Black colleges were in deep financial trouble, he noted, as were symphonic orchestras and general funding for musical culture. In the absence of public funds, the only beneficiaries of funding would be universities specializing in "academic experimentation"—atonal music at the top of that list—and "rock'n'roll," with its commercial revenue.[60]

Bernstein was inhabiting his two worlds: first, he was the esteemed star of musical institutions, whom television viewers could see on October 26 in Alice Tully Hall presiding over the inauguration of the Juilliard School of Music. Viewers saw first lady Patricia Nixon enter the hall to the strains of the national anthem performed by Leopold Stokowski and the Philharmonic; followed by Bernstein, who noted that the Julliard construction marked the climax of the Lincoln Center construction plans; and then John D. Rockefeller, who recalled Eisenhower's presence at the Lincoln Center ground-breaking ceremony a decade before.[61] Then in his second persona, he was the rebel Bernstein, the public-political, near-radicalized activist who served as master of ceremonies for a rally in Duffy Square by the Theater Community for Peace on November 13 and who joined the Moratorium to End the War in Vietnam in Washington, D.C., on November 15, marching with hundreds of thousands of others and addressing the crowd.[62]

## BLACK PANTHERS AND COINTELPRO

Whatever embarrassment had befallen Bernstein over his rejection of the black musicians paled next to his acute humiliation over the debacle of a Black Panther fund-raiser, not least its exploitation by Tom Wolfe and Bernstein's victimization by the FBI's Counter-Intelligence Program (COINTELPRO). The Panthers, a radical organization dedicated to protecting and upgrading the incomes and qualities of life of black ghetto dwellers, had lost several of its members in shootouts with police in California. Police raids on Panther households in Harlem on April 2, 1969, had uncovered pipe-bomb material, gunpowder, and various handguns, rifles, and shotguns.[63] On January 14, 1970, Felicia Bernstein, upset that the judge had set high bail amounts to keep the arrested Panthers in jail, each prisoner in solitary confinement, had organized a Black Panther legal-defense fund-raiser at the Bernstein apartment, the latest such party held by uptown liberal New Yorkers.

Many of the Bernsteins' friends were in attendance, among them the very rich and well-photographed members of the New York celebrity circuit, the liberal *New York Post* columnist Murray Kempton, and as well, *New York Times* columnist Charlotte Curtis, and essayist Tom Wolfe. The Panthers arrived in full leather gear with their leader, ("field marshal") Donald Cox. Bernstein arrived home when the party was under way and quickly ingratiated himself with Cox, answering "I dig absolutely" to Cox's pronouncement that "if business won't give us full employment, then we must take the means of production and put them in the hands of the people." The matter was duly reported by Curtis, and her column was followed on January 16 by an editorial in the *New York Times* castigating Bernstein for his "elegant slumming" with the Panthers, those "romanticized darlings of the politico-cultural set," as the editorialist dubbed them, members of a "so-called party, with its confusion of Mao-Marxist ideology and Fascist para-militarism," an affront to the dignity of serious-minded civil rights organizations.[64] Bernstein's party "might be dismissed as guilt-relieving fun spiked with social consciousness," but it "mocked the memory of Martin Luther King, Jr., whose birthday was solemnly observed throughout the nation yesterday."[65]

Bernstein did receive important support from King's widow, Coretta Scott King, who wrote him February 13 that she understood that his support for the Black Panthers was about freedom of expression, not

necessarily about the content of their program.[66] Bernstein went off
to Europe amid the swirl of negative press and appeared isolated and
humbled at a press conference in London on February 20, 1970, where
he apparently disavowed his support for the Panthers. The following day,
however, he reaffirmed that he was not supporting the Panthers, who "are
advocating violence against their fellow citizens, the downfall of Israel,
[and] the support of Al Fatah," but their civil liberties. "If we deny these
Black Panthers their democratic rights because their philosophy is unacceptable to us, then we are denying our own democracy."[67]

Meanwhile, the Bernsteins and other attendees at that party were
receiving letters that overwhelmed any of the positives of Mrs. King's
letter. In fact, some, if not the majority, of the letters were fictitious: on
February 25, 1970, J. Edgar Hoover authorized the FBI to compose letters pointing out the anti-Semitic positions held by the Black Panther
Party, signed by "A Concerned and Loyal Jew," and sent to attendees of
the Bernstein fund-raiser.[68] The attacks did not diminish: on October
20, 1970, the Jewish Defense League demonstrated in the street outside
Bernstein's apartment building, having decided against an earlier plan
to occupy the halls of the building.[69] Nor was this the end of Bernstein's
humiliation as a result of the Black Panther incident.[70] Six months after
the party, in June, Tom Wolfe published an article in *New York Magazine*
reducing Bernstein's politics to "radical chic" and seriously damaging
Bernstein's reputation. The writer continued the attack in a book later
that year.[71] *Radical chic* paralleled another term then in vogue, *limousine
liberalism.* The term sought to depict the concerns for the less well-to-do
by New York City Mayor John Lindsay and like-minded denizens of
Manhattan's Upper East Side Silk Stocking district, and the *New York
Times* editorialist saw the term as consonant with the "elegant slumming" indulged in by the posh Bernsteins.

Wolfe's characterization of a "radical chic" Bernstein was terribly insult-
ing and inappropriate. In any event, Bernstein was not about to vacate the
political sphere. In fact, he was about to take a turn into a realm soon to be
dubbed "Catholic chic."

## DANIEL BERRIGAN AND BERNSTEIN'S *MASS*

Bernstein had been working on *Mass* since the summer of 1969, having been commissioned by Jacqueline Kennedy in 1966 to compose a work for the premiere of the Kennedy Center in Washington, D.C.[72] Both the composition and the opening had been delayed, and by 1970, the pressure was on Bernstein to complete the project. His intention was to write a work that would probe moral-political questions of war and somehow meld these themes with those of the new ecumenical humanism and erotic emancipation into a theatrical form inspired by *Hair* and *Godspell*.

Meanwhile, he and Felicia had decided to stare down Tom Wolfe and the *New York Times* editorialists and hold another fund-raiser, this time for the defense of the Berrigan brothers, Daniel and Philip. The Berrigans, whom we met earlier in this chapter, were Roman Catholic priests; Daniel, the older brother, was a Jesuit, and Philip was a Josephite. Both were active in the Catholic Left, and both were heavily imbued with the ecumenism, antimilitarism, and respect for human dignity and human rights central to the ethos of John XXIII and the Second Vatican Council. The brothers considered their ministry to be much closer to the worker-priest movement in postwar Europe than to the traditional practice of delivering messages from above to parishioners below. Philip had taken his order's mission to aid black people quite seriously: he had participated in the Freedom Rides to Mississippi, worked with CORE (Congress of Racial Equality) and SNCC (Student Nonviolent Coordinating Committee), and marched from Selma to Montgomery. As a member of the Baltimore Five, he had expressed his opposition to the war in Vietnam by spilling blood on draft records on October 27, 1967.

Philip Berrigan, an early opponent of the war in Vietnam, had linked the poverty of the African American ghetto to the poverty of the third world, seeing both as the result of the emphasis on capital accumulation in American policy. Like Daniel, he had incurred the wrath of Cardinal Spellman, bishop of New York, a most vociferous proponent of the war.[73] Daniel Berrigan had been a rising star in the Jesuit order until he made his turn to radicalism by publicly honoring the life of a young man who, on November 10, 1965, had immolated himself at the United Nations to protest the war. Cardinal Spellman was infuriated and pressured the Jesuits into exiling Berrigan to Mexico, a step that backfired as fellow priests quickly organized themselves into a "Free Daniel Berrigan" movement. The Berrigans were soon exemplars to a generation of young, activist clerical and lay Catholics.[74] Daniel's activities continued apace. On January 31, 1968, he flew to North Vietnam with the historian Howard Zinn to obtain the release of three American airmen who were prisoners of war.[75]

In the draft-card protest of May 17, 1968, Daniel, Philip, and seven others—priests, brothers, nuns—invaded the Selective Service office in Catonsville, Maryland, seized some six hundred draft files, carried them out into the parking lot, and, in front of reporters who had been alerted to witness an undisclosed event, burned the files with homemade napalm. Philip Berrigan's statement in the parking lot was a cry to the nation's conscience:

> Today, May 17th, we enter Local Board No. 33 at Catonsville, Maryland, to seize Selective Service records and burn them with napalm manufactured by ourselves from a recipe in the Special Forces Handbook, published by the U.S. Government. We, American citizens, have worked with the poor in the ghetto and abroad. We destroy these draft records not only because they exploit our young men, but because they represent misplaced power concentrated in the ruling class of America. . . . We confront the Catholic Church, other Christian bodies and synagogues of America with their silence and cowardice in the face of our country's crimes. We are convinced that the religious bureaucracy in this country is racist, is an accomplice in war and is hostile to the poor. . . . Now this injustice must be faced, and this we intend to do, with whatever strength of mind, body and grace that God will give us. May God have mercy on our nation.[76]

The Catonsville Nine remained on the scene and were promptly arrested. They were bailed out of jail, put on trial on November 5, 1968, and found guilty after the judge permitted wide-ranging testimony about what had led the members of the group to their action. Each participant testified to his or her looking into the heart of U.S. power that supports right-wing death squads and regimes in Central America that napalm and encourage indiscriminate shooting, and police brutality. Each sought to confront members of the church about their passivity before, complicity or acquiescence in, or active encouragement of these practices. At issue was the very core of ethical life, the place where conscience is formed, emerging from the depths of inner doubt and conflict into the clarity of judgment and necessary action. The Catonsville Nine had undergone precisely this process in reaching their decision to act. The jury pronounced each of the nine guilty, but perhaps because of the group's principled actions, the judge gave the defendants relatively light sentences of up to two years. The Berrigans were on parole for over a year awaiting appeal, but on the day that their appeal was denied and they were to give themselves up, they fled. Philip was captured within days, but Daniel was on the lam for months. During his time underground, he read Eberhard Bethge's biography of Dietrich Bonhoeffer, entered into dialog with the activist psychiatrist Robert Coles, and popped up here and there to deliver sermons or talks, only to disappear just as the FBI showed up.[77] But in August, he was captured and imprisoned in the Danbury Federal Penitentiary.

Next came the events that would bring Bernstein back into the sights of the FBI. On November 27, 1970, while the Berrigans were still serving their sentence at Danbury, J. Edgar Hoover testified before the Senate Appropriations Committee that the Berrigans were plotting to kidnap Henry Kissinger, who was national security adviser at the time. The indictment that was handed down on January 12, 1971, formally charged Philip Berrigan, Sister Elizabeth McAlister, two other Roman Catholic priests, and two other individuals with conspiring with seven unindicted conspirators, including Daniel Berrigan, to kidnap Kissinger and blow up Washington's underground heating tunnels. The group was also charged with violating federal law by breaking rules about correspondence with prisoners. Dubbed the Harrisburg Five because their trial would take place in that city, the defendants were to be counseled by a team of attorneys that included Ramsey Clark and Leonard Boudin. To raise money for the Berrigan/McAlister defense, the Bernsteins threw open their home on the evening of May 10, 1971.

Meanwhile, Bernstein was also seeking advice from Daniel Berrigan on *Mass*. Some weeks before, on February 2, he had attended a preview of Berrigan's play, *The Catonsville Nine,* at the Good Shepherd Church in New York, a major venue for left-wing discussion.[78] On May 8, Berrigan agreed to meet with Bernstein on May 24 and entered into his notebook, "A project for the autumn unfolds, the opening of the Kennedy Center for the Performing Arts in D.C.; New York Philharmonic director Bernstein wants to come and talk turkey about my prose and poetry for a Mass on opening night. . . . Resistance can be a work of art, as Catonsville showed, and what extraordinary results on and off Broadway attended on that event! We'll have to see. . . ."[79]

Berrigan thus thought that Bernstein was going to compose a work of resistance, one that could bring the work of Catonsville to the popular stage. Two days later, on May 10, Felicia Bernstein ran the fund-raising party, and on May 24, Bernstein met with Berrigan at Danbury Penitentiary.[80] Berrigan wrote the following after Bernstein left:

Leonard Bernstein was here today. He seemed tired and harassed but gentle as a lamb. He said the press had coined a new word, "Catholic Chic" to describe the meeting last wk [*sic*], at which they raised 30 grand for the cause. He wants some help on a musical thing he's doing for opening of Kennedy Center in D.C. in September. I don't honestly know if I can be of any help but am willing to give it a try. In any case it was rewarding to be with such a good guy for an hour. He has some delightful theater music going for the opening. I'm not at all convinced it needs any embellishment. But we'll see. He seems quite awed by the prison thing, etc. Almost like waiting in a novitiate or an old time rectory. My own breeziness I hope helped lighten things to a degree.[81]

According to Berrigan's diary entry for July 4, Bernstein was studying Berrigan's "Sermon from the Underground of August 2, 1970," which included the following thoughts:[82]

We are told that, some thirty years ago, when the Nazis had occupied Denmark, the ministers of religion made an agreement among themselves that, week after week, they would mount their pulpits with a common project in mind. That is to say, they would go before the people with the word of God, in order to translate the lies of the times. . . . Week after week, the liars were unmasked. Week after week, the Jews were protected. Week after week, men, women, and children, went on living, supported in hiding, gotten out of the country, saved from the executioners.

Berrigan then appealed to the conscience of his countrymen:

Dear friends, how do we translate in *our* lives the bombing of helpless cities? How do we translate in our lives the millionth Vietnamese peasant perishing? How do we translate into the truth of our lives the one hundred thousandth village burned? How do we translate to our lives, in light of the Bible, the millionth refugee rounded up? How translate into the truth of this morning's text [Hebrews 11:1–40] the fifty thousand children napalmed? How translate the perfidy of the Gulf of Tonkin Resolution or the tiger cages at Song My?[83]

The sermon addressed the fundamental ethical question of the age: how is one to act in when one's government is committing atrocities? Thus, Berrigan's work was directly in line with Bernstein's own ethical orientation. Bernstein, it seemed to Berrigan, was now going to find inspiration in the sermon, seeking to give voice to the need for the present generations to make the world safe for their children. According to Berrigan, Bernstein had come up with a provisional title for the new work, "A Mass for the Unborn."[84]

The events that followed brought on the paranoia of the Nixon administration and the FBI. Berrigan apparently assumed that Bernstein was going to incorporate his sermon into *Mass,* because he asked himself, "What will Nixon think?"[85] To the FBI (whose agents surely would have read anything the Danbury inmate wrote), Berrigan's question could only mean that Bernstein was going to commit an anarchist or dadaist beau geste against the president. What did he have in mind? Now the administration felt some urgency to find out. To the humorless archconservative

Nixon, the multitudes of civil rights activists, antiwar demonstrators, Panthers, student "bums" rioting at campuses across the country, Maoists and Weathermen, hippies, and beats were collectively responsible for the unacceptably unruly state of America at the time. He had already unleashed the FBI to do something about them, and he and Hoover were certainly not going to stop their efforts now.[86] He had every need to succeed: the FBI was in the midst of an embarrassing humiliation because of its inability to stop publication of the Pentagon Papers, the first installment of which was released on June 13 and the rest after the Supreme Court lifted the injunction against further publication. Moreover, its agents were unable to find the Weather Underground members who were bombing corporate and governmental installations across the country in retaliation for the alleged Chicago police murder of Black Panther leader Fred Hampton and more generally, for the depredations committed by the U.S. government in Southeast Asia. Now came this alleged Bernstein plot, and the FBI was determined to avoid another humiliation. On July 12, Hoover sent a memo to the White House reporting that Bernstein had asked Berrigan to write an antiwar polemic in Latin for the *Mass*. "Important Government officials, perhaps even the President, are expected to attend this ceremony and it is anticipated that they will applaud the composition without recognizing the true meaning of the words. The source said that the newspapers would be given the story the following day that the President and other high-ranking government applauded the antigovernment song."[87]

In the FBI's narrative, Bernstein was an agent of the Berrigans. Members of what the FBI newly dubbed EASTCON Movement, coordinated by the Berrigans from inside Danbury, were drawing up plans for actions in three theaters of operation: first, the underground tunnels; second, the as-yet-undecided site of Kissinger's abduction; and third, the pit or stage of the Kennedy Center, this last to be the launchpad for Bernstein's (verbal? musical?) assault on the president.[88] This operation had to be thwarted. Thus, the authorities ensured that Bernstein was refused entrance to Danbury prison for a July 14, 1970, meeting with Berrigan, and the same memo advised Nixon to avoid the Kennedy Center on opening night, ostensibly to give wide berth to Jacqueline Kennedy and the Kennedy family.[89]

At least to Philip Berrigan, the FBI not only embellished the matter but also came to believe its own hype. As he later related, he had indeed thought up the idea of turning off the heat and electricity, but the idea of exploding the tunnels was pure embroidery by collusion of the FBI's informant, Boyd Douglass, and FBI officials. He and Elizabeth McAlister had indeed written each other about a "citizens' arrest" of Kissinger as a war criminal—another matter that the trusted Douglass had turned over to the FBI—but this idea was more in the realm of fantasy than reality, and in any event, no real plans were ever formulated.[90] As for Bernstein's role, the FBI came up with yet another hypothetical plot (beyond the first, rather sophomoric idea that Bernstein would get Nixon to applaud an antiwar message intoned in Latin), which is perhaps the one alluded to in an FBI memo of August 16, 1971: Bernstein supposedly had been toying with the idea of having the celebrant, the protagonist in *Mass,* yell "Fuck You!" during the mad scene.[91] Although neither the Latin text nor its English version had shown up in the dress rehearsal or the preview for Congress, FBI officials nevertheless cautioned that Bernstein could still insert the dangerous lines.[92]

Was the FBI's worry justified? Not only was this act as sophomoric a concept as the Latin-lyrics prank, maybe more so, but one cannot imagine Bernstein's ever taking such an idea seriously. Most likely, the idea was a running joke during the period of composition, not to be taken seriously for this work of art that had exercised and preoccupied Bernstein for months. Indeed, Bernstein would not have exploited Jacqueline Kennedy and the Kennedy family for a one-time cheap shot against Nixon. He owed a lot to the Kennedys, not least Jack's help in turning away the congressional investigation in 1956. They had honored Bernstein while they were in the White House and had turned to him in their hours of distress after the deaths of Jack and Bobby. In short, he was unlikely to do anything to jeopardize his relationship with Jackie Kennedy or his reputation as a serious musician and person.

In the end, if Berrigan had anything to do with *Mass,* it was in Bernstein's treatment of the Roman Catholic ceremony as a communal action of a spirited public.[93] Bernstein structured *Mass* within the framework of the traditional Roman Catholic rite but interspersed parts of the Jewish rite.[94] The major figures in *Mass* include the celebrant, a young man wearing "blue jeans and simple shirt" and his similarly dressed young congregants. The celebrant utters some caustic passages about the exploitation of the doctrine of purity of poverty to justify thievery, the destruction of whole species of animal life, imperialism, overpopulation, religion as once-a-week pew renting, and people who coerce others into religious belief. The Credo is punctuated by a Trope in which a solo baritone angrily asks God why a human being must die, a solo mezzo-soprano asks about the second coming, and another asks when the world will come to an end. A rock-singing soloist is ready to believe in as many gods as necessary to find a foundation on which to build his life.

This chaos seems to be driving the celebrant into mental breakdown: his call for prayer after the *Dona nobis pacem* is one of terror; he is struggling in voice and body, near crack-up. The stage directions demand chaos, "disarray," and "turmoil"—conveying emotional chaos in a long crescendo. Instruments burst into an already-frenzied vocal scene, rising in amplitude and forming a sound world fallen into cacophonic pandemonium. Suddenly the celebrant, holding the chalice over his head, calls all to order with a stentorian "Pacem!" repeated three times and then smashes the chalice to the floor.

The celebrant has gone over the edge, his voice almost a frightened child's, unable to grasp what he's done. "Haven't you ever seen an accident before?" he asks the crowd. Breaking another shard of the chalice, he remarks, "How easily things get broken," as if letting the crowd learn what it has been doing to the social fabric. The crowd does not deserve communion, he seems to be saying (an idea Berrigan apparently discussed with Bernstein).[95] The last section, Pax: Communion, the crowd members, shocked into recognition of what they've done to themselves and to the celebrant, come out of their silence to form communions and then, with the celebrant, move from the stage to enter communion with the audience. At the very end, a voice is heard: "The Mass is ended, go in Peace."

If critics writing in 1971 understood Bernstein's intention to make a political statement with *Mass,* they directed their criticism at Bernstein's excesses and the liberties he took with the Roman Catholic mass, or at the number of lyrics they found to be sophomoric, if not trivial and tasteless.[96]

But if we take Bernstein's political sensibilities into account and ask whether *Mass* provided the call to conscience demanded by the Berrigans and the Spocks, we can see that it had major shortcomings as a work of politically dissident or radical theater.[97]

The release of the Pentagon Papers that began on June 13, 1971, three months before the opening of *Mass,* was a staggering moment for the United States, exposing in a multitude of heretofore-secret documents how the Truman, Eisenhower, Kennedy and Johnson regimes had misled Congress and the public about the U.S. intervention into Vietnam. And although the collected materials did not extend beyond the Johnson administration, Nixon had every reason to expect that his administration would be tarred with the same brush as his predecessors. The papers revealed that each president had committed himself to the maiming and killing of tens of thousands of Vietnamese and Americans not to defend democracy but to preserve the United States' global hegemony. The idea that the United States was protecting democracy in South Vietnam, or virtually anywhere else in the world, was pablum for the masses.[98] As Under Secretary of Defense John T. McNaughton wrote on March 24, 1965, in a passage that has probably been the most-quoted text in the papers,

> We must have kept promises, been tough, taken risks, gotten bloodied, and hurt the enemy very badly. We must avoid harmful appearances which will affect judgments by, and provide pretexts to, other nations regarding how the U.S. will behave in future cases of particular interest to those nations—regarding U.S. policy, power resolve and competence to deal with their problems. In this connection, the relevant audiences are the Communists (who must feel strong pressures), the South Vietnamese

(whose morale must be buoyed), our allies (who must trust us as 'under-writers') and the U.S. public (which must support our risk-taking with U.S. lives and prestige).[99]

To the American reader of sensitivity, this last line was the most revolt-ing, because it reduced the American people, nominally the collective sov-ereign, to a passive, mindless audience that was expected to cheer on cue and willingly send its young into deadly fire, only to see these young Amer-icans return home in body bags and lie in state on the tarmac of Dover Air Force Base before being dispatched into the ground at Arlington.

As we read Bernstein's book for *Mass,* however, we begin to wonder who the enemy is in the work. Who drives the celebrant mad? The cacopho-nous youth? The Weathermen? Missing are Johnson, Nixon, McNamara, and Kissinger.

Bernstein knew that the times needed a work of art to represent the awful preoccupations of the age; its fundamental requirement, there-fore, was to set up dramatic tension between a celebrant representing a noble idea (such as that in Berrigan's sermon) and an antagonist of equal but negative gravitas (such as a Kissinger- or Nixon-like personage). But Bernstein's celebrant offers nothing from his pulpit that echoes either Ber-rigan's sermon or Bernstein's own speeches—nothing about napalm, mas-sive bombings, and other atrocities and war crimes; and nothing about the military-industrial complex that Bernstein believed had committed the United States to war in Vietnam. Nor did the composer invest the celebrant with the character and dignity that would make his collapse representative of a collapsed idea. The celebrant's foil was not a Nixon-like figure. It was street people, who not only lacked the mythic proportion of stiff-necked Hebrews with the golden calf but were at most a congeries of stereotyped youth complaining not so much about the war as about big city *Weltschmer-zian* alienation and rip-offs. When the celebrant has his breakdown, he seems more the victim of mental illness than of social and political condi-tions: his crack-up seems to stem from the selfishness and aimlessness of the crowd, not from the collapse of a noble ideal or grand myth.

To be sure, the work has an extraordinary range of rhythm and musical line and a wondrous play of musical-theatrical forces, including singers, full orchestra, organ, quadraphonically played tapes, and dance choreographed by Alvin Ailey and realized by his troupe. Many who attended performances in Washington or at Lincoln Center found the production a fine spectacle indeed. But the work did not develop its tragic dimension sufficiently to give expression to the calls to conscience demanded by the Berrigans and the Chomskys and the Arendts. Absent from *Mass* were the representations or even direct allusions to the great horrors of the age that would have given depth and meaning to the work. Thus did *Mass* fail to bear the weight of the crises it sought to take on. Neither Nixon nor Hoover would have had cause to worry had they known of the work's emphasis on mawkish feel-good sentimentalism.

Despite the harmlessness of *Mass*, Nixon and his aides saw red when they encountered the name Bernstein. Perhaps they were looking beyond *Mass* to Bernstein's politics, including his aid to the Panthers, his meetings with the Berrigans, and his antiwar speeches, when they decided to add his name to the infamous list of "enemies" marked for special attack by the Internal Revenue Service or criminal COINTELPRO operations.[100] But for Hoover's death in 1972 and Nixon's departure in 1974, Bernstein would have been subject at a minimum to harassment and frequent audits and to civil, even criminal investigation. Between the COINTELPRO harassments and IRS investigations, life under such circumstances would have been more or less Kafkaesque—free to go about one's life but under official suspicion and even surveillance, and never knowing when or how the authorities would next strike. Such was what awaited one in the world as conceived by Nixon and Hoover, a possibility mercifully cut short by Hoover's death in 1972 and later, by Nixon's departure in 1974.

Before his departure, however, Nixon continued to make war, and Bernstein made plain his animus toward the president. On January 20, 1973, while Nixon was enjoying his second-term Inaugural, Bernstein was taking part in an anti-Nixon rally, the "Concert for Peace," at the Washington National Cathedral. Eugene McCarthy spoke to the twelve thousand people inside and outside the cathedral on the need to end the war, and Bernstein led a performance of Haydn's *Mass in Time of War.*[101]

## EPILOGUE TO THE LONG SIXTIES

Thus ended the long sixties, the period of liberal revival and cultural radicalism that began in 1960 with Kennedy's election and ended in 1973–74 with the Watergate hearings, the U.S. withdrawal from Vietnam, and Nixon's resignation. The era had begun with many on the left politically cynical and disengaged and ended in much the same way. With Kennedy's election, many people, Bernstein included, had thought a new political era had arrived. They were gradually disillusioned during Kennedy's one thousand days in office, but with his death and Johnson's buildup of the war came a cynicism compounded by mockery and nihilism. Then came 1965, with mobilization of the civil rights, student, women's, and antiwar movements, and an élan, sometimes even euphoria, swept the Left. In 1968, this optimism again gave way to cynicism, this time deeper if not bordering on rage, in reaction to the deaths of King and Robert Kennedy, the engineering of Eugene McCarthy's loss of the race for the Democratic nomination, and the ascension of Richard Nixon to the White House. The radical philosophical and theological probings and political and cultural activities that were supposed to restore the mythic-utopian promise of American life had proven naught against established power backed by a conservative populace. The civil rights movement was splintering, and the antiwar movement evanesced when Nixon ended the draft in 1973. The groups that had merged into the antiwar movement, such as the Students for a Democratic Society, were dissolving, or, like those that organized into the Weathermen, were destined to live a violent, and for some members, short life. Other groups, such as those focusing on gender questions and sexual liberation, survived and even got stronger. But these groups were now isolated from one other, no longer enjoying solidarity with other great political action groups and no longer forming into the great fronts and coalitions that worked to end the war in Vietnam. Watergate would give the nation a victory over a president prepared to violate fundamental civil liberties and otherwise usurp power, but few on the Left believed that Watergate damaged the financial, corporate, media, and political structures of power that pushed the United States into war, in Vietnam and elsewhere, to maintain and expand American hegemony.

During this period, Bernstein's upbeat vivacity, emergent with the Kennedy election and taking form in his *Kaddish* Symphony and *Chichester Psalms,* gave way in the mid-1960s to gloom about Kennedy's death and the serious intervention of American forces in Vietnam and then again in 1967, despair about the outbreaks of violence in the American cities. Bernstein's entrance into the political arena amid the moral and ethical renewal emergent with the rise of mass politics, and his work on behalf of the Eugene McCarthy campaign in 1968 may have raised him from general gloom, but by the end of the decade, he was once again brooding about American life, depressed, as Daniel Berrigan noted after Bernstein's visit to him in Danbury Penitentiary in 1970. For Bernstein, as for many progressives, political matters only worsened in the following years. By 1973, Bernstein had made his retreat from the political arena.

# CHAPTER FIVE

# Norton Lectures

## *1973*

Bernstein had been spending time in Vienna when he received an invitation to come to Harvard to deliver the 1973 Norton Lectures, an honor that had also been bestowed upon Copland and Stravinsky. Preparing the lectures would permit him to reflect on the formal requirements that make music so primal and fundamental to human beings. He would thus seem to be building a musical anthropology, but, in fact, researching and writing the lectures would allow him to develop a musical-political philosophy and a justification for his own musical practice. The series would also reveal something about his state of mind in the time of political drift that marked the termination of "the long sixties."

## TONALITY AND FOUNDATIONALISM

As Bernstein readied himself for the lecture series, he thought back to his Harvard days and his mentor, David Prall. Prall's 1936 book, *Aesthetic Analysis,* had been reissued in paperback in 1967, and Bernstein must have immersed himself in it, because something in the new introduction by Arthur Berger apparently caught his eye. Berger was meditating upon the ways in which a seasoned listener gains immediate access to the aesthetic surface of a musical work, and he quoted a passage of the linguistic theorist Noam Chomsky's *Aspects of the Theory of Syntax* about the model "speaker-listener." Chomsky argued that the human mind comes equipped with a grammatical apparatus that enables a child to develop the procedures necessary for the development of linguistic faculties. Berger declined to assume an equivalent set of innately held procedures for the understanding of music. He did worry, however, that Prall, because he had used the word *natural* in characterizing the tonal system, might have misled readers into thinking that tonality was the innately given basis for a musician-listener relationship.[1]

As he prepared to lecture, Bernstein decided to do precisely what Berger refused to do—namely, extend Chomsky's argument about verbal syntactical innateness to tonal music. Tonality, Bernstein argued, is innate to human beings; we crave it, and music becomes increasingly joyful and meaningful as composers use the tonal system—the "home" note and the dominant, the circle of fifths—to form modulations, variations, and inversions that create playful incongruities and ambiguities. Composers then spin out these elements, much like poetic metaphors, into musical dramatic and epic narratives, narratives that express enduring and universal values and passions.

Bernstein's argument was an attack on the atonalists, whom he deplored. Though he had used the twelve-tone system in his *Kaddish Symphony,* he did so only as a foil, a sign of social discord that resolves into tonality, signaling social concord. Arthur Berger, who was a partisan of posttonal music, was well aware of Bernstein's animus. He remembered Bernstein's turning to his audience at a Young People's Concert as he was about to conduct Schoenberg's *Pierrot Lunaire* with the advice, "You better open the window in advance. Pierrot always makes me sick and needing to open a window."[2]

Thus, it was to the amazement and consternation of those members of Bernstein's audiences and the Philharmonic musicians who knew him well that in the winter season of 1964, he scheduled works by avant-garde composers, including John Cage, whose work, *Atlas Eclipticalis,* is at once prepared, aleatory, and participatory, this last occurring as audience members muttered, wondered aloud, or otherwise reacted to the music and thereby became part of the performance. When the performance went off, the audience did not hear music in the traditional sense but a collage of disconnected and contingent sounds, precisely the effect Cage was after. Bernstein, to be sure, had little use for Cage's work, nor for that of other avant gardists such as Iannis Xenaksis, nor for that of Pierre Boulez, a leader of the posttonalists who, according to Bernstein, had virtually taken over American composition and academic musical life.[3] According to Bernstein, Copland, through his recent turn to serialism, had virtually committed compositional suicide.[4]

In truth, there was always an undercurrent of conservatism in Bernstein's musical politics, but his conservatism, as we shall see, was consonant with his progressive politics.

·    ·    ·

As Bernstein argued in a lecture in 1963, tonal music "is concerned with human expressivity, the mirroring of our inner lives in music."[5] He carried his anti-atonalism message to his lectures at Harvard in 1973. At the outset of the first Norton lecture, he presented his thesis that tonality is innate to human beings. It is the ubiquitous, "monogenetic" source of all music. At their most sublime, tonal musical works express fundamental universal human aspirations. The world for which tonality is a foundation is "a world where an octave leap upward implies a sense of yearning or reaching," but in the atonal world, it is only "an intervallic symbol." Whereas the tonally based composer would "base our forms on the concept of struggle and resolution," the atonal composer is "condemned to reveal ourselves as forever unresolved."[6] In this first Norton lecture, Bernstein discussed how European art music's tonal system passed from the late eighteenth century into the current crisis-ridden time. Mozart and Beethoven had created their extraordinarily rich works by composing delightful ambiguities and incongruities within strict tonal constraints. Later in his life, Beethoven began to exploit chromatic possibilities, and other composers followed suit, but always within tonal constraints.[7] By the late nineteenth century, however, Wagner and Debussy were stretching tonal constraints to the breaking point. As the twentieth century opened, Bernstein argued, musical expression was in crisis.

In fact, he said, two crises had emerged in the fin de siècle period, one intramusical, the other, extramusical. The tonal system had already been stretched intramusically—that is, within the culture of the compositional craft. But it now had to respond to the extramusical shocks of modernity and political upheaval. Mahler's effort to stretch tonality to its limits was in response to these extramusical shocks. He loaded his music with cataclysmic breaks that seemed to prophesy catastrophes, and, especially in his 9th Symphony, he even came close to breaking tonal constraint. In doing so, Bernstein believed, Mahler was not only saying good-bye to his own life but also giving up on a tonal system that could no longer express the convulsive European condition of his time.[8] Mahler died in 1911, but his younger colleague Arnold Schoenberg had already made a turn into atonality three years before.

Was atonality thus the wave of the future, the only way left to express catastrophe? Was tonality dead? No, argued Bernstein, there was good news: Igor Stravinsky found a way to express the terror of the age without departing from tonality—namely, by melding polytonal and polyrhythmic innovations into Russian folk music, as in *Petrushka* (1911) and *Le Sacre du printemps* (1913). These innovations permitted him to express with wild dissonances and the musical equivalents of fauvistlike color a prehistoric primitivism that reunited the audience with its mythic origins, with a Jungian "collective unconscious," which Bernstein called "Poetry of the Earth."[9]

Stravinsky was not alone in searching for new means of expression. Indeed, so were other early twentieth-century dadaists, surrealists, and futurists whose collective rush into pandemonium was stopped in its tracks in 1923 by a call to order: Stravinsky, in tonal music; Schoenberg, by a new twelve-tone method; and T.S. Eliot, in poetry all sought to rein in the developing stylistic chaos. Stravinsky, in Bernstein's view, organized tonal music's call to order through neoclassicism: a synthesis of older forms—renaissance, baroque, Viennese classicism—with modernistic polytonality and polyrhythm and a new eclecticism full of irony and ambiguity that delighted the ear but also expressed the terror of the age. In short, he argued, Stravinsky's compositional methodology, by combining older and modernist forms while maintaining ironic distance from them, yielded ambiguities that rescued music from atonal formlessness and satisfied the extramusical requirements of the century.

Bernstein concluded his chronology with a complaint that music today (1973) was in a new crisis, brought on by composers who seemed in thrall to atonality. Thus came his heartfelt plea for tonal music: to return us to the rich earth of our innate response, "those deep unconscious regions where the universals of tonality and language reside."[10]

## BERNSTEIN VERSUS ADORNO

Though Bernstein did not explain why this apparent hegemony of atonality had arisen, he did mention an influential book that favored Schoenberg's atonal route over Stravinsky's, "a fascinating, nasty, turgid book called *The Philosophy of Modern Music* by the German sociologist and aesthetician Theodore Adorno."[11] Adorno, a thinker of first rank, had studied composition with Alban Berg and had become virtual philosopher at the court of post–World War II atonality. His explanation for the rise of atonality can help us understand how Bernstein's championship of tonality fit into his political outlook.

Adorno suggested that the contemporary individual, or subject, lives in mutual estrangement from others within a seemingly democratic but in fact a totally administered society. The composer seeking to maintain his or her authenticity must express that estrangement while denying officially sanctioned and orthodox constraints upon musical expression. Tonality functions as political orthodoxy: it forces the composer into closure and reconciliation—that is, into a false ideology that affirms the legitimacy of the status quo and that is fed to the mass audiences of repressed subjects by the culture industry. Atonality is thus the weapon of resistance. But isn't tonality innate? No, Adorno argued. Tonality is a mere convention that reached its apogee in the eighteenth and early nineteenth centuries, the period stretching from Bach to Beethoven in his middle years (that is, up to circa 1814). This era saw the rise of bourgeois liberalism, when reconciliation of the striving citizen-subject with the nation-state collective seemed possible—in other words, before the reality of enduring estrangement became apparent. Thus, Beethoven could express his subjectivity as a struggle of musical motives versus dominant orthodox form. In a musical work, these motives develop, place strains on form, but then comes the resolution, the triumphant reconciliation of motive and form (tonal imperative).[12] In this way, the work conveys the potential for unity between the subject and totality, by which the individual feels fully integrated into the social order and as a citizen, enjoys the rights and security afforded by the protective state.

However, Adorno believed this ideology of unity was already waning in the early nineteenth century, and by 1814, as Beethoven entered his next, and as it turned out, late period, he came to recognize the hopelessness of such reconciliation. In this later period, he forged expression through abruptly juxtaposed fragments, giving his response to the forces of bureaucratic rationalization that pressed upon the individual's autonomy and to the commodification that reduced every value to a cash value. By midcentury, these forces had overwhelmed the social order. Thus, Wagner, in contradistinction to Beethoven, did not express character development as herculean struggle but instead as "renunciation—the negation of the will to life," which only aided the forces of aggressive nationalism and state power.[13] Wagner died in 1883, and before the end of the century, Mahler was resisting political authority's official myths and narratives (the "world course") by blowing up received form with shattering crescendi and other "breakthroughs," or by introducing musical banalities, such as marches, to break up the pomposities of convention that affirm the legitimacy and serve the interests of entrenched political power.[14]

Whereas Bernstein emphasized Mahler's reluctance to relinquish tonality, Adorno saw Mahler as an iconoclast ready to break with tonal

convention. Small wonder, then, that we find in Adorno a more continuous transition from Mahler to Schoenberg than in Bernstein. Adorno
believed that Schoenberg was acutely aware of the power of totalitarian
forces of repression and took the absolutely right step when he broke
into atonality to emancipate the expressive subject from repressive and
reactionary tonality. If this music had no public, so what? The very
emptiness of the concert hall validated Schoenberg's refusal to cooperate with the official culture industry. According to Adorno, Stravinsky, right behind Schoenberg in creating a new musical avant-garde,
did cooperate with the culture industry and thus became an unwitting
accomplice of authoritarianism. For example, as Adorno explains, during the second decade of the twentieth century, both the atonal Schoenberg and the tonal Stravinsky wrote music about clowns: *Pierrot Lunaire*
and *Petrushka,* respectively. But where Schoenberg takes us into the
subjectivity of Pierrot, Stravinsky looks at Petrushka from the outside.
We share Pierrot's mental universe, but we laugh at Petrushka. In the
end, we suffer with Pierrot as we sense his terror. With Petrushka, however, Stravinsky's "music does not identify with the victim, but rather
with the destructive element."[15] Stravinsky's sadomasochism is apparent
in *Le sacre du printemps,* in which the victim is sacrificed to the collective while the audience is assaulted by repetitive shrieks and unrelenting drumming. This element of "shock" grants the listener a sense of
participation in, and victimization by, power as well as immersion in,
and domination by, the collective. With Stravinsky, we have regression
into the Jungian tribal "collective unconscious," but not, as Bernstein
suggested, collective humanity's celebratory "song of the earth." Instead,
he focused on the product and effect of the subject's "dissolution of individual identity."[16]

The contrast between Adorno and Bernstein is clear: where Bernstein
finds Stravinsky's listener thrilled by new tonal ambiguities, Adorno finds
Stravinsky's listener depersonalized and benumbed by a music of shock
and repetition, sadomasochism and catatonia. And where Bernstein, in
his last Norton lecture, saw in Stravinsky's neoclassical *Oedipus Rex* an

example of wonderfully incongruous intertextuality, Adorno found manifestations of Stravinsky's antihistorical "will to style"—an egoistic artistic tendency that parallels the idea of a totalitarian will to power.[17]

In sum, for Adorno, the debate over tonality was less musical than extramusical, a matter of cultural politics. Adorno argued that tonality had become totalitarian and that atonality was the only way to preserve freedom in present, totally administered conditions. For Bernstein, tonality was innate and necessary for music to express universal yearning; atonality empties concert halls and thus cuts off the communal experience of musically expressed yearning and hope. For Adorno, music had to negate the legitimacy of the totally administered social order; for Bernstein, music should affirm the potential for progress and ultimately the potential for democratic reconciliation.

We need to understand the controversy over tonal foundations in music in the context of discussions about the status of other, epistemological, ethical, and aesthetic foundations. For over a century, such writers as Dostoevsky, Nietzsche, and Kafka had been writing about their apparent loss of faith in bedrock assumptions about the civilized social order and in the grand narratives about progress toward universal harmony fashioned by Plato and later by Enlightenment thinkers such as Jefferson, Condorcet, Kant, and Schiller. In line with these latter thinkers were twentieth-century scientists and philosophers who believed that human thought aligns perfectly with the logic of systems and laws of nature, language builds upon these elemental propositions about atomic facts, the sciences are unified, and we are progressing toward higher levels of ethical life. These assumptions, however, had been eroding by the work of Wittgenstein and Otto Neurath, for example—but the last assumption collapsed with Auschwitz. In 1958, W. H. Auden had argued that the poet and, for that matter, any thinker has "lost belief in the eternity of the physical universe," has "lost belief in the significance and reality of sensory phenomena," has "lost belief in a norm of human nature which will always require the same kind of man-fabricated world to be at home in," and must concede "the disappearance of the Public

Realm as the sphere of revelatory personal deeds."[18] Auden's arguments that the poet has no "sensual match to reality" and that there are no longer "universal norms" were only confirmations of what was long suspected. George Steiner, arguing in 1970, seconded Auden's pessimism, arguing that we have lost faith in the centrality of European liberalism as the engine of global belief in progress and in the powers of increasing literacy to guarantee civility. He concluded, "All these signify the end of an agreed value structure."[19]

In the absence of bedrock foundations from which to deduce a system of justice, anything goes: incivility, terror, torture, and totalitarian absolutism. And yet, as Bernstein believed, there is a universal given: the desire for freedom and peace. For millennia, music, tonal music, has had the role of sustaining and giving expression to this timeless and ubiquitous human desire. From this perspective, then, Bernstein's deeply felt plea—that we recognize tonality's innateness and return to it—had an element of the tragic: his was an anguished cry for the restoration of a lost civilization. Bernstein was simply unwilling to give up the struggle for progress articulated through the grand narratives. Adorno thought that those grand narratives were palliatives, illusions, and distractions that kept people from focusing on the realities still present in the world, such as a terrorizing impulse within the administrative and economic organizations of society that could easily turn into fascism. Adorno liked Kafka's quip that there is hope in the universe, but not for humankind; but behind that quip was Adorno's much darker note: "To write poetry after Auschwitz is barbaric." Tonal music is akin to an opiate whose administration would only dull the critical and oppositional faculties. "The concept of cultural resurrection after Auschwitz is illusory and absurd, and every work created since then has had to pay the bitter price for this. But because the world has outlived its own downfall, it nevertheless needs art to write its unconscious history. The authentic artists of the present are those in whose works the uttermost horror still quivers."[20] In short, for Adorno, an approach such as Bernstein's affirmed the legitimacy of deep structures of political power when it should deny them.

In 1961, Adorno encouraged serialist composers to stick to their post-Schoenbergian guns and break from all tonal, rhythmic, or other forms that would be imposed a priori upon expression.[21] For Adorno, a true music "in the image of freedom" would be unrecognizable to anyone but composers and cognoscenti.

To Bernstein, such hermeticism was anathema. He held that music has a universal responsibility to dramatize and give epic dimension to narrative form. Behind all his years of lectures at Brandeis, on *Omnibus,* at Young People's Concerts, and before Thursday evening Philharmonic concerts ran his long-standing social agenda: to create and recreate a communally engaged audience. The audience is all we have left of lost community and the only surviving element of the left-wing progressive's dream of a community of sweet friendship and mutuality. This progressivism found realization in the 1940s with the formation of the United Nations and in the 1960s with the radical music of Dylan and the Beatles, music that was coterminous with the Mahler revival and its expressions of horror over social catastrophe. People, Bernstein would be arguing, show up at concerts because they are starved for a communal moment of authentic subjectivity, in which each can take his or her trip into interiority within the sound world of a work of musical art and shed his or her official persona: the concert reminds audience members of that possibility, if only for a moment before they separate and go back to their private lives. But a catalyst is needed to transform a collection of ticket purchasers into an "intelligent organism," someone who can embody and exhibit the powers of impassioned music.

## MAGUS AT THE PODIUM

Bernstein could not depart from the idea that tonality and morality were bound together and that atonality and loss of faith were likewise paired.[22] In fact, he suggested that tonally based music has a role to play in the civilizing process, an idea that goes back to Plato and Christian and Renaissance thinkers and that is still cherished today in many philosophic circles.

This idea is worth further exploration here because it lies behind a good deal of Bernstein's ethics, and, far-fetched as the connection may appear at first, tells us something about his podium manner.

The theory of a tie-in between aesthetic and ethical realms got under way with the discovery, supposedly by Pythagoras in the sixth century B.C., that harmonious musical intervals—the tones of octaves, thirds, fourths, and fifths—could be produced by plucking at a stretch of string pinched into similar, congruent lengths. This extraordinary discovery, that physical and musical harmony are congruent, seemed to be a key to the structure of the universe and led Plato to write in his *Timaeus* of a Demiurge that creates the universe by spinning out spiritual and material stuff in a harmonious numeric series to form the World Soul, which contains the fixed stars, the planets, the sun, and the moon, each in its own concentric orbit around the inert earth, as well as all the lesser beings—human, other animal, vegetable, and mineral.

If the earth and its denizens are imperfect and finite, humans can nevertheless live in harmony with the cosmos about them and with their fellows and themselves if, as Plato indicated in his *Republic,* they create a potentially perfect and harmonious ethical polis, or city-state. This city-state must be designed to promote in its citizenry contemplation of beauty, moral purpose, and mutual demand for and pursuit of justice. No dissonance or disharmony should disturb this well-formed city, and therefore the theory of *paideia,* or the education of the young, must exclude anything that would contribute to imperfection and disharmony, such as musical dissonance. In such surroundings, the well-balanced person grows up in sympathetic vibration, in harmonious consonance, with his or her social, political, natural, and cosmic surroundings.

Over the centuries, many of Plato's texts were lost to Western thinkers, but those that survived came to be interpreted within church doctrine. Thus, in the Middle Ages, the church took a Platonic turn by banning the performance of the so-called *diabolis in musica* or Devil's Chord, the discordant interval consisting of three whole steps (e.g., C to F-sharp). Plato's *Symposium,* rediscovered by late fifteenth-century Renaissance theorists, had an enormous influence on the arts. Its translator Marsilio Ficino held that if one would forgo mundane delights and instead contemplate the hierarchy of eternal ideas, one would bask in an ecstatic flow of love via mystical union with the Godhead. But for Ficino and other Renaissance scholars, Plato's texts were in fact secondary to those believed to predate even the Hebrew Bible, those of the Egyptian sorcerer, or magus, Hermes Trismagistus. These texts of ancient wisdom revealed how the powers and forces that emanate from the stars could be harnessed to benefit human beings. The Renaissance magus, armed with this ancient astrological knowledge, could, by various forms of incantation, recitation, and musical performance, enable the individual to receive certain emanations from the stars while blocking out others and thus enhance that person's physical and mental health.[23] Thus, the magus could bring down to his client a certain Jovial gravity or Venusian eroticism, tempered either by Apollonian "grace and smoothness" or a more Mercurial "strenuousness," by making such music during the times that Jupiter, Venus, or Mercury are, respectively, near Apollo, the Sun.[24]

But what music? According to the scholars D. P. Walker and Francis Yates, the ancient Orpheus composed the music that could transport audiences, but unfortunately for the Renaissance magus, no notated music had come down from Orpheus's time.[25] A century after Ficino, French theorists of the Académie de poésie et de musique, modeled after Ficino's Platonic Academy, attempted to replicate the effects of the ancient music by, for example, measuring each note to a precise fit with each utterance of a carefully developed or quoted text.[26] Using this technique, they prepared a concert for the wedding of Duc Anne de Joyeuse and the monarch's sister-in-law in Paris in 1581.[27] Behind this moment, however, was a political idea: that of finding the magical methods to align the state to the stars. The main figures in this movement included the British astrologer to Queen Elizabeth, John Dee, and the magus-courtier Giordano Bruno.

By the turn of the sixteenth century, belief in the astrological foundations of music and morals was disintegrating for a variety of reasons, such as evidence that the texts of Hermes Trismagistus did not date back to the time of the ancient Hebrews but were written after the death of Jesus. But perhaps more importantly, the scientific revolutions brought about by Copernicus and then Galileo were seriously challenging if not dismantling the older astrology-based cosmology and the numerical mysticism that underlaid the Platonic and Neoplatonic worldviews. And yet, even as number was demystified and the belief in the powers of magi was scorned and ridiculed, some forms of the old outlook held on here and there. Late eighteenth-century Masonic lore certainly found musical expression in Mozart's *Magic Flute,* with the idea of the magus as wise conciliator.

Enter Richard Wagner, who in the late 1840s and early 1850s, proposed that music was the vehicle that would create the bond between the individual and the larger but lost historical German community. According to Wagner, if the German language had become so encrusted and distorted by official language, musical theater—that is, dramatic poetry expressed within epic and symbolic music—would bind together the German race and bring it back to its ethical life. To any number of Germans, not least young Friedrich Nietzsche, Wagner was the magus-tragedian who would create the sound worlds and mythic moments that would pull Germans into recognition of their destiny.

Within twentieth-century musical circles, many people, not least Bruno Walter, adored Wagner's music but had come to disdain tendencies toward German nationalism. Walter, in his 1935 address to a Viennese audience, "About the Moral Powers of Music," had sounded a rather ironic note by arguing that if listening to great music made people moral, musicians would be very moral indeed! But Walter was after something more solid, something that made tonal music necessary to audiences. Tonal music conveys the struggle to resolution, dissonance finding consonance, and striving forms finding rest and peace. Atonal music cannot deliver this message to the audience because it has no home key and therefore denies its listeners rest and peace. But tonal music offers "moral uplift"; it takes listeners into the heart of a human being's emotional life, where once again resolution is the goal. Finally, he said, tonal music brings an audience into a community.

The powers of music that made us a society, a "togetherness" is the highest proof of the presence and intensity of her moral powers, and this community does not only pertain to those who are making music: it pulls those who listen into the same magical circle. Whether there are five or two thousand, all are seized in the same manner, carried up to the same heights of sensation. Music makes them a group. I often feel how she grabs us with the powers of her magic, a form of mystical absorption, a melting together, an experience of becoming one. In the current of love, that envelopes [*sic*] us in music, the bonds of individualism; that, on this earth, have condemned us to the life-long imprisonment of our lonely soul, have carried us up to the eternal realm of music, where we become one in a boundless unity with the eternal (all), and get a glimpse of heaven. And the words of the dying Faust are appropriate for such big moments of musical association: "In anticipation of such great happiness, I enjoy now this highest moment."[28]

Bernstein, some thirty-eight years later, posed much the same argument. The audience is a community; its members, enlivened by tonal music of the highest quality, thereby share in the contemplation of the highest ethical values. And in the absence of real political community, the concert hall is the only surrogate for reenacting, if only symbolically, the ethical polis.

And indeed, in 1973, with the great communities of the 1960s gone, defeated, dissolved away, the concert hall once again had to serve its ancient function of secular ecclesia. Bernstein thus held to a sentimental notion lingering after centuries of keen certainty and then dissolution. Deep within his outlook was the idea of the conductor as a modern magus who transforms inert musical notation into a force that galvanizes orchestra and audience. This magus creates a unifying sound world by fashioning tonal music into perfection of form—beauty—within the concert hall. Everyone within this world absorbs this music on a preinterpretive level such as to elevate, unite, and harmonize them into community.

In other words, a public, ethical life—a political community—comes into being, at least on the plane of aesthetics, but with the promise of a leap onto the plane of ethics. For Bernstein, the performance of tonal music remained important because it offered the listener emancipating trips into his or her consciousness and narratives that reminded audiences of the potential for a joyful community of authentic subjects. Such was Bernstein's hope, which he communicated by his exuberance at the podium, a much-misunderstood element of his performances. His critics only saw exhibitionism when they should also have seen an ecstatic celebrant translating the enrapturing tonal sound world into physicality, into dance. This transport could occur in the concert hall, wherein musicians, conductor, and audience could reenact in imagination the idea of participation in the ethical polis that had inspired Greek audiences in the fifth century B.C.

Bernstein was not in his rhapsodic mode when he concluded his Norton Lectures. The joyful polis was only a regulative idea, a way to measure the existing state of affairs. For Bernstein, as for progressives in general, that state of affairs was far from joyful.

## BERNSTEIN AND THE
## MAHLER GENERATION

From the late 1960s on, Gustav Mahler's work came to occupy a high place within the classical music canon, due in the greatest part to Bernstein's promotion. The filled concert halls in cities across the world; the massive festivals; the acceleration in the number of recordings; the number of biographies, discographies, and analyses, some of which are multivolume masterpieces in their own right; the illustrated coffee-table books; the published conference papers; the Mahler societies and Web sites—all attest to Mahler's prominence.

The composer had not always been so revered. In the decades between his death in 1911 and the 1960s, Mahler enjoyed a mixed reputation. For Schoenberg, Webern, Berg, and other members and followers of the Second Viennese School, Mahler was a hallowed revolutionary, not only as musician but as social critic: as Berg's disciple Theodore Adorno wrote, Mahler had broken through eighteenth- and nineteenth-century symphonic custom by inserting fanfares and other jolts into the musical flow, as if he were breaking through the patina of bourgeois illusion.[29] Mahler's innovations in instrumentation; his mix of voice and instruments; his open forms and play with tonality—these and many more such innovations made him an exemplar to these and other radical composers. Others were not so certain of Mahler's importance: in 1940, Aaron Copland wrote that Mahler's music was "long-winded, trite, bombastic; he lacks taste, and sometimes he plagiarizes unblushingly."[30] Indeed, for decades, Mahler's music had only a small audience.

Before the war, and until the boom started in the 1960s, conductors such as Mengelberg, Walter, Klemperer, Scherchen, Rodzinski, Rosbaud, Furtwaengler, and Mitropoulos had kept Mahler's music alive. Though only sixteen commercial recordings of Mahler's works were released between 1924 and 1940, the 1950s saw, on average, five commercial recordings each year.[31] The number rose with the introduction of the LP in 1958, which made the mammoth symphonies seem less forbidding to consumers who had no doubt been intimidated by the ten or more double-sided 78s needed for just one hour's music.

Bernstein's association with Mahler's works went back to 1948, when he performed the Symphony no. 2, *Resurrection,* at Tanglewood.[32] He conducted many of Mahler's works for the Mahler centennial celebrations that started in 1960, and he recorded for Columbia (now Sony) the first complete Mahler cycle, finishing in 1967. During these years, Bernard Haitink for Philips, Rafael Kubelik for Deutsche Grammophon, and Georg Solti for London had entered the fray, so by 1972, music buyers had a choice of four Mahler cycles on sale. Meanwhile, the overall yearly average of commercial releases rose to eleven for the period 1960–70, with an upward leap between 1966 and 1971 of sixteen, on average, per year. Bernstein continued conducting Mahler with the Vienna Philharmonic in the 1970s and 1980s, and along the way, recorded a second complete cycle of the Mahler symphonies on film for Unitel and a third complete cycle on CD for Deutsche Grammophon. Not only was he Mahler's champion, but also Mahler, dead since 1911, seemed to play an important role in Bernstein's life. What accounts for Bernstein's association with Mahler? And what was the composition of the audience that sustained that Mahler boom and thus responded to and encouraged Bernstein to remain Mahler's champion?

Bernstein, like Mahler, was Jewish, was a composer, and conducted both the New York and Vienna Philharmonics. Mahler died in 1911, seven years before Bernstein was born, but had a symbolic if not mythic place in Bernstein's heart, given that Bernstein had been handed the baton by Mahler's protégé Bruno Walter on November 14, 1943. But there were other reasons for this affinity, not only for Bernstein but for his generation, certainly for those who formed the audience and recording market for Mahler's works. Who were these new consumers of this heretofore-obscure music? What compelled them to rush to Mahler?

The argument that the LP itself made Mahler's works accessible to the home listener does not suffice to explain the works' rise from near obscurity to popularity and their ability to fill concert halls across the world. Certainly, the answer must lie in the music's appeal to its audience. Mahler's music is generally known by its juxtaposition of the elevated and the vernacular, the mystical and the banal; in it, brutal marches dissolve into rhapsodic and surreal reveries, and sweet lyrical lines are broken by ironies, parodies, and grotesqueries. In Mahler, we hear protracted, bittersweet suspensions that dissipate as a shimmering violin holds on for measures or as wind lines are offset with sparkles from the celeste, harp, or glockenspiel. These effects are far from the conventional resolutions offered by earlier masters. In such fashion does the protagonist in "Der Abschied" from *Das Lied von der Erde* disappear into all-consuming, all-embracing, eternal nature. So too does the musical persona fall into the sleep/lullaby episodes in the Ninth Symphony.

Anyone listening to the drama in these works experiences something emotionally searing. Perhaps this feature is the key to the Mahler boom: the public that was forming around Mahler's works in the late 1950s and early 1960s, and which grew in the next years, found in this music the expression of unresolved or irresolvable preoccupations with the destruction of a civilization and with unbounded pity and grief, none of which could find expression in the unbroken lyrical lines and forceful and clear resolutions of traditional symphonic forms.

The bulk of the Mahler-consuming public in the 1960s and early 1970s was fully mindful of the catastrophes wrought when the Nazis took command in Europe. Some experienced the terror of fascism and the war directly; others fought in the war; those born in the middle of this period might not have fought but lived through the terror or watched events unfold; all experienced the catastrophe in one way or another. In the postwar decades, their sensibilities were dominated by the horrors of genocide, as well as by McCarthyism and Cold War rhetoric. They lived and worked within economies dominated by massive industrial-financial and state-bureaucratic power blocs, within spatial arrangements dominated by suburbanization, and within a public sphere dominated by voracious commercialization. Small wonder, then, that they were preoccupied with existential and Freudian reflections on the individual's isolation and spiritual discontent. They needed a music that expressed itself in first-person singular and that was outside the orthodox discourses of ideological, patriotic, and nationalistic affirmation and triumphalism. This generation was desperate to avoid falling into cynicism, narcissism, and nihilism. It needed to connect, or reconnect, with its roots in the intellectual, artistic, and musical culture of prefascist Europe and to express empathy with the victims of the European catastrophes. This music therefore could not celebrate victory in the heroic fashion of Beethoven.

Mahler's music fulfilled these requirements for nonheroic biographical and epic representation. First, those who have more than a passing acquaintance with Mahler's life and music know how profoundly his literary and intellectual interests informed the early symphonies, and how he found expression for his own life in his later symphonies and in *Das Lied von der Erde*.[33] Second, because he was virtually exiled by the anti-Semitic protofascists in Vienna, thus making his victimization a harbinger of the catastrophe to befall European Jewry, the music can be enlisted in a narrative of genocide, the murder of a people and its culture.[34] Third, the sudden and massive upheavals in Mahler's works permit the music to represent the immanence of the catastrophic into contemporary life— seemingly providing an apt trope for the decades beyond World War II, as Bernstein suggested. As Bernstein said, Mahler's time had come.[35] We can little wonder, then, at Bernstein's affinity for and championship of Mahler's music.

# CHAPTER SIX

# Bernstein at Sea

## *1974–1990*

By 1974, the "long sixties" had come to an end. The American war in Vietnam was over, and Nixon had been ousted from office, but the Right was in resurgence, fed by resentment about the feminists' and blacks' drives for equal rights, the urban ghetto uprisings that had left cities ablaze, the loss of the war, and economic woes. Of these factors, the last was accelerating the mobilization on the Right. By the early 1970s, small-business owners, suffering falling rates of profit and increasing rates of bankruptcy, had organized antitax revolts that started in earnest in Michigan and California but soon spread across the nation. This rightward tendency further accelerated with the petroleum crisis spurred by the increase in prices by the Organization of Petroleum Exporting Countries (OPEC) at the end of 1973. The ensuing shock wave of unemployment, starting in the auto and steel industries in 1974, left bankruptcies and further collapse in its wake, wiping out savings, causing panic, and inducing even more movement away from the already-weakened ranks of liberalism.

Nevertheless, even as the Right gained strength, the feminist and gay-liberation movements seemed full of energy, the former especially galvanized by the Supreme Court's 1973 ruling on abortion rights in *Roe v. Wade.* But the two sexual-liberation movements did not have the benefit of synergy like that of the civil rights and antiwar movements only a few years before. Whereas the latter movements thrived on the comradeship of hundreds of thousands of like-minded people, these sexual-political movements were more or less on their own, each seeking its redresses largely in legislatures and courtrooms rather than in the streets. As the multitudes that had demonstrated against the war vacated the public sphere, many a "reradicalized" progressive such as Bernstein now fell back into relative quiescence.

In short, the overall mood of radicalism so prominent in the 1960s was disappearing. For example, the avant-garde artworks that had provided so much "shock of the new" in the early 1960s were being absorbed and marketed by the fashion and culture industries.[1] In November 1973, Susan Sontag noted, "With Whitman's dream of cultural revolution discredited, all we have left is a sharp-eyed, witty despair."[2] In 1974, Pauline Kael, powerful articulator of film-generation criticism, lamented the loss of political impulse in the film industry, now hopelessly taken over by financially profitable entertainment values.[3]

Perhaps a sign that Bernstein had joined the general retreat from political engagement was his agreement to compose for Robbins's ballet *Dybbuk,* a work of kabbalistic mysticism that, unlike *Kaddish,* stayed clear of the ethical concerns of the Hebrew prophetic tradition that might align with contemporary political issues. Even the FBI found nothing new to add to Bernstein's dossier.[4]

By 1975, Bernstein was busy with new creative projects. To celebrate the upcoming American Bicentennial celebration in 1976, he scheduled a number of performances of American music, and with lyricist Stephen Jay Lerner, composed a musical theatrical work, *1600 Pennsylvania Avenue,* which opened on Broadway on May 4. The work was an attempt to survey the practice of slavery and racism over the course of American history by focusing on the reflections of a black couple that works in the White House for assorted presidents, from Washington through Theodore Roosevelt. According to Arthur Laurents, Bernstein and Lerner set out to create a work that would rescue from "Nixon's mark of Cain . . . a country they loved passionately," but the show turned out to be, "in sum, an unstructured, ambitious mess."[5] The Broadway run lasted only a few weeks. But a far stronger statement was in the works.

## SONGFEST

Bernstein's long search for a compositional method by which to express his socially responsible outlook was evident in remarks he made during a United States Information Agency (USIA) film interview in 1977. No composer, he mused, can express his political position through his music alone because musical notation has no correlative verbal translation. At best, a work of music can be a "time capsule" in that its style reflects the period of composition.[6] The transcript of the interview shows Bernstein struggling with these ideas, but as he talked his ideas seemed to sharpen. Artists, he argued, are particularly sensitive to attempts at censorship and take action not only in public demonstrations but also in their art. Through style, a composer can register reaction to present political conditions. Interestingly, his examples were composers—he did not mention Schoenberg, Berg, and Webern by name—who adopted atonality to express the upheavals of the earlier years of the twentieth century. Thus, a composer can express his or her resistance to political or cultural orthodoxy through musical forms that discomfort and disturb.

In fact, Bernstein concluded, art can stimulate and enliven listeners. The key to politically significant musical expression is to discover an appropriate musical form: it may contain atonal music but must be centered in tonality—the sole means, he argued, whereby music can communicate to the American public.

That Bernstein had been searching for a new form was apparent from his struggle to conceptualize his new work, *Songfest*—a composition that set music to poems by Americans from Puritan times to the 1950s—which he had hoped to finish during the bicentennial year but which other matters had kept him from finishing on time. By the time the work finally premiered on October 11, it had gone through a number of subtitles, including "Six Characters in Search of an Opera" and "Notes for an American Opera"—evidence of his unrest.[7] The work was supposedly a celebration of American song, but most of the poems that he selected celebrated or memorialized the marginalized and the forgotten, people to whom much of the official self-congratulatory hypernationalist mythology had little meaning or significance. Bernstein made quite clear his ambivalence about American culture and politics by introducing the piece with the kind of stylistic revolt that he had discussed in the USIA interview, a jarring and off-putting horn and snare-drum fanfare that explicitly rejected the military triumphalism that conventionally symbolizes American patriotism. He followed this fanfare with a prelude, a chorale set to lines from Frank O'Hara's "To the Poem," written in 1952 or 1953, that verbally underscores his dissentient stylistic intervention: "Let us do something grand just this once. Something small and important and un-American."[8] Some years later, Bernstein would explain to audiences in Munich and Paris that by "un-American," O'Hara meant "not . . . *anti*-American, but simply not flag-waving, not patriotically boastful. It is a kind of American paradox: grand, small, unimportant—but also a bit self-mocking and without chauvinism."[9] Indeed, O'Hara's text seemed to be precisely about writing a poem about the unheroic day-to-day life, very much his genre. But the House Un-American Activities Committee, of course, dominated the period of the poem's composition, and one could not mistake the term's reference, especially as underscored by Bernstein's music. The line was a double entendre, a piece of political speech that was as heavy with irony and defiance as it was expressive of literary form.

Bernstein followed the O'Hara piece with Lawrence Ferlinghetti's "The Pennycandystore Beyond the El," a wistful recounting of painterly images—a cat on a counter full of candy, an erotic awakening, a kind of moving still life of leaves falling and dying—set in twelve-tone whimsy with a light touch. Next was Julia de Burgos's "A Julia de Burgos," in which a young woman proudly declares her independence from stereotype, convention, and patriarchy, pounding out her defiance in Falla-like rhythmic accentuation. In contrast, the next song is a long-lined melodic setting of Walt Whitman's "To What You Said," a poem its author left out of *Leaves of Grass* because it dealt with the impossibility of love between men, which Bernstein communicated in tones of deeply melancholic resignation to unending injustice. Setting this poem must have been terribly important for Bernstein, not only because of the sentiments he shared with the poet but because it made a statement about his own America. The song's sorrowful opening fanfare alludes to the fanfare at the beginning of the cycle, thereby lending overall unity to the whole cycle, and at the same time reinforces the work's criticism of an uncritical, self-righteous bicentennial celebration. The bitter sentiment is reinforced by a haunting melody in the low strings and woodwinds played over a relentless ostinato rhythm, as steady as a heartbeat. A solo voice—in concert with the chorus—intones tenderly and compassionately of men robbed of normal human joy, compelled to deny their impulses for love save for stolen moments. Suddenly, the sense of sober resignation is interrupted by biting sarcasm: "I introduce that new American salute," angrily sung over a brutal roll of the snare drum, symbol of the jackboot, that belies the uncritical fife, drum, flag, and fireworks of bicentennial pageantry.

Bernstein next turned to poems about racial discrimination—"I, Too, Sing America" by Langston Hughes and "Okay, 'Negroes'" by June Jordan—in a composite work of two voices. The optimism of Hughes, certain of coming racial equality, is countered by Jordan's belief that racism will persist unless blacks take action. Two poems about marriage follow, set for a trio of women's voices: "To My Dear and Loving Husband," a personal statement by the seventeenth-century Puritan Anne Bradstreet; and, in contrast to this affirmation of marriage, Gertrude Stein's "Storyette H. M," an ironic if not sarcastic statement about marital discontent.[10] E. E. Cummings's ironic "If You Can't Eat You To" deals with profound poverty, set by Bernstein in an ambience reminiscent of the Juliet de Burgos piece. Conrad Aiken's "Music I Heard with You" is a poem of grief for a beloved who has died. Bernstein set rather sinuous music to Gregory Corso's "Zizi's Lament," an ironic expression of an unhappy person unable to find joy. Edna St. Vincent Millay's "What My Lips Have Kissed" is a tragic remembrance of lovers killed in World War I; the music descends to accompany the thoughts of these lost young men, touches an incongruous note of whimsy or nonchalance that turns back into its theme of memorial to dead lovers, the narrator reaching down into her vocal depths to express her sense of utter devastation.

*Songfest* ends with a setting of Edgar Allen Poe's "Israfel." The archangel enchants all of creation with his song, expects all songs to at least attempt to mimic his own passion, but knows that earthbound mortals can never soar to his angelic heights. This ending does not aim to resolve the whole: even as it speaks to the magnificence of song, it only underscores its composer's melancholic outlook in those years of the mid-1970s.

## MALAISE AT HOME, PROBLEMS IN ISRAEL

As we have seen, for some years, Bernstein had centered his conducting career on the Vienna Philharmonic, his repertoire consisting largely of Beethoven and Mahler. Since 1972, he had been filming his second complete Mahler cycle for Deutsche Grammophon and the German film company Unitel; he would finish the cycle in 1977.[11] His agenda was filled more with conducting than with composing. President Jimmy Carter's July 1979 so-called malaise speech echoed Bernstein's state of mind in those days. In the speech, Carter reflected on the enormous impact of the second, 1979, OPEC shock on the American economy, marking the end of the United States' decades-long dependence on low-cost oil. Carter announced a program of energy conservation and the development of new energy sources but also went beyond the sheer economic impact of the oil crisis to speak of a loss of spirit in the American public, a loss of confidence and of faith in American institutions such as family, government, and churches— thoughts paralleling Bernstein's.

Most troubling to Bernstein at the moment, however, were recent problems in Israel. Bernstein had long been a devotee of the Jewish state, visiting in 1947, even before independence.[12] In October and November of 1948, he had conducted performances across Israel, sometimes in areas subject to cannon bombardment.[13] At one point, he was offered the position of music director of the Israel Philharmonic (which he turned down).[14] In 1950, he was invited to perform in Washington, D.C., for visiting Israeli president Chaim Weizmann.[15] Over the years, he returned frequently to perform with the Israel Philharmonic Orchestra, most memorably conducting with soloist Artur Rubinstein the Beethoven Piano Concerto no. 5 for the inauguration of the Mann Concert Hall in Tel Aviv; he also toured with the orchestra in the United States, made numerous recordings with the orchestra, and filmed a performance of Mahler's *Das Lied von der Erde* for Unitel in 1972.[16]

Bernstein's support for the Jewish state stemmed from his ethnic and religious sentiment as much as historical fact: the Israelis were survivors of a European Jewish culture that had remained alive over the millennia-long diaspora from its ancient homeland. Jews had been coming back to Palestine for centuries, their numbers increasing greatly from the late nineteenth century and early decades of the twentieth century but accelerating in the decades straddling World War I. By the late 1930s, the Jewish population in Palestine was some 400,000, and by 1947, Jews numbered 650,000 in the total population of 1.3 million.[17] Jewish presence had long worried Arabs concerned about their own livelihoods and power and about British plans to divide Palestine into two states, one Jewish and one Arab. Many Arab leaders who were offended both by British power and Jewish presence became supporters and admirers of Hitler. Arab violence against Jews became commonplace: Jews were attacked, sometimes murdered. Antagonisms only intensified with the arrival of thousands of survivors of the Holocaust who were taking up permanent status.

War seemed inevitable. The Jewish population was politically and institutionally well organized: the socialists, anarcho-syndicalist kibbutzniks, and progressives who formed the majority of the Jewish population had formed a democratic government in the years immediately following World War I. Empowered by the example of the heroic Warsaw Ghetto uprising and rallying themselves with a cry of "Never Again!" the Jewish populace and government organized a military force whose numbers were small but imbued with zealously developed morale. Thus, the Jews proved victorious when the Arab Palestinians attacked them on November 1947. They were again victorious when, immediately upon Israel's being declared an independent state, May 15, 1948 (with recognition by both the Soviet Union and the United States), they faced mass invasions by the Arab League.

To themselves and to Jews everywhere, not least Bernstein, here was a tiny populace representing the six million people who had only a few years before inhabited thriving Jewish communities from Vilna, Warsaw, and Krakow to Vienna, Prague, and Budapest; from Rhodes and Thessalonica and Bucharest to Rome, Paris, Berlin, and Amsterdam, but who had been murdered by the Nazis and their allies.[18] Here, in Israel, these survivors were now constituting a state of their own to ensure their security. For those who were religiously observant, the new state presented an opportunity to reconstruct their ancient traditions and customs. For the secular, it provided a land wherein to reconstruct the classical European philosophical, literary, musical, and ethical civilization that the Nazis had hoped to destroy.

Over the succeeding years, Israelis had to withstand unrelenting acts of Arab terrorism. Many were killed. In 1967, the Israelis, under intense pressure of blockade and a massing of Egyptian troops, went on the offensive and attacked Egypt and Syria. Victory brought Israel control of the West Bank, the Gaza Strip, and the Golan Heights, from which Syrian bombardments and sniper attacks had been commonplace. In 1973, Egypt and Syria suddenly invaded Israel on Yom Kippur, the highest holy day, with virtually the whole Jewish population in synagogue or otherwise in retreat. For a few days, the fate of the Israelis seemed in jeopardy. The bloodbath long promised by the Arabs seemed imminent. The Israelis, however, turned the tide and within two weeks inflicted enormous casualties upon the Arabs. But in 1977, a new government headed by the right-winger Menachem Begin adopted a policy demanding permanent occupation of the West Bank not only for security and strategic purposes but to encourage the formation and expansion of Jewish settlements in these territories; this policy of annexation expropriated Palestinians from their homes, villages, and means of livelihood.[19]

On June 21, 1979, Bernstein, along with a number of other Jews with impeccable credentials as supporters of Israel, including Saul Bellow, law professor Alan M. Dershowitz, and the literary critic Alfred Kazin, published a petition that was read in an outdoor meeting in Tel Aviv calling for an end to the West Bank settlement policy. The American group argued that "a policy which requires the expropriation of Arab land unrelated to Israel's security needs, and which presumes to occupy permanently a region populated by over 750,000 Palestinian Arabs," was "morally unacceptable, and perilous for the democratic character of the Jewish state."[20] Bernstein and his fellow petitioners got nowhere: the twin impulses of antiterrorism and expansionism proceeded to dominate Israeli politics in the coming years.[21]

## A QUIET PLACE

On November 14, 1980, Bernstein celebrated Aaron Copland's eightieth birthday, leading a performance of *A Lincoln Portrait* with Copland narrating. The evening was a bittersweet moment for Bernstein and Copland, because only a few days before, the conservative Ronald Reagan had won the presidency. The electoral and ideological base of post–World War II liberalism was collapsing with the decline of the massive industrial economy and the concomitant decline of union membership. By the mid-1970s, formerly prosperous northeastern and midwestern heavy-industrial towns were failing, their residents migrating to the Sunbelt that stretched from the Carolinas to Southern California, leaving behind boarded-up homes, shopping malls, and schools. A politics of resentment was growing among white, heretofore Democratic voters who were increasingly upset with policies promoting racial integration and preferences for blacks in employment and other workplace areas. The conservative media exploited other so-called wedge issues to create moral panics, thereby to whip up voters' concerns about the various immoralities and injustices supposedly result-ing from the sexual liberation of heterosexuals, lesbian women, and gay men. Many of the attacks upon feminists and gays came from evangeli-cal and fundamentalist leaders, who preached their messages to audiences in church and especially to Americans sitting at home in front of their television sets. The turn to religion was a most startling social fact: only a few years before, sociologists and theologians had been discussing the decline in the number of religiously observant Americans. By the middle to late 1970s, this new movement of evangelical groups and antitax pro-ponents had made Nixon's "silent majority" a reality. In a climate of anxi-ety induced by the moral panics, oil-price increases, high inflation, Soviet gains overseas, and Iranian hostage taking, this conservative populace elected Reagan president.

According to Reagan, government was the real domestic enemy, whereas liberals and progressives argued that his outlook was a cover for proposals to grant tax relief to those in the higher earning brackets and to cut social spending while increasing defense spending. Certain not to rise in the Reagan budget were appropriations for research to combat AIDS, which was a most pressing issue for Bernstein. Not only was the adminis-tration failing to address the AIDS epidemic, but also, as Bernstein bitterly noted in a June 1983 speech, the religious Right was proclaiming AIDS to be God's punishment for gay men's supposed sinful depravity.[22]

That one could publicly and openly contemplate issues of homosexual-ity in the early 1980s was testament to the development of the gay-libera-tion movement. Since the 1969 Stonewall incident in New York, when gay men, upset with harassment by police officers, started a melee that spurred efforts across the nation to protect their rights, many gays had been com-ing out of the closet.[23] Indeed, Bernstein had left Felicia in 1976 to live with his same-sex lover. He returned to her a year later when she became ill and remained at her side until her death in 1978, but after his mourning period was over, he went on to live an erotically full life. He had long been preoccupied with the issues of war and peace, but now, he was focused on the marginalization of gays as well.

Could the complexities of gay men's living within difficult familial situations and subject to more general stigma be expressed in operatic form? In 1980, according to the writer and director Stephen Wadsworth, Bernstein, apparently at loose ends, decided to concentrate on themes that were clearly troubling him personally. He asked Wadsworth for a libretto, a sequel to his 1952 *Trouble in Tahiti,* for a serious opera rather than an operetta or Broadway musical.[24] At this juncture of his life, he needed to compose a serious and significant work, perhaps his long-hoped-for but unrealized major American opera.

Wadsworth's libretto for the new work, *A Quiet Place,* focuses on the later strains and struggles within the family of Sam and Dinah from Bernstein's *Trouble in Tahiti.* The sequel—recalling the couple's dream of a garden of peace, a "quiet place"—is set thirty years later. Dinah is dead, killed in an auto accident.[25] Returning home from the funeral are Sam's children, Junior and Dede, and her husband, François. Junior is a psychotic homosexual in mutual alienation with Sam, and François is Junior's former lover. Ancient family tensions quickly come to the surface, but over the course of this dark and somber work, the grieving and enraged Sam is finally able to make a tenuous connection with his son, his daughter, and his son-in-law: reconciliation proves difficult but possible.

The score is manifestly darker than Bernstein's earlier music. Absent are the moments of joy and buoyancy that found expression in *Age of Anxiety* and the musical theater works, such as *On the Town, Wonderful Town, Candide, West Side Story,* and *Mass.* The jazzlike moments that do occur represent psychosis at worst, irony at best. The problem with the work is the libretto. Is the work about a family in disarray, or is it social criticism? If the latter, then Dede's apparently incestuous relations with Junior and her marital arrangements with Junior's former lover, François, work at cross-purposes to, and distract from, the intended commentary on sexual politics. The opera has been largely forgotten, although a suite composed from Bernstein's score has given this often-powerful music a deserved life of its own.

## JEREMIAH

In the summer of 1983, Bernstein became increasingly agitated about Reagan's new militarization programs. The president framed this new arms race as a response to events set in motion in the early 1970s. In the wake of the Vietnam catastrophe, the public had become reluctant to sanction involvement in international adventures, and the Soviets, who were enjoying large inflows of money due to petroleum exports as OPEC raised petroleum prices, were not only able to raise incomes at home but to fund overseas activities in the Middle East, employing Cuban troops in Africa and providing aid to such revolutionary groups as the Sandinistas in Nicaragua. To counter these Soviet advances, Congress had earlier acceded to Jimmy Carter's wish to increase military spending in support of his Carter Doctrine to secure flows of oil from the Persian Gulf. Carter's program entailed a massive military buildup, including the construction and placement of MX missiles that could enter the stratosphere and let loose a number of smaller missiles, or MIRVs. Moreover, to counter the Russians' installation of intermediate (as opposed to intercontinental) missiles targeting Western European targets, the Americans, with NATO's agreement, were installing their own, Europe-based missile system aimed at the Soviet Union. Reagan entered office with the idea of upgrading the American military investment, including funds to accelerate missile construction, and to pay expenses with moneys that previously had supported programs benefiting the poor, the working classes, and the elderly.

In March 1982, Bernstein joined many other Americans who were angered by Reagan's nuclear buildup in a movement to support the Kennedy-Hatfield Congressional Nuclear Freeze Resolution.[26] In March 1983, Reagan announced the start-up of the new Strategic Defense Initiative, or "Star Wars" program, which would send billions of dollars to military contractors over the coming years. On August 25, in an address to a crowd gathered to inaugurate the Leonard Bernstein Outdoor Theater in Lawrence, Massachusetts, Bernstein noted that the costs of a nuclear weapon could be devoted instead to the construction of libraries and schools.[27] At the end of the year, Bernstein's anger with the Reagan administration's missile program led him to a bitter confrontation with Derek Bok, the president of Harvard University. Bok had written a foreword to *Living with Nuclear Weapons,* a study by a team of Harvard professors who pointed out that inasmuch as everyone of consequence knows how to build nuclear weapons, nations could never have the certainty of universal disarmament, so they should remain armed. Outraged, Bernstein wrote Bok that he would no longer donate money to Harvard. We may know how to visit terror of all kinds upon others, he wrote, but that does not mean that we must commit ourselves to a technology of terror.[28]

On December 31, 1983, Bernstein spoke again about antinuclear action and peace causes at the Cathedral of St. John the Divine in New York. Never before had he sounded so much the Hebrew Old Testament prophet as he did in this address, arguing that mankind had now moved beyond "fratricide," "mass homicide" and "genocide" to "geocide, the murder of the world itself." This Jeremiah lamented the superficial cant of headlines about coming economic upturns—"all hypocrisies, falsehoods"—which hid the fact that millions were living in poverty and privation and others were mortgaging themselves into deeper debt in order to live well. "The truth, alas, are Famines, Drop-outs, Lip-Service in high places, Global Poverty, and the affluence of a Credit-Card economy," a "hypocritical superstructure" of multinational corporations and "super nation-states" that lives off arms buildups and war preparation. Real peace would permit nations to unleash the technology and funds necessary to eradicate disease, poverty, and illiteracy. He closed with Bernard Shaw's remark "The worst of crimes is poverty," adding that "the best of solutions to that crime is peace." As an introduction to a performance of *Urlicht* from Mahler's *Knaben Wunderhorn,* in which a child sings of his longings for the eternal bliss of Heaven, he said, "This music reflects the pure innocent child in each of us, the child that longs for, and believes in, the supreme miracle of peace."[29]

Bernstein was taking up a new idea for a work he hoped would be his masterpiece opera. In his "Sermon on Political Involvement" on January

25, 1985, he spoke of his dreamed-of opera once again, but, remarkably, this time it was no longer an American opera. In tones resonating with his understanding of the prophetic in Mahler's work, he said that this opera would have a chronological narrative that would brood over the catastrophes from Hitler's time to the present—"when so many of those danger signals from half-a-century ago are again flashing and ringing and beeping with alarming frequency." To prepare for this work, he had been studying personal accounts from the ghettos and the loci of genocide and the work of the "propaganda machines" in propagating anti-Semitism, which was "as rife today as ever, and all over the globe."[30]

On April 23, 1985, he wrote about Journey for Peace, his forthcoming tour with a youth orchestra; his love for both country and "planetary neighbors"; and his plans for an international musical body to play his Symphony no. 3, *Kaddish*, "a prayer for the dead, yet one which literally speaks not of death, but of life, of peace, and of sublime praise."[31] Five days later, on April 28, he performed in Alice Tully Hall, memorializing Marc Blitzstein, dead some twenty-six years, noting, as he was about to play Blitzstein's *Zipperfly*, that this "masterpiece" was "the very essence, in its crazy deeply quirky way, of Marc's proletarian soul, of his communality with the suffering and ever hopeful human race."[32] He was clearly upset about Reagan's visit to the Nazi cemetery at Bitburg, which had been arranged by German Chancellor Helmut Kohl; a letter on May 23 from Edward M. Kennedy documents that he, too, found the visit "unconscionable."[33] During July and August, Bernstein undertook the Journey for Peace concerts with the European Community Youth Orchestra, playing his *Kaddish* and other works in London, Athens, Hiroshima—where the concert took place at the ground zero site on August 6, the fortieth anniversary of the dropping of the atomic bomb—Budapest, and Vienna. He was preoccupied with Reagan's militarization programs. Thus, during a videotaping for a performance of Shostakovich's 9th Symphony with the Vienna Philharmonic on October 31, Bernstein commented upon the centrality of the antihero in postwar comedy and tragedy, noting that the composition shares cause with those works of film and literature that celebrate the unassuming, ever-victimized man in the street.[34]

The idea of the antihero appealed to him: a year later, on November 6, 1986, Bernstein and Jerome Robbins began collaborating on a revival of their failed 1968 antiheroic piece, *The Race to Urga*. Bernstein's notes indicate that he insisted that the work emphasize the ubiquitous and unceasing murder of working-class or racial or ethnic underdogs. He was as excited by the prospect of searching for a new form as he was by the opportunity to update Brecht's social message. He believed that he and his collaborators were "ethically duty-bound to reach an affluent public at all costs, and by all means." His exhilaration was apparent: the work was going to be "a new and great and unprecedented theatre-piece."[35] "Are we making an ethical point as well as a political one? Sure we are: after all, didn't Brecht make them [the coolies and guides] white and yellow? Sure, but isn't the class struggle universal? A MAN HAS BEEN KILLED. What man? Does it matter who, or what his importance, as if he's a grain of sand in a vast population?" A workshop for the production started in April 1987, but his euphoria collapsed when, a month later, Robbins dropped out.[36]

Bernstein's conducting career was in high gear. He was still performing and recording with the Vienna Philharmonic, his repertoire taken up with Beethoven, Mahler, Schumann, Brahms, and his own works.[37] On August 22, he conducted his last Salzburg Festival concert, with a program consisting of Mozart's Symphony no. 29 in A Major, K. 201; Jean Sibelius's Symphony no. 5 in E-Flat Major, op. 82; and his own Symphony no. 1, *Jeremiah*. He continued to concertize and record in fall and spring—Mozart and Sibelius, and much more Mahler and Beethoven.

All this while, Reagan had been using his bully pulpit to make conservatism so commonsensical and liberalism so much the object of ridicule and contempt that by 1988, the Democratic nominee, Michael Dukakis, dared not utter the now tainted "L" word lest he lose support. Meanwhile, the Republican presidential nominee, George H. W. Bush, openly disparaged "tax and spend liberalism" and broadcast the infamous Willy Horton ad loaded with coded symbols of racism.

Writing in the *New York Times* on October 30, an outraged and exasperated Bernstein pointed his finger at his fellow citizens, Dukakis included, to remind them that progressive liberals were the ones who had ended slavery and won workers' rights; that the "tyrants" who oppose liberalism included the fomenters of the Red Scares of 1919 and the post–World War II period; that modern tyrants would build up the defense budget at the expense of socially necessary programs such as health care and "cultural pursuits."[38] Bernstein's remarks were quite extraordinary in those days of liberalism's nadir, and the essay was a high point in Bernstein's long years of public political engagement with his fellow citizens.

Matching his anger was despair: on November 21, 1988, the eve of the twenty-fifth anniversary of the death of John F. Kennedy, Bernstein answered a letter from Martha Graham about her plan to rework her forty-year-old *American Document,* suggesting a "new element in American Document, 'assassination.'"[39]

He worried about Bush's election in 1988 for yet another reason: he feared that it would ensure low priority for AIDS care and low federal spending on medical research and that it would encourage those who continued to preach that AIDS was God's payment for homosexual sin.[40] Indeed, Bush did not disappoint conservatives, giving them support for their 1987 attack on the autonomy of the National Endowment for the Arts (NEA) in determining who receives grants. An NEA-funded gallery show in North Carolina contained a work by Andres Serrano entitled *Piss Christ* that upset right-wing senator Jesse Helms, Republican of North Carolina. When, shortly thereafter, the NEA funded photo images by Robert Mapplethorpe of gay men in various sadomasochistic poses, Helms and several of his colleagues in Congress demanded an overhaul of the NEA. The Bush administration fell in line and revoked an NEA grant for an exhibit in New York, *Witness: Against Our Vanishing,* that dealt with the politics of AIDS. Bernstein was disgusted by these actions, and on November 15, 1989, he refused Bush's offer of a National Medal of Arts.[41]

Bernstein's apogee as a public figure occurred with the fall of the Berlin Wall in late December 1989. Under Brezhnev, the creaky Soviet machinery had survived only as the Soviets sold oil, purchased wheat, and otherwise participated in the global market; but they had become vulnerable to the vagaries of global economic and political forces. Thus, as the price of oil fell in the early 1980s, so too did the inflow of cash that had been sustaining the economy.

By the mid-1980s Soviet president Gorbachev was planning programs—glasnost, or transparency within Soviet institutions, and perestroika, political and economic reform—racing against economic collapse and bureaucratic consolidation. So long as Reagan and the American hard-liners were pushing a new arms race, the Soviet military-industrial consortia could demand a distribution of budget moneys equivalent to those of the Americans. They might not get it all, but matching expenditures by the two superpowers meant that the Soviets would spend a much higher percentage of total wealth (measured as gross domestic product) on defense than would the Americans. The long-standing American policy to force the Soviets to spend themselves into bankruptcy was finally paying off.

But Reagan had a change of mind. At Geneva in 1985 and then in Reykjavik, he embraced Gorbachev's plans, thereby angering American hard-liners and pulling the rug out from under the antiglasnost/-perestroika Soviet hard-liners who had depended on American intransigence to justify their own military/imperial programs. Reagan may not have been mentally agile at the time, but he rose to the larger business, giving Gorbachev and the Soviet military confidence that the Americans would not jump on them as they were about to pull out of the satellite countries and thereby would not weaken these states, which the Soviets saw as their buffer-zone defense. Thus, the Soviets were able to begin their pullout from the European satellite countries and Afghanistan. In short order, one after the other communist regime collapsed, and in October 1989, down came the Berlin Wall. On December 23, and then December 25, Bernstein led an orchestra of East and West Berliners to perform Beethoven's Ninth Symphony in celebration of the reunification of Europe.

.  .  .

Matters were different at home. Bernstein was sick at heart over the collapse of American progressivism, the resurgence of reactionary sexual politics, the sloganeering and patriotic pandering of the new militarization and support for right-wing dictatorships cum death squads, and the demagogic rhetoric being put forth to justify the shift in the burden of taxation from the well-to-do to the middle and poorer sections of the populace. He had lost the inspiration that could find realization in an American work. During the 1970s, he had already spent much of his time in Vienna, Mahler's Vienna, essentially living in exile from the country that he loved profoundly but that had seemed to betray itself time and again.

By the late 1980s, Bernstein was experiencing malaise similar to that he had experienced in the mid-1960s and again after 1968. He would never again find the sense of optimism and progress that he had experienced in the last years of the 1930s and up to the late 1940s. By the 1970s, having been betrayed by his own government, humiliated, blacklisted, chronically threatened by congressional investigators, presidential and FBI saboteurs, agents provocateurs, and complicit journalists; seeing his hopes dashed by John F. Kennedy's, Martin Luther King's, and Robert Kennedy's assassinations and by the cynicism of the American political machinery; having become distraught over the war in Vietnam and the avaricious military-industrial complex that stole funds from socially useful projects, Bernstein was spending increasing time traveling across the Atlantic to perform in Europe, especially with the Vienna Philharmonic. He was adulated everywhere, the toast of Vienna. By the late 1980s, however, he was no longer in good health, having to rush off the podium at the end of a piece to breathe from an oxygen tank and to take a drag on a cigarette before going back to take his bows from adoring audiences.

Bernstein conducted the New York Philharmonic in October 1989 and the Vienna Philharmonic in New York in March 1990—each turning out to be his last performance with a beloved orchestra.[42] He had been diagnosed with mesothelioma, an inevitably fatal form of lung cancer.[43]

On May 29, 1990, he sat in his room in the Intercontinental Hotel in Prague, across from the Jewish Museum, and wrote to his long-term business manager Harry Kraut essentially his valedictory address, a poem that he entitled "Finalizing the Deal, I Believe You Call It," hoping for just enough time "to write 'That one Important Piece.'" He was not afraid of death, he wrote, only "of hurting / Someone I love, and then / Of not writing my Piece / Before my Not-to-Be."[44]

This piece, this "important piece," seemed terribly significant to Bernstein. What it might have been—what he had in mind, or in the back of his mind—is the subject of the next chapter.

# CHAPTER SEVEN

# Understanding Bernstein

## THE UNREALIZED MASTERWORK

The myriad photos of Bernstein that appear in coffee-table books show a man of great charm and buoyancy—at the podium, an impassioned magus; in public, a self-confident notable; at home, a happy husband and father.[1] Indeed, these picture-book images would seem to fit a man who had achieved canonical status, commoditized by the culture industry but as well knowing how to exploit its power.

There was, as we have seen, another Bernstein: the man who brooded over what he considered his failure to compose a masterwork of lasting importance. He knew he had such a work in him, but he never got around to creating it. Why he did not fulfill this project is a question that has intrigued many of his friends and critics, who, over the years, have offered various explanations to account for it. I contend that the answer to this question is of great importance, not only for understanding Bernstein but also for understanding the culture in which he was a leading figure.

The most common explanation for Bernstein's failure to compose a masterwork was that he spread himself thin: had he concentrated upon composing rather than diverting his energies into orchestral conducting, piano performance, and administration, he might well have succeeded in composing works that realized his highest aspirations. The locus classicus of admonishments to concentrate on one activity was Koussevitzky—ironic in light of the present discussion—who in 1944 told his young protégé, flush with the success of *On the Town,* to stop composing and focus on conducting.[2] Two years later, questioned about the potential for his multifaceted career to diminish his artistic potential, Bernstein explained that whether he conducted or performed at the piano or composed for the concert hall or the Broadway theater, he concentrated all his energies exclusively on the task at hand.[3] In 1948, Marc Blitzstein warned him that he needed to decide between composing and conducting.[4] Bernstein apparently had other ways to avoid composing: according to his biographer (and Columbia Records producer) Paul Myers and tenor Jerry Hadley, Bernstein's gregarious nature kept him from seeking the solitude necessary for serious composition. He squandered much of his time, they claimed, in pursuance of friendship and love.[5] In short, according to these arguments, Bernstein was his own worst enemy: had he habituated himself to the requisite hours of intense and sustained composition, he might well have honed his compositional talents and produced his desired masterpiece.

However, despite the intensity with which Bernstein embraced all his musical and other pursuits, he did compose substantially. Virgil Thomson wrote in 1968 that "Strauss, Mahler, and Leonard Bernstein . . . had always conducted; they needed money; and they wrote music like windmills."[6] Without making comparisons to the catalogs of Strauss and Mahler, we must acknowledge that Bernstein's catalog includes a substantial and varied number of compositions: among others, three symphonies; two major song cycles and a number of songs; a choral work of four movements; seven works for musical theater, including two operas and an operetta; a film score and a number of scores for ballet. Judging by volume alone, the assumption that Bernstein tended toward dissipation falls short of explaining his missed potential as a composer.

A second explanation for Bernstein's frustration is that though Bernstein composed a considerable amount of music, he was incapable of producing large-scale works of substance and that when he tried to do so, his work could not meet his intentions. Thus, Mstislav Rostropovich wrote that Bernstein was a brilliant theatrical composer, but that "when Lenny tried to become a deep composer, like Mahler, or, for example, like Beethoven, then it was perhaps not so successful for his composition."[7] Leon Botstein and David Denby have argued that Bernstein, especially in his serious concert and operatic works as opposed to his popular theatrical works, was incapable of composing music of an expressive power equal to the power of his ideas, or that the ideas themselves were superficial. In 1983, Botstein wrote,

> In his serious music, especially of late, Bernstein is in search of profundity. Yet what he achieves is only grandiose gesture. He has conducted and listened to Mahler and Verdi too many times; he has read too much Shakespeare, Yeats, and Dostoevsky; he has felt moved too often by religious and political beliefs. The serious music is a barrage of heartfelt emotions, the tortured, longwinded, richly orchestrated ramblings of one man's public contact with the angst of life, the power of nature, the sorrow of death and pain. All is cast in vicarious musical language on the scale of Beethoven, Mahler and Shostakovich. The sentiment is sincere but commonplace. The art is secondhand. Bernstein's serious music, at its best, is reminiscent of an exuberant adolescent who, lacking confidence in himself, uses impressive mannerisms, clichés, and gestures to pour out his heart.[8]

David Denby has advanced a similar charge:

> In his symphonies, a natural lyrical impulse got overtaken by the hectoring political stances that had surrounded him as a young man. Bernstein was influenced first by the popular-front attitudes of the thirties and later by the resistance to McCarthyism and the struggles against racism and anti-Semitism, all of which imbued liberalism with a high ethical fervor. The Holocaust and the birth of Israel extended these emotions into a mood of redemptive anger. He was a liberal who took things personally, and he confused "speaking out" with politics. Unfortunately, he began to confuse it with art, too.[9]

Whatever we are to make of Denby's critique of Bernstein's supposed "confusions" about how he conducted his political life, the essence of his and Rostropovich's and Botstein's charges is that Bernstein should not have attempted to compose music that expressed philosophic or religious or, for that matter, political themes and that when he did so, the results were grandiose and superficial.

How well does this argument stand up? One can certainly find kitsch and histrionic excess in, for example, the mad scene in *Mass,* where the celebrant's dramatic, show-stopping chalice smashing is totally disproportionate to his whimpering that follows, or in certain moments of Oedipal excess in *Kaddish.* But the match between powerful social-critical ideas and musical expression in much of *Kaddish,* or in *Age of Anxiety,* or in *Songfest,* does not result in imbalance or superficiality. If one listens to the music with an understanding of the profundities of the texts, one will find the music equal to its expressive tasks. In short, the arguments that Bernstein did not have the talent to fulfill his compositional program fall short of sufficiency. Indeed, these arguments are flawed from the outset. Bernstein's inability to realize his masterpiece did not stem from a lack of talent: such would have been the case had he found his libretto or other narrative form but then failed to compose commensurately. But, I suggest, his frustration was due to his inability to find the right libretto or other such narrative in the first place.

I will discuss this contention shortly, but I must first consider another hypothesis: that Bernstein's hopes to compose a work of profound social significance were blocked by fears of being "outed" as a gay man. One could draw this conclusion from the work of Nadine Hubbs, which deals primarily with the period of the 1930s through the 1950s. She suggests that when Bernstein joined the Thomson-Copland group in the late 1930s and early 1940s, he accepted Thomson's programmatic position that gay composers should avoid responding to political events with their music, lest they open themselves up for exposure. As evidence of Bernstein's acquiescence in this pact, Hubbs offers this "credo attributed to Leonard Bernstein":

> This will be our response to violence
> To make music more intensely,
> more beautifully,
> more devotedly than ever before.[10]

Hubbs provides no documentation of these lines, so we have no evidence that they were Bernstein's. And if they were, we have no idea when he uttered them, nor in what context. Further, they in no way reflect a hard and fast lifelong commitment to avoid engagement with political events. The argument that Bernstein's supposed sexually induced repression might have been responsible for his compositional disappointment raises another problem as well. As we have seen, Hubbs argues that motivation for the pact was to protect its adherents from potentially career-ruining and humiliating exposure by conservatives. This worry deepened during the so-called Lavender Scare that ran concurrent with the McCarthyite Red Scare of the 1940s and 1950s, when homosexuals were persecuted as potential security risks. If this argument has merit, then we would expect Bernstein to have withdrawn from political life and taken refuge in the aesthetic realm. Though he indeed took flight from political activity in the 1950s, the evidence I have presented here overwhelmingly suggests that Bernstein was under attack because of his actively espoused left-wing politics. By the middle 1960s, Bernstein had returned to public political life, speaking out against American foreign policy. If fear of exposure of his homoeroticism were keeping him politically mute in his music, he certainly would have remained mute in his speech. Finally, by 1976, when he was composing his "Notes for an American Opera," which we recall was a subtitle for *Songfest,* and was thus thinking seriously of composing his dreamed-of work of substance, he had come out of the closet and thereby preempted anyone who would expose his homoeroticism. In the end, then, I think we must reject the notion that Bernstein's fear of exposure of his homoeroticism inhibited his compositional powers. Indeed, the power of his music for *A Quiet Place* of 1983 was clear demonstration that issues of homosexuality were not going to inhibit his creative potential.

Two critics, Wilfred Mellers and Joseph Horowitz, take us onto different terrain, suggesting that historical and social causes might lie at the root of Bernstein's frustration. Mellers made the following comment about Bernstein's supposed failure to compose significantly after *West Side Story:*

The dissipation of Bernstein's creativity seems indeed, almost a moral tale that has more than personal significance. We cannot merely say that he has not "had time" to create, for no true artist ever put anything before creation. If he has found more satisfaction in the various roles he has decided to play so brilliantly, that is at least in part a comment upon the society that has produced him. *A failure in creativity, we have seen, is also a failure in love;* and that is why American civilization—as the music of Blitzstein and Gershwin has told us—is still "waiting" for the Promised Land.[11]

Where Mellers only suggests that something must have gone awry in Bernstein's relationship with American society and inhibited his creativity, Horowitz probes further and identifies certain historical and social forces that affected Bernstein's creative impulses. Horowitz argues that in the mid-1960s, Bernstein fell into a malaise because "his compositional output had diminished in quantity and importance."[12] Moreover, he suggests that Bernstein could not make contact with the new popular culture. Bernstein was depressed about the state of America after Kennedy's assassination and the state of affairs that he called "The Twentieth Century Crisis" in his Norton Lectures. "We know at a glance," Horowitz concludes, "that the twentieth-century crisis is also Bernstein's crisis, with a history of its own."[13] Horowitz, however, neither amplifies nor extends his discussion of this crisis, which, as we have seen, Bernstein variously identified as loss of faith, horrific war, periodic genocide, or intellectual anomie.

Nonetheless, Horowitz's argument, when developed, yields greater power to explain Bernstein's frustration than those that focus solely on his supposed idiosyncrasies or artistic shortcomings. Indeed, as I have attempted to illustrate in this book, any attempt to understand Bernstein the composer must take into account the fact that he responded directly to the moral climate and social-political milieu in which he lived. And this conclusion provokes a question central to any effort to identify the sources of Bernstein's frustrations: what type of work did Bernstein hope to compose? Given the evidence available to us, we can conclude only that he wanted to write a work in an operatic or closely associated form that would offer Americans a mirror in which to see themselves and capture the loss of faith and diminution of ethical concern in contemporary American life. This work would plunge composer, performers, and listeners into the deepest and most fundamental recesses of human spirit, where, as Bernstein said in the Norton Lectures in 1973, consciousness and feeling meet in "those deep unconscious regions where the universals of tonality and language reside."[14] This music would concern matters close to him—not least the crises in liberalism's acquiescence in the neo-imperialism of the Johnson era, its fragmentation during the 1970s, and its increasing irrelevance, and loss of dignity and millions of adherents in the 1980s. Only the most masterly music could successfully carry the weight and sweep of such an epic of dramatic narratives and tensions. But to compose such music, he clearly needed a libretto or a program that narrated this loss of liberal faith and loss of civic ethical life, either directly or by implication through the work's plot, themes, and allusions. Bernstein needed as well to know that he had an audience that would respond to his ethical challenge. He apparently never found this mix of narrative and audience, and we need some cultural diagnostics to understand why.

## THE SOCIAL OPERA AND
## THE SOCIAL NOVEL

Bernstein first formulated the idea for a socially critical opera in the heady days of the New Deal. In 1938, when Bernstein was at Harvard, the composer Roger Sessions wrote that the composer of a new, "vital opera" must know that "in a period such as ours, so sharply defined by clear historical and social forces, the truly relevant dramatic material should always in some way reflect those forces, either directly, or by analogy or implication."[15]

Anyone reading Sessions in those days knew immediately that this prerequisite for a vital American opera was identical to that for the politically engaged fiction of the period—especially as expressed in the social novels of Theodore Dreiser, Sinclair Lewis, and John Dos Passos, wherein characters from a variety of walks of life react to social and economic forces.

Lewis and Dos Passos, for example, were following Balzac, Zola, and Dreiser in synthesizing extant reportage and other forms of documentation to show the effects of great economic transformations on representative types. Their panoramic depictions of social life became master narratives from which other writers and artists drew to produce variations in literary, dramatic, plastic, operatic, and other forms. Though the social novel need not always precede other imaginative genres in building master narratives, at least since the nineteenth century, when this form of novel came into being, it has been the primary artistic form by which members of society can understand the social order, its varieties of manners, motivations, and ethical codes, and its distribution of wealth and power. Thus, from the core of the American social novels of Dreiser and Dos Passos, other artists—such as playwright Clifford Odets; choreographer Martha Graham; photographers Paul Strand, Dorothea Lange, and Walker Evans; painter Ben Shahn; and novelist John Steinbeck—went on to explore various forms of social and economic injustice. This critical engagement found a ready audience in an American public that shared these artists' aesthetic, moral, and political sensibilities. Sessions expected similar sensibilities in a composer of opera.

Anyone looking for an American opera that was a model for Sessions's manifesto need go no further than Marc Blitzstein's *The Cradle Will Rock.* Blitzstein dramatized for working-class audiences the way in which economic power elites were taking control of virtually every institution of modern life, including police forces and the communications media, turning these forces into apparatuses of dictatorial government. *Cradle* was especially close to Bernstein's heart. He knew the composer and the work intimately, knew for whom it had been composed and the social forces that it exposed.

In February 1948, we recall, Bernstein had been conducting a revival of *Cradle* when he announced that he was going to write a "great American opera." That month was also precisely the moment when the progressive Left thought it had in the quintessential New Dealer, Henry Wallace, the candidate who could successfully challenge Harry Truman for the presidency of the United States. Progressives thought that Wallace would restore FDR's struggles against economic concentration and reverse Truman's bellicose foreign policy. Wallace's message seemed to be working, for at that point in the campaign, he seemed to be gathering enormous support from millions of voters yearning for a return to the egalitarianism and internationalism of the New Deal. As Blitzstein had a decade before, Bernstein now intervened in the moral and political arena to inspire this apparently massive audience to recognize its place in the social order and thus to struggle against the great social forces of war and injustice. Bernstein could not have expected to compose his opera before the November election, but with support for Wallace supposedly building, he planned to compose for the mass movement that would sustain this restoration of the New Deal spirit.

Bernstein's inspiration to compose that opera died in November 1948 when the work's putative mass audience deserted the Progressives to vote for the Democrats. Whether these voters were upset about communists within the Progressive Party or feared that Republicans would win the election, virtually this whole mass base that Bernstein thought he was going to inspire, and which was motivating his compositional program, simply evaporated. Truman's discourse of business-labor-agriculture-government conciliation and the need to combat communism at home and abroad monopolized the rhetoric that formed public opinion. Progressives, virtually enveloped by the all-pervasive Cold War culture, ridiculed by anticommunist liberals and the popular media, and facing blacklisting, went into inner migration or sought to work through the crisis by toning down their criticism.[16] Progressivism was disintegrating.

## DISSOLUTION OF THE
## PROGRESSIVE IMAGINATION

We can understand what happened to the progressive imagination after 1948 by turning to Bernstein's contemporaries Arthur Miller, born in 1915, three years before Bernstein, and Norman Mailer born in 1923, five years later, both among the most self-conscious of the progressive writers, and along with Bernstein, members of *Life*'s April 1949 gallery of "communist dupes" (see chapter 2). Both Miller's and Mailer's work in the period after Truman's election in 1948 through the McCarthy years show the chilling effects of Cold War culture. Before that election, Miller had not hesitated to confront political and economic power. His 1945 novel, *Focus,* and his 1947 play, *All My Sons,* were direct assaults upon racism and big-business criminality, respectively. But after the 1948 political debacle, his work shifted away from its earlier realism and his hard-hitting political engagement. In his 1949 *Death of a Salesman,* Miller cast the play's major protagonist, Willy Loman, in the mold of a minor Babbitt who sings the slogans and spouts the commercial wisdom of the prevailing mythos of the economic order, only to wind up trashed by the imperatives of the profit motive. But Miller diffused the progressive social-critical plot line by crossing it with a salacious and audience-arousing subplot in which Willy and his lady friend are caught by his son Biff in the hotel room in Boston. This second, scandalous subplot thus raised the possibility that Willy was not the victim of capitalist logic as such but of his moral failure. Had Willy remained faithful to his wife, Biff would have become a well-off football player and Willy would have become a contented father, grandfather, and happy pensioner. Family catastrophe, in other words, would have trumped the logic of capital. Or did it? In fact, despite Willy's infidelity, the play left little doubt that his tragic fall was due to the relentlessness of business logic. Miller next set about to expose the Red Scare inquisition, but indirectly: his *Crucible* of 1953 was a condemnation of the McCarthyite investigators but only by analogy to the seventeenth-century Salem witch hunts. Audiences, of course, had no problem understanding Miller's point. Indeed, by placing events in seventeenth-century Salem, the playwright allowed audiences to gain critical and emotional distance and to see more clearly how unethical and tyrannical authorities, swept up in or manipulative of moral panic, could force innocent people into betraying each other. Miller's 1955 *View from the Bridge* continued his attack on that repressive system, this time focusing on the morally bankrupt informer, motivated by sexual jealousy. By the time he wrote these last two plays, Miller, otherwise unable or unwilling to confront the McCarthyite system head on in his theatrical work, had nevertheless fulfilled his fundamental ethical intention: to depict how we should live when we face such a system. However, at this point, 1955, Miller seemed set to withdraw from that project, writing that he would no longer follow the example of the most important of social dramatists, Henrik Ibsen, for whom a play was an "arraignment of social evils." That approach, Miller wrote, "was later taken up by left-wing playwrights whose primary interest was the exposure of capitalism for the implied benefit of socialism or communism. The concept is tired and narrow, but its worst effect has been to confuse a whole generation of playwrights, audiences and theater workers."[17] As we will see, Miller was moving away from his progressively oriented American social plays to works focusing on more private spheres and European settings.

We can also see this diminution of political discourse in the work of Norman Mailer after the 1948 Progressive defeat. His social novel, *The Naked and the Dead,* which he wrote while the progressive movement was gaining strength and published before the November 1948 election, was a panoptic accounting of representative Americans fighting in the South Pacific, not only against the Japanese but also against overarching natural forces and American military power hierarchies. At one point in the book, Lieutenant Hearn, a Harvard-educated intellectual (like Mailer himself), predicts that American postwar civilian life will be shaped by unaccountable corporate power allied with protofascistic repressive forces. But post 1948, with Cold War rhetoric in full bloom, Mailer's progressive outlook started to lose its focus. His *Barbary Shore* (1951) occasioned Marxist speeches about the structure of power, but the characters, including a Soviet spy, an FBI agent, and a woman of sultry mien, are hermetically enclosed within an apartment building in Brooklyn, physically and psychologically locked away from the American scene. His *Deer Park,* begun in 1952, concerned a Rossen-like screenwriter who is blacklisted when he refuses to testify on colleagues before the House Un-American Activities Committee, then turns around and does testify, only to see himself reduced to a hack.[18] But Mailer, like Miller in *Salesman,* crossed his political narrative with sensationalistic forces of sexual power and victimization and thereby weakened the politically significant plotline. As with Miller, so with Mailer: in the decade after the progressive defeat of 1948, neither sought to run totally from the politically repressive forces that had gained hegemony in American culture and neither took flight into pure aestheticism, but neither could nor would confront these forces head on.

What can we determine about Leonard Bernstein's stance? Before the Truman victory in 1948, we recall, he had courted the idea of an operatic adaptation of Maxwell Anderson's radical play *Winterset.* He dropped that project but went ahead with his setting of Auden's existentially profound but apolitical *Age of Anxiety,* which premiered in 1949. In 1952, already on the State Department and CBS blacklists, he was hardly in a position to expose his career to further jeopardy. Planning an upcoming festival of the arts at Brandeis University, where he was teaching, Bernstein remarked to Irving Fine, his close friend and collaborator, that the best path was to produce either light works or works of darker speculation and avoid works focusing on the real social forces operating within American society:

> We discovered at the last festival that we are not living in experimental times: that our times are cautious in the extreme: that we are not producing real tragedy. On the other hand we are not producing real satire either; the caution prevents it, all the fear prevent it; and we are left, at the moment, with an art that is rather whiling away the time until the world gets better or blows up. Good and Evil are still valid and oft-used subjects in the abstract (Billy Budd and The Rake), and will always be the best subjects; but since our time doesn't major in this field, let's be amusing, or pretty, or diverting. This is, I think, a theme (the whole question of abstraction in painting arises with it, and the various literary and philosophical cults of despair or of passivity.)[19]

Bernstein had been learning his lessons: the social criticism in his *Trouble in Tahiti,* about to premiere at the Brandeis festival, was not the sort of work that would provoke new attacks upon him. The following year saw the introduction of his *Wonderful Town,* a romp without social-critical content. By 1956, Bernstein had gained enough confidence to take a risk, and he agreed that his collaborator Lillian Hellman should include some lines of political satire within their *Candide*. But Hellman's lines were far less biting than those Arthur Miller had composed for *Salesman, Crucible,* and *View from the Bridge*. Bernstein's *West Side Story,* premiering the following year, was a lamentation about juvenile ethnic gangs, a highly topical focus in the mid-1950s. In short, the playbooks and lyrics that Bernstein set to music in those years were at most outré, but not so radical as to bring him to the attention of the blacklisters.[20]

The weakening or even the disappearance of political discourse from imaginative and speculative thought in the early Cold War period is most apparent in perhaps the era's most important novel, Saul Bellow's 1953 *The Adventures of Augie March*. The world of the novel is virtually open-ended, with Augie finding almost innumerable paths to social success. Bellow does provide colorful and intensely portrayed descriptions of the immediacy of personal life, placing Augie within thick family connections, love relationships and betrayals, smarmy Chicago business dealings, and other varieties of human foible. But in contrast to the worlds of Miller's and Mailer's protagonists, Augie has no direct or indirect relationship to the system of inquisition, betrayal, and blacklist. Instead, Augie's conversations and meetings are first-person narrative close-ups, followed both by his reflections on what he has learned from wise men like his first exemplar, Einhorn, and by speculations about the metaphysics of the human condition. These meditations never engage a middle ground between the personal narrative and metaphysical rumination—that is, to the concrete social American landscape in which individual lives play out amid structures and political and economic power relations. This ground remained outside of Bellow's frame of reference and outside of the orthodox view of a freewheeling American society.

To be sure, mainstream sociologists and political scientists in the 1950s pointed to social forces operating within the nation. But unlike Depression-era forces that would produce economic breakdown and the potential for authoritarianism, those of the postwar era—although they created conformism, alienation, and rebellion, especially among youth—did not threaten the stability of American life. Economic depression was now ruled out as government experts ensured high employment and low inflation. Social equilibrium was the result of compromises reached by myriad business, labor, agricultural, and other voluntary associations through negotiation and bargaining or brokered by the political parties and the organs of government.

With the liberal order secured, with public rhetoric promoting the openness of American possibility, and with the swarming of everyday social relations, upward and geographic mobility, and infinite foibles of the denizens of the republic, we cannot be surprised that in 1961, the writer Philip Roth, born in 1933 and coming of age in the early Cold War years, could conceive only of a variegated and amorphous America with no discernible core or structure.[21]

By the early 1960s, then, the critical imagination had been shorn of its progressivism and become domesticated. Not only had it submitted to discipline by the orthodoxy, but it had abandoned the large-scale canvas of societal life for the smaller unit or psychological portrait. Novelists and playwrights explored the interior life, private life, domestic life, neighborhood life, regional life, and corporate life, but in all these works, as one surveyor wrote, "society itself has vanished."[22] In short, the politically grounded American social text—novel and play—had disappeared during the Cold War years. Miller's 1963 *After the Fall* did expose some of the world of the inquisitorial HUAC investigations, but this focus was largely incidental to the work's central concern, the protagonist Quentin's attempts to make sense of his preoccupations—with his parents, with the witch hunts and his relationship with Elia Kazan, with the Nazi concentration camps, and with his marriages, among them to a woman unmistakably like Miller's ex-wife, Marilyn Monroe. His 1964 *Incident at Vichy* dramatizes a heroic act in Nazi collaborationist-led France; it also made clear that he was continuing his turn away from inquiring into the deeper forces affecting American ethical life. In this regard, Miller was quite representative of American playwrights: in 1966, Harold Clurman, a most sensitive observer and practitioner himself, said that the "cooling of social fervor" occurring with the war's end had turned into a "freeze." If the postwar plays of Miller and Tennessee Williams "sounded a more subdued and introverted variation on the plays of the thirties," soon thereafter playwrights had given up trying to identify the social origins of contemporary problems, instead seeking their sources in the familial and the oedipal. "The age of conformity and McCarthy terror," Clurman concluded, "drove men of sensibility into themselves."[23] As Mailer said the same year, the American creative imagination, both mainstream and progressive, had retreated into the "microcosm in American life."[24]

But when McCarthyism disappeared in the 1960s, when HUAC had been dissolved and the blacklist ended, why didn't the progressives' critical social narrative make its return? The answer lies in the nation's shifting economic structure, which had been developing during the 1950s. The progressives of the New Deal and the postwar period assumed a society in which malefactors (employers, financial manipulators) victimized whole classes and groups (workers, black people). By the early 1960s, however, who were the victims? Unionized and increasingly prosperous blue-collar workers, with new cars, homes, and paid vacations now identified themselves as members of the middle class. They no longer thought of themselves as victims of a deeply flawed and cleaved social structure. Granted that many in the working classes remained demoralized, apathetic, and apolitical, the greatest number, those most powerfully organized, confidently anticipated incremental increases in wages and salaries. In broader economic terms, unemployment was relatively low, inflation was minimal, profits were up, and financial institutions were regulated. Moreover, Johnson's poverty programs, the Civil Rights Act of 1964, the Voting Rights Act of 1965, and the overall effects of a continuous economic boom started to bring black people into the mainstream. In short, domestic American life was governed by policies that seemingly brought social forces under control. If any gnawing feelings remained about out-of-control social forces, they were in the arena of international Cold War politics and the nuclear arms race.

Indeed, left-wing critics no longer saw a society deeply fissured by economic class issues but were concerned instead about an overbureaucratized, overcommoditized America obsessively building weapons of mass destruction, if not carrying out murderous warfare. These writers, frustrated and bewildered by a seemingly happy and content, if not smug, American populace, turned to irony compounded by caustic, angry cynicism. Theaters staged Beckett's and Ionesco's absurdist works, while Joseph Heller's *Catch 22* (1962), Stanley Kubrick's *Dr. Strangelove* (1965), and Thomas Pynchon's *Crying of Lot 49* (1966) offered profoundly cynical views of American Cold War culture.

Then, in the middle of the 1960s, explosive events came as if out of nowhere. Still stunned by the shocks of the Kennedy assassination, the now-daily reports of carnage in Vietnam, and scenes of American cities burning, progressive artists were traumatized. As we remember from John Gruen's 1967 interview with Bernstein, the composer had fallen into compositional paralysis (see chapter 4). This paralysis and inability of creative artists to depict America's social turmoil astonished progressive critics—thus Robert Brustein's shocked reaction to Arthur Miller's 1968 play about a family feud, *The Price:* "Torn by riots, seething with violence; our disgraceful involvement in the Vietnam conflict is making large numbers ashamed of being American. Our sense of reality is disintegrating, our illusion of freedom faltering, our expectation of disaster increasing—yet Arthur Miller, the most public-spirited of dramatists, continues to write social-psychological melodramas about Family Responsibility."[25]

## LATE 1960S: REVIVAL OF THE SOCIAL TEXT?

Nevertheless, the events tearing American society apart were beginning to find some representation in the American creative imagination. From the ranks of the universities arose a new master narrative about an America ready to send hundreds of thousands of American draftees into war to support right-wing despots and subvert and overthrow left-wing democracies, all to ensure the free flow of global capital. This new critical outlook spurred multitudes to hit the streets and march against the war in Vietnam. Mailer, as we have seen, took part in the prelude to the great march on the Pentagon in October 1967. His 1968 report on the march, *Armies of the Night,* with its vast array of characters coming face to face with brute power exercised by their own government, seemed to be a template for a new social literature.[26] The turmoil reenergized Bernstein, washing away his demoralization and apathy of 1967. Now, in the revolutionary spring and the summer of 1968, and with the backdrop of the radical events in Paris, Rome, and Prague, he was campaigning for Eugene McCarthy and supporting the antiwar candidacy of Paul O'Dwyer for the New York senatorial race. His intellectual powers revived as he lectured mass audiences about the unholy concentration of powers within the imperialistically aggressive military-industrial complex and the victimization not only of the Vietnamese but also of young Americans. As Eugene McCarthy and Robert Kennedy won primary races, he and many others believed that millions of voters were going to turn away from Johnson's handpicked candidate, Hubert Humphrey, and thereby radicalize the Democratic Party.

This euphoria, as we all know, was short-lived. The assassination of Robert Kennedy in June of 1968, coming on the heels of King's murder earlier in the year, was crushing enough. But by August, Humphrey's victory over McCarthy, engineered by the Democratic Party machine, and the police riot at the conclusion of the Democratic convention brought home the fact that hopes for a progressive revival were a pitiful illusion. The progressives' claims that the huge buildup of military spending had decimated spending for education, housing, and health care had fallen on deaf ears, at least those of the great majority of voters then riding the economic boom. Many members of the heavily unionized blue-collar population that was nominally the core of the progressive revival's base had long adopted middle-class and politically orthodox values and bore a deepening animus for the antiwar, civil rights, and counterculture movements that had arisen during the decade. If they bore any anger about the war in Vietnam, it was only about how it was waged, not about claims of its moral and ethical legitimacy.

That the election had offered no real choice between Hubert Humphrey and Richard Nixon save the outright racist George Wallace was the clearest indication of the collapse of left-wing hopes of the late 1960s. The war not only went on unabated, it worsened, and the progressive imagination was once again traumatized. In his *Slaughterhouse Five* (1969), Kurt Vonnegut located a sense of stunned incredulousness in his mind-shattered protagonist, Billy Pilgrim. The returned serviceman and dramatist David Rabe gave voice to the rage on the left, writing in his play *Sticks and Bones* (1970) of the inanities of an Ozzie and Harriet America, blind to the atrocities committed in its name.

During this period of leftist contestation, Bernstein set out to conceptualize his *Mass*. But whether because of procrastination or an inability to find the time, he was late in composing it. Judging by Daniel Berrigan's comments in his diary about their talks in Danbury Penitentiary in May 1970 (see chapter 4), Bernstein certainly had in mind a radical political piece. By September, however, the work he finally staged fell far short of that plan. Perhaps he lost his clarity of thought—and perhaps dissipated his potential for artistic inspiration—amid the ideological divisions and confusion wrought by fractious, schismatic, and sectarian groups such as the Weathermen, Maoists, and Black Panthers. In any event, torn by competing demands—seeking to honor Jackie Kennedy, compose an exposé of Nixon and the war-making bureaucracy, honor Berrigan (a model for an earlier version of the celebrant?), indict the schismatic groups that had failed so terribly in 1968, and ensure financial success for the production—Bernstein wound up composing not high political drama but midcult pop melodrama.

## TWENTIETH-CENTURY CRISIS

The landslide victory of Richard Nixon over the antiwar and antimilitary-industrial Democratic candidate George McGovern in November

1972—Nixon won every state save Massachusetts—seemed the final blow to progressive hopes for an audience receptive to an imaginative work of radical criticism. No doubt this defeat only added to Bernstein's malaise. He had been spending less time in America, conducting abroad with the Vienna Philharmonic, and his interests in American music had been waning as well, as witness the fact that he had virtually nothing to say about American music in his 1973 Norton Lectures outside of a nod to Ives's *Unanswered Question*. He subsumed the American crisis into the larger "Twentieth Century Crisis"—the title of his fifth lecture. Bernstein noted a number of "prophets of our struggle": "Freud, Einstein and Marx have also prophesied, as have Spengler and Wittgenstein, Malthus and Rachel Carson—all latter-day Isaiahs and St. Johns, all preaching the same sermon in different terms: mend your ways, the Apocalypse is at hand. Rilke said it too: 'Du müsst dein Leben ändern' [You must change your life]."[27]

But his comments quickly turned back to the American crisis, in which people have sought, rather than political engagement, any number of artificial "antidotes" to catastrophe: "Logical positivism, existentialism, galloping technology, the flight into outer space, the doubting of reality, and overall a well-bred paranoia, most recently on display in the high places of Washington, D.C. And our *personal* antidotes: making it, dope, subcultures and counter-cultures, turning on, turning off. Marking time and making money. A rash of new religious movements from Guruism to Billy Grahamism. And a rash of new art movements, from concrete poetry to the silences of John Cage. A thaw here, a purge there. And all under the same aegis, the angel of planetary death."[28]

Bernstein, in his own prophetic voice, argued that a crisis had enveloped America but that Americans, instead of following Rilke and changing their lives, instead of facing up to the tasks of understanding and combating the sources of danger, were escaping into this welter of disengaged, novel, idiosyncratic, and individualistic ideas and beliefs and thereby side-stepping inquiry and activity against the neglectful, aggrandizing, and war-making tendencies that were taking the world into catastrophe. These supposed disengagements with sociopolitical reality had become the subject matter of *Mass*—a far cry, we will remember, from the attack on the perpetrators of the war, who seemed to be Bernstein's subject when he discussed the work with Berrigan in Danbury Penitentiary. For Bernstein, then, the current crisis was multisided, born of a society consumed with fads and consumer gluttony that was unready to understand or deal with the destitution of the American inner city and was largely uncritical of the latest of twentieth-century catastrophes, the war in Vietnam.

Bernstein was hardly alone in his sense of doom. As the 1960s turned into the 1970s, writers' images of American culture grew darker and apocalyptic, and their narrative landscape zeroed in on the ungovernable, sociopathic, and surreal zones, such as those in Philip K. Dick's *Do Androids Dream of Electric Sheep?* (1968), Barry Malzberg's *Beyond Apollo* (1972), and Thomas Pynchon's *Gravity's Rainbow* (1973).[29] Their works suggested that humanity was controlled by vast impersonal structures and a runaway technology driven by its own imperatives and virtually impervious to human intervention. These forces were imprisoning all—at least the middle classes—within a sinister but seemingly benign, virtually victimless totalitarianism, in which the supposedly victimized were ignorant of their plight. For Mailer, this totalitarianism was identifiable only by its symptoms and effects. Its "crucial characteristic," he wrote, is "a moral disease which divorces us from guilt," one that paralyzes the critical faculty such that we are "incapable of facing back into the accumulated wrath and horror of [our] historic past."[30] In short, this benign totalitarianism was the cause of, and then was aided and abetted by, the political disengagement of the American middle-income classes that formed the bulk of the American public and electorate.

To be sure, millions of people stood outside the American consensus. They were the marginalized and the exploited whom Bernstein sought to champion. In his 1976–77 *Songfest,* for example, Bernstein composed for two audiences: first, those too smug in their patriotic celebratory high, and second, those inspired by the feminist, lesbian, and gay-liberation movements. His goal was likewise twofold: to jolt the first audience out of its complacency while he commemorated and celebrated the second. In O'Hara's verse "let us do something Un-American" through most of the poems that Bernstein set in *Songfest,* there issued forth declarations of pain, frustration, or anger by people marginalized by a noncaring mainstream. If Bernstein had associated *Songfest* with his ambition to compose a great American operatic work—recall its provisional subtitles "Six Characters in Search of an Opera" and later, "Notes for an American Opera"—then had it been composed, that opera would more than likely have centered on a narrative of injustice within the American historical trajectory. He had already experimented with the idea of a work that would structure events in historical sequence, with his adaptation of Wilder's *Skin of Our Teeth* and *1600 Pennsylvania Avenue.* Perhaps he had an epical work in his mind as a next step after *Songfest.*

## FRAGMENTATION ON THE LEFT: IDENTITY POLITICS

In any event, Bernstein did not develop these themes, nor those of *Songfest,* into a unified text. The fact that he did not construct a new text from *Songfest*'s material may be symptomatic of the era's growing politics of identity, in which the old liberal-left coalition, already weakened by the entry of its main constituency into middle-income brackets, was in the middle 1970s undergoing even more erosion and fragmentation with the rise of new groups, including blacks, feminists, and gays, that were seeking equality of employment, their fair share of governmental resources, and, in general, social legitimacy.

From the mid-1930s on, the more powerful constituents of the Roosevelt coalition of unionized blue-collar workers; Jews; urban, middle-class professionals; and Catholic ethnics had more or less remained in force, supplying votes to local, especially urban, state and national Democratic Party candidates and remaining the mass repository of New Deal progressive memory and sentiment. But sentiment alone does not explain why the coalition endured. Over the years, Democrats and Republicans had together formed so called interest-group liberalism, in which business, labor, and other strong interest groups formed cooperative alliances with congressional powers and executive-branch agencies to obtain federal largess in the form of revenue, or favorable legal and administrative protection and regulation.[31] Because each alliance sought continuity and aggrandizement, these groups saw individual and mutual interests in a government that expanded to meet their needs rather than one with a nonexpanding budget that would force them to compete for their shares. Because of this economic realism, the myriad organized interest groups were able to create the equilibrium that prevailed through the 1960s.

With the economic downturn and deindustrialization of the 1970s, and a growing tax revolt across the country, established interest groups now sought to exclude newcomers from feeding at the governmental trough, which threatened to become a nongrowing, even shrinking pool of resources. Among the excluded were the post–Vietnam-war feminist, gay, race-based, ethnic, and environmental groups. Without a unifying force such as the economic victimization that had united the members of the old Roosevelt coalition or the mutually beneficial compact that had united the postwar interest-group liberal coalition or the civil rights coalition or the anti-Vietnam-war movement, each of these newer groups had to organize itself more or less independently of the others. Each had to argue its own cases in court, or articulate its own positions before electorates or legislative and congressional committees, or otherwise seek its own solutions to its own set of problems.

But this fragmentation on the left paralleled fragmentation of a different sort within the older coalition. First, long-standing support for the Democrats—and for that matter, for the Republicans—was eroding as various personal loyalties passed from political parties to interest groups. In addition to this erosion of party support were the effects of the media on the older party organizers.[32] Massive declines in union membership due to deindustrialization, the movement of jobs to the nonunionized South, and new social policies in the cities were also adding significantly to the erosion of the liberal coalition.[33] The established liberal-ethical coalition that still had a connection to New Deal progressivism was falling apart.

This long-developing fragmentation of a public constituency that had been more or less liberal reached its critical point with the presidential election of 1980. Many people who had voted for the Democratic Party in previous elections were now alienated by the newly mobilized groups promoting identity politics, angry about the growing size and intrusiveness of government, and young enough to have no sentimental alliance with, or even memory of, the New Deal, and thus little sympathy for the liberalism of earlier decades. As a result, they were ready to leave the Democratic fold, and millions left for good.[34]

To progressives, novelist Philip Roth's 1961 vision of an amorphous and multivariate American society now seemed on the mark. Thus, Mailer admitted in 1979, "Ever since *The Naked and the Dead* there's always been a part of me that's been a social novelist and I have become more and more frustrated over the years because I've never found a way to write a large social novel. I always wanted to and never found a story as simple as that, that lent itself naturally to a large social novel."[35] In the absence of such a "story" or master narrative of people under attack or unifying to meet a challenge, no social critic, neither a Mailer nor a Bernstein, could find the means to write a social text—a script or libretto—that would capture the nation's drift from its progressive and liberal roots into a political culture of short-attention-span entertainment, sound bites, and commercialism. When the conservative victory of 1980 was consolidated four years later by Reagan's landslide victory, the potential source of inspiration for Bernstein's long-sought masterpiece, pointing audiences to a revival of their long-buried progressive ideas, disappeared.

In 1982, Mailer was finally on his way to writing a social novel, but he set it not in contemporary America but in ancient Egypt. Asked why, he explained that the grounding moral ideas with which he had formed judgments about present-day America were now out of date, useless in helping him form a "vision that would comprehend everything."[36] Thus did Mailer testify to the disappearance of the old progressive outlook. His hope to write the great American novel had been dashed. As for Mailer, so too for Bernstein: he never initiated his project to compose a powerful American opera because he could not find a libretto that would capture the essential fault line in American society. His "Notes for an American Opera" remained only notes. His 1983 opera, *A Quiet Place,* was a last-gasp effort at an American opera, but that idiosyncratic, psychological, and familial-oriented work was a far cry from the large themes that would have inspired him to fulfill his great ambition. Frustrated, his attention turned from American themes with the aborted *Race to Urga* and to conducting, recording, and teaching.

In sum, Bernstein's compositional frustration had its roots more in the evolving American social fabric, from the beginnings of the Cold War to his death in 1990, than in his supposedly limited talents, his idiosyncrasies, his habits, and his psychological dispositions. The effects of the McCarthy period on progressive artists virtually expunged questions of the structure of political power from social discourse in the first two decades of the Cold War and through the 1980s and eroded the New Deal social ethic. The great changes in the American social, political, and economic structures from the 1960s through the 1980s fed the continuing fragmentation of the American electorate. They crippled the progressive imagination's attempt to create a clarified vision of American society beset by identifiable economic and social forces that could be brought under control by an ethically charged people united behind its democratically responsible government.

In his 1988 *New York Times* Op Ed column, "I'm a Liberal and Proud of It," Bernstein spoke to an American liberal polity that had forsaken its progressive heritage and, as far as he was concerned, had lost its confidence and its dignity. In the midst of the conservative revival, his cry was in vain. He knew that the things that might have inspired him, the fabled moments of the mass-based antifascist New Deal of the late 1930s, were long gone, and their apparent revivals in early 1948 and 1968 had turned out to be mirages. Indeed, his own preoccupations had shifted from American themes to the destruction of European Jewry. In the 1970s, he had tried in vain to adapt André Schwarz-Bart's *Last of the Just* as an opera libretto.[37] Now, in the very late 1980s, he was busy researching the European Holocaust for a new opera.[38]

In May 1990, as we remember from the previous chapter, Bernstein was acutely ill in a hotel room in Prague, not far from the Jewish cemetery and the memorials to the dead, lamenting his failure to write the masterwork that would consecrate his legacy as a composer and as a social critic. On June 5, 1990, he performed Beethoven's Ninth in Prague and then returned to Tanglewood, where his career had begun, to lead a memorial honoring Koussevitzky. On August 14, he conducted Copland's Symphony no. 3 and on August 19, Beethoven's Seventh and the *Four Sea Interludes* from the work he had inaugurated at Tanglewood so long ago, Britten's *Peter Grimes*.

Later that month, Arthur Laurents, Bernstein's collaborator on *West Side Story* and the failed *Race to Urga* and a longtime close friend, visited Bernstein:

> I could see the pain hit him; it was unbearable. I wanted to duck. He would gasp—freeze frame, pause, take a breath—not a deep breath because a deep breath started coughing—pause again; then a rueful shake of his head and off he would go, picking up the conversation at a full clip. . . .
>
> "You'll lick it," I said. "You've always been lucky."
>
> He gave me a look. "Not this time."[39]

Less than two months later, on October 9, 1990, Bernstein announced his retirement from public performance due to ill health. He died at home on Sunday, October 14, with family and friends nearby.

# A Man in Dark Times

Bernstein never deserted his progressivism. In the 1940s, he had continued to hold to the idea that an enduring Popular Front might realize in peacetime the wartime utopian goals of a united humankind. Like so many other progressives, Bernstein learned the price of not toeing the line set by the orthodox Cold Warriors. He was blacklisted, but he was lucky: the liberal humanists who operated the machinery of the cultural Cold War got him off the blacklist without most of the public's knowing he had been on it, years before the blacklist era came to an end and, in fact, while others were still being victimized. He also knew how to take advantage of the American cultural media's need to create and fetishize stars for commodification's sake. He was everyone's "Lenny."

But Bernstein brooded about those "dark times" when, as Hannah Arendt wrote, following Bertolt Brecht's poem "To Those Born Later," malign forces operate and the citizen must make choices of relatively great consequence.[1] To disengage from politics and take flight into other realms, such as the aesthetic or the scientific domains, would be craven; to confront these political forces alone was quixotic or even suicidal. Lone individuals might manage to remain ethically connected to their fellows by remaining mindful of the evil and malignant power. They do not forget the dark times, and one such individual was Leonard Bernstein.[2] Once off the blacklist and safely established as music director of the New York Philharmonic, he could have easily taken an inner migration into sheer aestheticism and into purely private issues of the inner life or the family. Instead, he retained and acted upon his progressive impulses.[3] He appeared in political rallies and meetings from the 1960s until his death in 1990; he was a member of the Committee for a Sane Nuclear Policy (SANE) and participated in the civil rights and anti–Vietnam war movements; and he pointedly refused to accept George Bush's invitation to the White House because of cuts in federal funding for the arts. He intervened, in short, to defend the progressive heritage from its detractors and to shore up liberals demoralized by the conservative onslaught. Some of his celebrity service work was of relatively symbolic significance—for example, his appearance in Montgomery to meet the marchers who had come from Selma—next to the heroic activities of others. But the authentic Leonard Bernstein, not the celebrity, quietly sought out Daniel Berrigan in Danbury Penitentiary, knowing full well that he would invite FBI inquiry. And true to form, J. Edgar Hoover, ever frustrated in finding evidence to arrest Bernstein for denying Communist Party membership in his 1954 affidavit, tried to destroy him in the early 1970s. Bernstein survived, but the "dark times" prevailed, and over the next nearly twenty years, until his death in 1990, he continually sought to express in musical form the deep contradictions in American culture.

·   ·   ·

Bernstein's optimism was that of an extrovert, but in his later decades, this upbeat aspect of his personality cohabited with the darker, prophetic vision of a Jeremiah contemplating America gone off track, if not, at times, gone mad. He was not a prophet-philosopher with a systematic body of thought, though he tried to create one in his Norton Lectures at Harvard in 1973.[4] But he did attempt to express his philosophic outlook through his music, and in this form, he did think profoundly. In his attempt, mistaken as it was, to ground tonality within the innate capacities of the human mind and thereby provide evidence of its universality, he sought a common aesthetic ground on which humanity might find common incantation and expression. He had formed this universalistic outlook at the family dinner table in the Hebrew prophetic declarative voice of his father. He may have upset his father by not taking on a rabbinical voice in the synagogue, but his concert halls were in a sense gathering points for congregations, ecclesia, assemblies wherein his voice might light in his audience a glimmer of that lost tribe, united humanity. He composed a lot of music that has entered the concert-hall canon and musical theater and reaches a wide and receptive audience. But by his own assessment, Bernstein never found the text by which to compose music that would break the hearts of his fellow Americans and let them gain a glimpse into their history and their potential for social renewal. That text remained, as we know, elusive. But Bernstein did find one means for prophetic expression. His predecessor Mahler had stretched music to its heartbreaking incantation, and Bernstein had found in Mahler's music the long narrative of catastrophe and terror that had engulfed European civilization in the first half of the twentieth century and seemed to go on endlessly. Mahler spoke for his generation about the loss of belief in enlightened and progressive values. And so in conducting Mahler, perhaps more so than any other composer, Leonard Bernstein the ecstatic magus was able to communicate to orchestra and audience his own tragic vision.

# NOTES

General Note about FBI Citations:

The citations to Federal Bureau of Investigation files in these notes refer to the extensive "Leonard Bernstein" dossier kept by the U.S. Department of Justice, which was supplied to me by the American Civil Liberties Union and parts of which are available in the Leonard Bernstein Collection, Personal Business Papers, box 946, folder 1, "Proskauer: FBI files 1950–1970." The file numbers are coded by location. Thus, files whose numbers begin with BS contain materials from the FBI's Boston office; HQ, from the main office in Washington, D.C.; and NY, from the New York office. The batch I received from the ACLU was divided into numbered sections, which I cite here for the reader's convenience, though section numbers may not apply to other collections from the dossier. The FBI file citations herein use the following shorthand:

"Supplemental Release" refers to the file "Supplemental Release Resulting from Consultations with Department of Justice Criminal Division, Department of State, Central Intelligence Agency."

"Administrative Appeal" refers to the file "Supplemental Release Resulting from Administrative Appeal."

"FBI Summary" refers to "Summary of File References." These summaries are compilations of reports of Bernstein's activities and other materials that were placed in his file over the years.

## INTRODUCTION

1. Robert Moses, "Remarks on the Groundbreaking at Lincoln Square," in *Empire City: New York Through the Centuries,* ed. Kenneth T. Jackson and David S. Dunbar (New York: Columbia University Press, 2002), 737.

2. "President Turns Earth to Start Lincoln Center," *New York Times,* May 15, 1959, 1, 14.

3. See, for example, Joan Peyser, *Bernstein: A Biography,* rev. ed. (New York: Billboard, 1998); Humphrey Burton, *Leonard Bernstein* (New York: Doubleday, 1994); Meryle Secrest, *Leonard Bernstein: A Life* (New York: Random House, 1994); and Paul Myers, *Leonard Bernstein* (London: Phaidon, 1998). In addition to these works are two earlier biographies: David Ewan, *Leonard Bernstein* (West Philadelphia, PA: Chilton, 1960); and John Briggs, *Leonard Bernstein* (Cleveland: World Publishing Co., 1960).

4. Secrest, *Leonard Bernstein,* 173–74.

5. Peyser, *Bernstein,* 245n.

6. Ralph Blumenthal, "Files Detail Years of Spying on Bernstein," *New York Times,* July 29, 1994. Blumenthal wrote, "The F.B.I. documents, 666 pages of reports on Mr. Bernstein, were made available yesterday in Los Angeles by the American Civil Liberties Union of Southern California, which had obtained them from the bureau under the Freedom of Information Act."

7. I received this information from Mark Eden Horowitz, archivist of the Leonard Bernstein Collection in the Library of Congress.

8. Meyer, *Leonard Bernstein,* 83–84.

9. Norman Lebrecht, *The Maestro Myth: Great Conductors in Pursuit of Power* (New York: Citadel Press, 1993), 179.

10. Quoted by Amos Elon, "A Fugitive from Egypt and Palestine," *New York Review of Books,* February 1999.

11. Bertolt Brecht, "To Those Born Later" ("To Posterity"), in *Bertolt Brecht: Poems, 1913–1956,* ed. John Willett and Ralph Mannheim with the cooperation of Erich Fried, trans. John Willett (London: Methuen, 1976), 318–20.

## 1. YOUNG AMERICAN

1. "I'm not a musician, I'm really a rabbi." Quoted by Charles Rosen in *Piano Notes: The World of the Pianist* (New York: Free Press, 2002), 120. See also Walter Wager, "Bernstein—A Teacher Too," *New York Times,* July 11, 1972.

2. Leonard Bernstein, *Findings* (Garden City, NY: Anchor Doubleday, 1982). The essays are, in order, "Father's Books," 13–14; "The Occult," 26–35; and "The Absorption of Race Elements into American Music," 37–100.

3. Burton Bernstein, *Family Matters: Sam, Jennie and the Kids* (New York: Summit, 1982), 22–38, 53–65.

4. Ibid., 38–53. Burton notes that Jenny was working at the mill in 1912 when the workers went out for the great Lawrence strike called by the International Workers of the World but that Jenny, while sympathetic, did not participate in the strike. Ibid., 48.

5. Ibid., 13.

6. Ibid., 194–95.

7. Save for a reference to the family's apparent veneration of FDR, Burton offers no discussion of family political sentiments. Ibid., 81. However, from that reference and Leonard's writings, we can assume that the Bernsteins were no different from the tens of thousands of other Jewish families that looked to Roosevelt as protector. One can catch a sense of the threat American Jews felt from homegrown Nazis in Philip Roth's *The Plot against America* (New York: Houghton-Mifflin, 2004).

8. Ironically, Samuel and his family joined a conservative synagogue that featured organ music. Paul Myers, *Leonard Bernstein* (London: Phaidon, 1998), 16.

9. According to Rexford Tugwell, a member of Roosevelt's brain trust and undersecretary of agriculture from 1933 to 1937, Roosevelt thought MacArthur "the second most dangerous man in America" after the Louisiana demagogue Huey Long. *The Democratic Roosevelt* (Garden City, NY: Anchor Books, 1957), 349.

10. Bernstein, "The Occult," in *Findings*, 26–33. The line "Plato makes Eros the center of all emotions" may have found expression in Bernstein's work of 1954, *Serenade*.

11. William R. Trotter, *Priest of Music: The Life of Dimitri Mitropoulos* (Portland, OR: Amadeus Press, 1995), 87–88. Bernstein may not only have imitated Mitropoulos's conducting style, as Trotter suggests; he may also have caught another bug from the conductor: Mitropoulos was in those days one of the few champions of the composer Gustav Mahler. As we shall see, Bernstein not only performed Mahler but led the so-called Mahler boom that started in the 1960s and persists into the twenty-first century.

12. D. W. Prall, *Aesthetic Judgment* (New York: Thomas Y. Crowell, 1929), 57–82. On Prall's influence on his circle at Harvard, see Andrew Rindfleisch, "An Interview with Arthur Berger," available by applying to the author at

Department of Music, College of Arts and Sciences, Cleveland State University, 2121 Euclid Ave., Cleveland OH 44115-2214. See also Arthur Berger, *Reflections of an American Composer* (Berkeley: University of California Press, 2002), 246 n1.

13. Leonard Bernstein, *The Unanswered Question: Six Talks at Harvard* (Cambridge, MA: Harvard University Press, 1973), 3–5. Two years later, Bernstein revealed his embrace of Prall's outlook to an audience at the Curtis Institute: "Our sense of truth must be interdisciplinary, and our sense of beauty must be expansive, even eclectic." "Speech at Curtis Institute for its 50th Anniversary, 28 February 1975," Writings, Leonard Bernstein Collection (LBC), box 90, folder 4, Library of Congress, Washington, D.C.

14. Prall, *Aesthetic Analysis* (New York: Thomas Y. Crowell, 1936), 64, 70. But Prall also made room for the idea that tonality is only a convention. See *Aesthetic Analysis*, 65, and *Aesthetic Judgment*, 238, where he states quite clearly that "Tonality is . . . a matter of convention."

15. Prall, *Aesthetic Judgment*, 182, 339–351.

16. For Marc Blitzstein's and Samuel Barber's reactions to Copland's *Piano Variations*, see Howard Pollack, *Aaron Copland: The Life and Works of an Uncommon Man* (New York: Henry Holt, 1999), 182 and 192, respectively. See also Morris Dickstein, "Copland and American Populism in the 1930s," in *Aaron Copland and His World*, ed. Carol Oja and Judith Tick (Princeton, NJ: Princeton University Press, 2005), 88.

17. See Aaron Copland and Vivian Perlis, *Copland: 1900 through 1942* (New York: St. Martin's/Marek, 1984), 191–92; and Mark Stevens and Annalyn Swan, *De Kooning: An American Master* (New York: Alfred A. Knopf, 2004), 193. Thus, the gregarious and charismatic Bernstein, by dint of his close association with Copland, was only one or two degrees of separation from these circles.

18. Van Wyck Brooks, *America's Coming of Age*, rev. ed. (New York: B. W. Huebsch, 1915; repr., Garden City, NY: Doubleday, 1958).

19. Brooks wrote of a new, modern Young America in *America's Coming of Age*, 118–25, 154–59. See also Van Wyck Brooks, "On Creating a Usable Past," in *The Early Years*, rev. ed., ed. Claire Sprague (Boston: Northeastern University Press, 1993), 219–26.

20. Paul Rosenfeld, "An Hour with American Music" (1929), reprinted in *Musical Impressions: Selections from Paul Rosenfeld's Criticism*, ed. Herbert A. Liebowitz (New York: Hill and Wang, 1969), 249.

21. Liberals seek to secure and protect the equality of civil rights, civil liberties, and economic liberty and to bring about welfare and labor legislation that can help raise the standards of living of the poor, the aged, and those unable to

work. They also support the rights of workers to organize unions to bargain collectively on their behalf. Progressives are liberals who emphasize a greater role for government in reaching liberal goals, including policies to regulate business and otherwise to plan the economy to ensure what they consider a more just distribution of incomes and economic development.

22. For a Harvard musical ditty in the academic year 1938–39 entitled "Oh the Land of the Free," Bernstein extolled Ickes while damning his attacker, chairman of the recently formed House Un-American Activities Committee Martin Dies, as a veritable "Nazi in disguise," Writings, LBC, box 70, folder 9.

23. Kristi Andersen, *The Creation of a Democratic Majority, 1928–1936* (Chicago: University of Chicago Press, 1979).

24. Consider the resemblance between John Dewey's progressive outlook and evolutionary and democratic Marxism: "Our institutions, democratic in form, tend to favor in substance a privileged plutocracy." The "cooperatively organized intelligence" behind the New Deal signaled that the public mind was coming to realize the possibilities of organized social control that would "socialize the forces of production, now at hand, so that the liberty of individuals will be supported by the very structure of economic organization." John Dewey, "Renascent Liberalism," in *Liberalism and Social Action* (New York: Capricorn, 1935), 88. This article was reprinted in V. F. Calverton's widely read anthology, *The Making of Society: An Outline of Sociology* (New York: The Modern Library, 1937), 735–47. The first quotation is on 741; the second, on 743.

25. "Even before the inception of the 'Red Decade,' social concerns made their appearance in modern dance. Graham's *Revolt,* which premiered in 1927 (a year that witnessed huge rallies in Union Square to protest the execution of Sacco and Vanzetti), like her *Poems of 1917: Song Behind the Lines, Dance of Death,* and *Immigrant: Steerage, Strike,* both of 1928) were harbingers of a trend that would become dominant in the 1930's." Lynn Garafola, "Toward an American Dance: Dance in the City," in *New York: Culture Capital of the World, 1940–1965,* ed. Leonard Wallock (New York: Rizzoli, 1988), 159.

26. Marc Blitzstein, "Coming—The Mass Audience!" *Modern Music* 13, no. 4 (May–June 1936): 25.

27. John Houseman, *Run-Through: A Memoir* (New York: Simon and Schuster, 1972), 257.

28. Copland and Perlis, *Copland,* 183.

29. Nadine Hubbs argues that Copland was following Virgil Thomson in producing the prairie motifs. *The Queer Composition of America's Sound* (Berkeley: University of California Press, 2004), 39–42.

30. Anthony Tommasini, *Virgil Thomson: Composer on the Aisle* (New York: W. W. Norton, 1997), 80.

31. Aaron Copland, *Our New Music* (New York: McGraw Hill, 1941), 165.

32. Roger Sessions, "To Revitalize Opera," *Modern Music* 15 no. 3 (March–April 1938): 150.

33. Virgil Thomson published remarks in the *New York Herald Tribune* on December 15, 1940, that represent the progressive outlook in those years: "The three great theater-pieces of [Mozart's] maturity, *Die Zauberflöte, La Nozze di Figaro, and Don Giovanni,* are all of them celebrations of . . . faith and fellowship, of what we should call liberalism or 'leftism' and what the eighteenth century called Enlightenment." Also, "The nearest thing we know to eighteenth-century Enlightenment is called today liberalism or leftism." Virgil Thomson, *The Musical Scene* (New York: Alfred A. Knopf, 1945), 74, 76.

34. See, in general, Harold Clurman, *The Fervent Years: The Group Theater and the 30s* (New York: Da Capo, 1983).

35. Ibid., quoted on 78.

36. On October 3, 1938, Bernstein wrote Copland that he "saw the Group Theater bunch today and they all asked for and about you. Odets, true to form, thinks the Salon Mexico 'light,' also Mozart except the G Minor Symphony. That angers me terrifically. I wish these people could see that a composer is just as serious when he writes a work, even if the piece is not defeatist (that Worker word again) and Weltschmerz and misanthropic and long. Light piece, indeed. I tremble when I think of producing something like the Salon." Correspondence, LBC, box 114. Reproduced in Copland and Perlis, *Copland,* 249.

37. Prall, *Aesthetic Judgment,* 162.

38. Ibid., 160–61.

39. Ibid., 164.

40. Ibid.

41. Ibid., 165.

42. Leonard Bernstein, "Boston Carries On," *Modern Music* 15, no. 4 (May–June 1938): 239.

43. Bernstein, *Findings,* 45.

44. Of the two recordings made of *The Cradle Will Rock,* the original cast recording narrated and accompanied on the piano by Blitzstein himself, American Legacy Records T 1001, excerpts on Pearl, compact disc, 0009, is far more in the spirit of Weill than is the 1964 Broadway-musical version, MGM compact disc SE4289-2OC.

45. Houseman, *Run-Through,* 254–78.

46. He received financial backing from Prall, the poet Archibald MacLeish, and the liberal historian Arthur Schlesinger Sr. See Humphrey Burton, *Leonard Bernstein* (New York: Doubleday, 1994), 53.

47. Eric A. Gordon, *Mark the Music: The Life and Work of Marc Blitzstein* (New York: St. Martin's Press, 1989), 178.

48. Decades later, Bernstein may have been alluding to the John Reed Society when he told a group that he had "joined anti-Fascist leagues and marched against Franco, Hitler" and "the [1938] takeover of Czechoslovakia." "Speech on Anti-Semitism, Friday, November 30, 1979, at Metropolitan Synagogue." Writings, LBC, box 91, folder 23.

49. Office Memorandum, May 21, 1946, entry 100–8895–18 P17, FBI file BS 100–17761.

## 2. THE FORTIES

1. The two works were released on compact disc in 1998 by Pearl under the title *Leonard Bernstein, Wunderkind,* GEMS 0005.

2. Aaron Copland to Mrs. Grant, March 17, 1940, General Correspondence, Serge Koussevitzky Archive, box 13, folder 21, "Copland, Aaron, 1940–1944," Library of Congress, Washington, D.C.

3. Humphrey Burton, *Leonard Bernstein* (New York: Doubleday, 1994), 69.

4. Bernstein to Fritz Reiner, August 27, 1940, Northwestern University Music Library, Fritz Reiner Library, quoted by Philip Hart, *Fritz Reiner: A Biography* (Evanston, IL: Northwestern University Press, 1994), 64. Bernstein wrote Reiner that Koussevitzky's assignment "gave a great lift to my Weltanschauung." Apparently, Bernstein had to mollify Reiner, whose feelings were hurt by his student's apparent transfer of loyalty to Koussevitzky; these feelings were exacerbated by Bernstein's seeming dig that with Koussevitzky, he could actually conduct performing musicians, whereas with Reiner, he had to shadow conduct—that is, without musicians. Ibid., 65.

5. Bernstein to Helen Coates, November 11, 1940, Correspondence, Leonard Bernstein Collection (LBC), box 13, folder 2, Library of Congress, Washington, D.C.

6. David Diamond, Prelude and Fugue no. 3 in C-Sharp Minor, Leonard Bernstein at the piano, January 1940, New York, New Music Recording, 78 rpm, NMR-1611. The official Bernstein discography is accessible at www.leonardbernstein.com/discog.html.

7. Agnes De Mille, *Promenade Home* (Boston: Little, Brown, 1958), 11.

8. Bernstein befriended a number of jazz musicians over the next years. His pianistic techniques astounded Teddy Wilson, who quickly recognized young Bernstein's gifts and even took a few lessons from him! Teddy Wilson, with Arie Ligthat and Humphrey van Loo, *Teddy Wilson Talks Jazz* (London: Cassell, 1996), 80. He also befriended the drummer Gene Krupa, with whom, in 1947, he debated the question "Has Jazz Influenced the Symphony?" The debate, published in *Esquire* that year, is republished in Robert Gottlieb, ed., *Reading Jazz: A Gathering of Autobiography, Reportage, and Criticism from 1919 to Now* (New York: Pantheon, 1996), 774–84.

9. Martin Gilbert, "Churchill and the Holocaust: The Possible and Impossible," in *Proceedings of the International Churchill Societies 1992–93,* 25th Anniversary International Conference, U.S. Holocaust Memorial Museum, Washington, November 8, 1993, www.winstonchurchill.org/i4a/pages/index.cfm?pageid=605.

10. *New York Times,* December 26, 1941.

11. Elizabeth Wilson, *Shostakovich, A Life Remembered* (Princeton, NJ: Princeton University Press, 1994), 148–49.

12. Burton, *Leonard Bernstein,* 99.

13. Office Memorandum, May 21, 1946, FBI file BS 100–17761. The FBI document notes that the press that printed the program had done work for a number of communist organizations.

14. Both articles appeared in the July 14, 1943, edition of the *New York Times.*

15. Paul Bowles, *Paul Bowles on Music,* ed. T. Mangan and I. Hermann (Berkeley: University of California Press, 2003), 82–83, 123–24, 134–35, respectively.

16. Leonard Bernstein, *Sonata for Clarinet and Piano,* David Oppenheim on clarinet, New York, Hargail, 78 rpm, MW 501; and Pearl, compact disc, GEMM CD 9279.

17. For full listings of Bernstein's performances with the New York Philharmonic, see Philharmonic Society of New York, *Bernstein Live at the New York Philharmonic,* accompanying the ten-compact-disc set, Special Editions NYP 2003; and Howard Shanet, *Philharmonic: A History of New York's Orchestra* (Garden City, NY: Doubleday & Co., 1975).

18. Peter Manso, *Brando: The Biography* (New York: Hyperion, 1994), 113.

19. D. M. Ladd to the Director, March 3, 1949, p. 4, FBI file HQ 100–360261, section 1.

20. Burton, *Leonard Bernstein,* 104.

21. Paul Bowles, "Bernstein's First." *New York Herald Tribune,* March 30, 1944, reprinted in Paul Bowles, *Paul Bowles on Music,* ed. Timothy Mangan and Irene Herrmann (Berkeley: University of California Press, 2003), 174.

22. Bowles claimed that the symphony "outranks every other symphonic product by any American composer of . . . the younger generation." He noted a "sustained atmosphere of mystery and beauty" that found favorable contrast with a "brutality of harmonic and sonorous treatment of the contemporary American school." By "harmonic brutality," he meant the ability "to create summary handling of . . . psychological effect" (*Paul Bowles on Music*, 173–74). The Russian qualities that were plain to Bowles were downplayed by Bernstein and by his biographer Humphrey Burton. Burton follows Bernstein's 1944 program note (Bernstein, *Program Book, Pittsburgh Symphony Orchestra*, January 28, 1944. See Burton, *Leonard Bernstein*, 125). Bernstein removed the work from its immediate, wartime context to grant it the conceit of timelessness. Burton sees the work as emblematic of Bernstein's American Jewishness. Although at one point he claims that Bernstein wanted to depict his "anger at the way [the Jewish historical] legacy was destroyed by persecution," he immediately insists that Bernstein did not have Nazi persecution in mind because he had composed much of the "Lamentation" in 1939, "years before the Nazis put into operation their 'Final Solution.'"(125–26). But Bernstein, as we have seen, only sketched this part in 1939, and the final version of "Lamentation" was "greatly changed" to fit with the preceding material written in 1942. In sum, Bernstein may have been writing for the ages, but as Burton himself makes clear (126), the work as it was performed in 1944 clearly sought to memorialize the terrible catastrophe suffered by European Jewry.

23. Dawn Powell, *The Diaries of Dawn Powell: 1931–1965*, ed. Tim Page (South Royalton, VT: Steerforth, 1995), 232. By "powers-soon-to-be," was Powell alluding to the circle of gay musicians led by Virgil Thompson and Copland and including Bernstein, Paul Bowles, David Diamond, and recent inductee Ned Rorem, which supposedly was gaining an iron grip on New York musical life? Rumors of such power, if not hegemony—thus its appellation "Homintern"— within musical circles certainly circulated in those years. Nadine Hubbs, *The Queer Composition of America's Sound*, 156, 158. But if Bernstein was empowered by that group, it was because his work, in collaboration with Robbins, had been received with great enthusiasm by ballet audiences.

24. Bowles, *Paul Bowles on Music*, 190.

25. *Fancy Free, Ballet*, Ballet Theater Orchestra, February 6, 1944, Decca, 78 rpm, DA 406; and 33 rpm, DL 6023, 7512. The label Varèse-Sarabande issued the recording at 33 rpm, VC 81055. Releases on compact disc include MCA Classics 10280 and Pearl 0005.

26. Marshall Berman, *On the Town: One Hundred Years of Spectacle in Times Square* (New York: Random House, 2006), 74–81.

27. Ibid., 81.

28. Julius Mattfield, ed., *Variety Musical Cavalcade, 1620–1969: A Chronology of Vocal and Instrumental Music Popular in the United States,* 3rd ed. (Englewood Cliffs, NJ: Prentice-Hall, 1971), 549.

29. *New York Times,* April 14, 1944.

30. S[pecial] A[gent] [blank], in a May 21, 1944, Office Memorandum in FBI file BS 100–17761, reports that Bernstein appeared in "An Evening with Paul Robeson, Leonard Bernstein and Muriel Smith, Carmen in Carmen Jones, with Samuel L. Barlow, presiding, at the Boston Opera House, Huntington Ave., Sunday, May 14, 1944 at 8:30 pm, under the auspices of: The Joint Anti-Fascist Refugee Committee, the Council on African Affairs" (cited as 100-7908-510A). The memorandum contains a second entry citing the following report by the *Boston Herald* (no date): "Bernstein delighted the audience by shifting from Brahms to boogie woogie in a neat encore" (cited as 100-6947-107).

31. On September 30, 1944, Bernstein accepted an invitation by telegram from Lily Pons asking him to sponsor and attend the opening of a "Russian war relief exhibit of Nazi photographs depicting fascism in operation to be held Oct. 16 1944, sponsored by the American Society for Russian Relief." Personal Business Papers, LBC, box 983, folder 16, "American Society for Russian Relief, Inc."

32. Datebook, November 20, 1944, LBC. Penciled out but legible because in pen: "Testimonial dinner in honor given by Joint Anti-Fascist Refugee Committee. Colonial Room Copley Plaza–Boston, December 4, 1944." Bernstein attended a dinner of the committee in Westchester County, New York, on December 15, 1944. Ladd to Director, March 3, 1949, p. 6. On December 19, 1944, Gail Kelvin, executive secretary of the JAFRC, wrote Bernstein to thank him for his speech. Personal Business Papers, LBC, box 1002, folder 16, "Joint Anti-Fascist Refugee Committee." Demonstrating the recent licensing by the federal government, correspondence from the Boston chapter of the JAFRC to Bernstein bore the imprint "President's War Relief Control Board reg. No. 539," Personal Business Papers, LBC, box 1002, folder 16, "Joint Anti-Fascist Refugee Committee."

33. LBC, box 1008, folder "Nation."

34. Ladd to Director, March 3, 1949, p. 15.

35. Letter from Paul Robeson, February 12, 1945, Personal Business Papers, LBC, box 1016, folder "Spanish Refugee Appeal of the Joint Anti-Fascist Refugee Committee."

36. "A highly confidential and reliable source having access to the records of the Joint Anti-Fascist Refugee Committee" reported that Bernstein's "name . . .

appeared on a proposed list of permanent persons for the National Campaign Committee of the Spanish Refugee Appeal of the Joint Anti-Fascist Refugee Committee of New York City in 1945." FBI Summary, December 13, 1950, p. 17, FBI file HQ 100–360261, section 1. The file also records a reference to a *Washington Post* ad, February 27, 1945, Veterans of Abraham Lincoln Brigade, "For America's Sake: Break with Franco Spain." Ladd to Director, March 3, 1949, p. 8.

37. Ladd to Director, March 3, 1949, p. 8.

38. Dorothy Parker to Bernstein, February 28, 1945, Personal Business Papers, LBC, box 1016, folder "Spanish Refugee Appeal." Printed at the bottom of the letter is the notice "The Committee [JAFRC] is licensed by the President's War Relief Control Board."

39. *On the Town: Four Dances*, On The Town Orchestra, February 3, 1945: RCA Victor, 78 rpm, M 995, DM 995. The recording was also offered on 33 rpm (CAL 196, CAL 336) and 45 rpm (CAE 203). Releases on compact disc include RCA/ BMG 09026 609152 and Pearl 0005.

*Symphony no. 1, Jeremiah*, St. Louis Symphony Orchestra; Nan Merriman, mezzo-soprano, February 14, 1945, St. Louis, Kiel Opera House, RCA Victor, 78 rpm, DM 1026. RCA/BMG reissued the recording on 33 rpm: RCA Victor SMA 7002 and RCA Camden CAL 196. Releases on compact disc include RCA/BMG 09026 61581 and Pearl 0005.

40. Burton, *Leonard Bernstein*, 140.

41. Aaron Copland, Serge Koussevitzky et al. to Bernstein, April 13, 1945, Correspondence, LBC, box 16, folder "Copland." The National Council of American-Soviet Friendship was soon to appear on the attorney general's list of communist front groups.

42. Datebook, LBC.

43. FBI Summary, December 13, 1950, p. 27.

44. *Daily Worker,* September 25, 1945, 12: Bernstein is listed as one of a "Thousand Artists and Writers" supporting the Committee for the Reelection of Benjamin Davis to the New York City Council, headed by Paul Robeson. On September 30, a statement by the Artists, Writers and Professional Division of the Davis Reelection Campaign to the New York City Council lists Bernstein as a sponsor. His photo appears with those of Margaret Webster, Lena Horne, Hazel Scott, Joan Tetzel, and Teddy Wilson.

45. "In 1945, when the Committee to aid Ben Davis was being considered, I was officially advised by Davis and by Jack Stachel that Leonard Bernstein was an adherent of the Communist Party. I had previously been advised to the

same effect by Alexander Trachtenberg and V. J. Jerome though I do not recall at the moment on what occasion. Again in 1945, I was officially advised by Jack Stachel of Mr. Bernstein's agreement to submit to Communist discipline when his associations with the Joint Anti-Fascist Committee was up for consideration, that being necessary for me to be advised upon an [blacked out]." The document ends with the reference number 100–360261–7. FBI file HQ 100–360261, section 1.

46. Letter from the American Committee for Spanish Freedom, November 21, 1945, Personal Business Papers, LBC, box 1016, folder "Spanish Refugee Appeal."

47. Leonard Bernstein, "The Arts Belong to the People," Writings, LBC, box 71, folder 8.

48. "City Symphony a 'Complete Fraud' As City Venture, Bernstein Says," *New York Times,* November 19, 1945.

49. "Orchestra's Head Chided by Mayor," *New York Times,* November 20, 1945.

50. Ladd to Director, March 3, 1949, p. 5.

51. "Tickets sold for $2.50 each and about 100 or more people attended the musicale." Ibid.

52. See Howard Fast, *Being Red: A Memoir* (New York: Bantam Doubleday, 1990), 145–52.

53. Datebook, LBC.

54. Bernstein to Helen Coates, May 9, 1946, Correspondence, LBC, box 13, folder 6.

55. Eric A. Gordon, *Mark the Music: The Life and Work of Marc Blitzstein* (New York: St. Martin's Press, 1989), 289.

56. This "intelligence" was gathered by "technical surveillance," which could include wiretaps and garbage sifting. Ladd to Director, March 3, 1949, p. 7.

57. Datebook, LBC.

58. FBI Summary, December 13, 1950, p. 4.

59. "City Symphony Concert," *New York Times,* September 23, 1946.

60. Leonard Bernstein, "Program Note" (1947), in *Facsimile: Choreographic Essay for Orchestra* (New York: Jalni Publications, 1988), 1.

61. Datebook, LBC.

62. FBI Summary, January 22, 1952, p. 30, FBI file NY 100–99895, section 1.

63. Bernstein shared his duties with cochairman Ferdinand C. Smith, "who was then an official of the National Maritime Union." Ladd to Director, March 3, 1949, p. 5.

64. For immediate postwar Left fears that the Vatican and the American Catholic hierarchy was preparing to come to Franco's support, see, among others, the widely read Left writer George Seldes, *The Catholic Crisis* (New York: Julian Messner, 1945). With the end of the war, the FBI revived its attack upon allies of Republican Spain, dormant since 1940, arresting Abraham Lincoln Brigade veterans and charging them with recruiting soldiers to fight overseas wars. The charges were dropped. Robert Gid Power, *Secrecy and Power: The Life of J. Edgar Hoover* (New York: Free Press, 1987), 235. By 1946, it was apparent that the FBI was going after the Joint Anti-Fascist Refugee Committee, set up primarily to help Spanish Loyalists exiled in France and elsewhere. Thus was Bernstein entered into a new enemies list of the bureau: On February 13, "a highly confidential and reliable source having access to the records of the Joint Anti-Fascist Refugee Committee" reported that Bernstein's "name . . . appeared on a proposed list of permanent persons for the National Campaign Committee of the Spanish Refugee Appeal of the Joint Anti-Fascist Refugee Committee of New York City in 1945." FBI Summary, December 13, 1950, p. 17.

65. Leonard Bernstein to Helen Coates, February 9, 1946, Correspondence, LBC, box 13, folder 6.

66. Leonard Bernstein to Helen Coates, February 9, 11, and 16, 1946, Correspondence, LBC, box 13, folder 6. According to Fritz Reiner biographer Philip Hart, "Arthur Judson constantly urged his artists to avoid anything remotely associated with political sentiments that might offend the business power structure." *Fritz Reiner,* 58.

67. FBI Summary, December 13, 1950, p. 43.

68. Ibid., 3.

69. Ibid., 4.

70. Ibid.

71. Margaret Webster to Bernstein, March 18, 1946, Spanish Refugee Appeal of the Joint Anti-Fascist Refugee Committee, Personal Business Papers, LBC, box 1016, folder "Spanish Refugee Appeal."

72. FBI file BS 100–17761–1, March 24, 1946. Also invited was Donald Ogden Stewart.

73. FBI Summary, December 13, 1950, p. 43.

74. *Daily Worker,* December 5, 1946, 8.

75. Bernstein's memo is on a letter from the Progressive Citizens of America dated February 4, 1947, Personal Business Papers, LBC, box 1012, folder "Progressive Citizens of America." Ickes and Eleanor Roosevelt disliked Truman and had hoped to replace him on the 1948 Democratic ticket with Eisenhower

and the New Dealer Supreme Court justice William O. Douglas. Ickes did not support Wallace only because of the communist presence in the Progressive Party and held his nose as he gave his support to Truman, doing so only because the loss of votes to the Dixiecrats on the Right and the Progressives on the Left could have resulted in a victory for the Republicans. See T. H. Watkins, *Righteous Pilgrim: The Life and Times of Harold L. Ickes, 1874–1952* (New York: Henry Holt, 1990), 848–49.

76. Ladd to Director, March 3, 1949, p. 5. For the genesis of the Loyalty-Security Program, see Carl Bernstein's interview with Clark Clifford in Carl Bernstein, *Loyalties: A Son's Memoir* (New York: Touchstone, 1989), 195–206.

77. FBI Summary, December 13, 1950, p. 52. The letter was recovered by a "Los Angeles Confidential Informant [blocked out] which was a trash cover" [*sic*]. Supplemental Release, FBI file HQ 360261–8. FBI agents commonly sifted through the garbage of subjects under surveillance.

78. See Clifford Odets, *The 1940 Journal of Clifford Odets* (New York: Grove Press, 1988), index references to Hanns Eisler.

79. See Hanns Eisler, *A Rebel in Music: Selected Writings,* ed. Manfred Grabs, trans. Marjorie Myers (New York: International Publishers, 1978); and *Composing for the Films* (New York: Oxford University Press, 1947). Eisler thanked for their help the philosopher and Second Viennese School associate Theodore Adorno, Odets, the director Jean Renoir, and Harold Clurman, as well as the poet/playwright Bertolt Brecht, with whom Eisler worked on songs and operatic works. Ironies abound: Eisler received funding from the Rockefeller Foundation to support his work on this book.

80. See the testimony of Ruth Fischer before HUAC in Eric Bentley, ed., *Thirty Years of Treason (Excerpts from Hearings before the House Committee on Un-American Activities, 1938–68)* (New York: Viking, 1971), 71.

81. See Hanns Eisler's testimony before HUAC in Bentley, *Thirty Years of Treason,* 86.

82. Quoted in Aaron Copland and Vivian Perlis, *Copland Since 1943* (New York: St. Martin's Press, 1989), 90. Copland later wrote about his exchanges with Clurman: "I agreed to lend my name for the Eisler benefit. While I was working on *The Red Pony,* I heard from Harold again (17 February 1948): 'How do you like Hollywood these sour days?' Later (March), he wrote, 'I'm glad that you're for Wallace . . . the [Eisler] benefit 'tho far too long, went off well. Good reviews by D. D. [David Diamond] and V. T. [Virgil Thomson] but poor Eisler is still in a jam. Olin Downes is trying to get Toscanini to get Eisler a visa.'" Ibid., 90.

83. On Bernstein's invitation to Eisler, see his Datebook, December 1, 1947, LBC. On his signing the petition to Attorney General Tom Clark, see *Daily Worker,* December 17, 1947, cited in FBI Summary, December 13, 1950, p. 72, FBI file HQ 100–360261, section 1. According to information the FBI received from a "New York confidential agent," "The letterhead of the 'Committee for Justice for Hanns Eisler,' 1 West 89th Street, New York City, dated February 11, 1948, listed Leonard Bernstein as co-chairman of this committee." Ibid., p. 76. For Bernstein's performance in the concert for Eisler at Town Hall on February 28, 1948, see ibid., p. 75. See also Datebook, LBC.

84. "The roster for the flight . . . included Danny Kaye, Gene Kelly, Paul Henreid, Evelyn Keyes, Jane Wyatt, Marsha Hunt, June Havoc, Geraldine Brooks, Richard Conte, . . . Ira Gershwin, as well as the Bogarts, [screenwriter Philip] Dunne, and [director John] Huston. A number of independent producers, notably David O. Selznick and Walter Wanger, worked quietly behind the scenes to back the effort." A. M. Sperber and Eric Lax, *Bogart* (New York: William Morrow, 1997), 366. Bernstein's membership in the Broadway branch of the Committee for the First Amendment was reported by the *Washington Evening Star.* Ladd to Director, March 3, 1949, p. 9. Bernstein later added his name to those of, among others, Garson Kanin, Ruth Gordon, Deems Taylor, Howard Taubman, Marc van Doren, Goodman Ace, and Paul Strand, to deplore the decision of the Hollywood studios to capitulate to the House Un-American Activities Committee and to institute the blacklist. The joint letter was published on December 1, 1947. FBI Summary, December 13, 1950, p. 69.

85. Sperber and Lax, *Bogart,* 378.

86. The studio heads' "Waldorf Statement" is reprinted in L. Caplair and S. Englund, *The Inquisition in Hollywood: Politics in the Film Community, 1930–1960* (Garden City, NY: Anchor Press/Doubleday, 1980), 445; and in Ellen Schrecker, *The Age of McCarthyism: A Brief History with Documents* (New York: Bedford/ St. Martin's, 1994), 215–16.

87. *Daily Worker,* December 1, 1947, 3, quoted in FBI Summary, January 22, 1952, p. 35. This act was prescient, for Bernstein's name would cross the desk of Daniel T. O'Shea, an "ultraconservative" who left Hollywood in 1950 for CBS, where he "ran the tightest blacklist in the entertainment industry." Sperber and Lax, *Bogart,* 396.

88. FBI Summary, January 22, 1952, p. 54. There appears as well a memo for the director from the Office of Chief of Naval Operations, Washington, D.C., dated June 6, 1947, with the subject line "Report on Maritime and Union Activity": "Leonard Bernstein was listed as a sponsor of a National Youth Lobby which

was scheduled to be held in Washington, D.C., June 16, 1947. The purpose of the lobby was to speak to Senators and U.S. Representatives on behalf of Federal aid to education." FBI Summary, December 13, 1950, p. 58.

89. Virgil Thomson, "Lively Revival" (November 25, 1947), in *A Virgil Thomson Reader* (Boston: Houghton-Mifflin, 1981), 300–301.

90. Leonard Bernstein, *Findings* (Garden City, NY: Anchor Doubleday, 1982), 131.

91. Paul Moor, "Leonard Bernstein: Ceiling Unlimited," *Harper's Magazine,* February 1948, 142.

92. Burton, *Leonard Bernstein,* 171. The quotation is from an interview with Bernstein in the *Houston Post,* January 4, 1948, and cited in Burton, 171 and 552n.

93. Kirk H. Porter and Donald Bruce Johnson, *National Party Platforms, 1840–1964* (Urbana: University of Illinois Press, 1966), 436–47.

94. James A. Hagerty, "Big Aid to Wallace Is Seen in Victory of Bronx Protégé," *New York Times,* February 19, 1948.

95. *New York Times,* February 20, 1948, 14.

96. According to the FBI memorandum, Bernstein was cited in an article in the February 7, 1948, *German-American* as one of "prominent Americans [who] had declared themselves against President Truman's policy in Germany." FBI Summary, December 13, 1950, p. 75.

97. *New York Times,* February 24, 1948.

98. FBI Summary, December 13, 1950, p. 75.

99. *New York Times,* March 8, 1948.

100. FBI Summary, December 13, 1950, p. 75.

101. An April 17, 1948, article in the *New York Journal American* states, "Leonard Bernstein, a conductor and a member or sponsor of eight Communist fronts including the Council of American-Soviet Friendship, was one of the signers of a protest sent to President Truman concerning American interference in the Italian elections." FBI Summary, December 13, 1950, p. 80.

102. An FBI memorandum from February 2, 1948 quotes a Yergen article that "states that on February 2, 1948, there took place the annual meeting of THE COUNCIL ON AFRICAN AFFAIRS. The business of the meeting and the adjourned meeting which followed consisted solely of the disgraceful fight of the Communists against me and their efforts to get control of the Council and use it for their own treacherous purposes. The communist high command had handed over the task of character assassination to PAUL ROBESON, DOXEY WILKERSON AND ALPHEUS HUNTON. These men had the unfailing help of LEONARD BERNSTEIN and others who were placed on the Council membership by the proposals of ROBESON, HUNTON AND WILKERSON." FBI Summary, January 22, 1952, p. 27.

103. See Martin Bauml Duberman, *Paul Robeson* (London: Pan Books, 1989), 256–57, 330–31. In May 1948, Yergen was dismissed from the council.

104. Leonard Bernstein, "Dialogue And . . ." (April, 1948), reprinted in *Findings,* 113, 116–17.

105. Bernstein to Marcuse Family, March 19, 1948, Correspondence, LBC, box 37 folder "Marcuse, Philip, Barbara ('Babs') & Philip, Jr."

106. See David Caute, *The Dancer Defects: The Struggle for Cultural Supremacy During the Cold War* (Oxford: Oxford University Press, 2003), 387. Bernstein to Helen Coates, May 3, 1948, Correspondence, LBC, box 13, folder 8.

107. Bernstein to Helen Coates, May 5, 1948, Correspondence, LBC, box 13, folder 8.

108. Leonard Bernstein to Shirley Bernstein, May 5, 1948, Shirley Bernstein Papers, LBC, folder 1 of 6.

109. "'Notables Score Bill as Police State Move.' This article reflects that the conductor, LEONARD BERNSTEIN was among those persons who joined leaders of the Civil Rights Congress in scoring the Subversive Control Act of 1948, which was sponsored by the House Committee on Un-American Activities." *Daily Worker,* April 26, 1948, 3. The memorandum also notes, "The Civil Rights Congress is an organization declared by the Attorney General as coming within the purview of Executive Order 9835." FBI Summary, January 22, 1952, p. 71. (The pagination stops after p. 69.)

110. Ibid.

111. On black leaders' outlook on Robeson, see Duberman, *Paul Robeson,* 324–25.

112. See Samuel Lubell, *The Future of American Politics,* 2nd ed. (Garden City, NY: Anchor/Doubleday, 1956), 219–22; Herbert S. Parmet, *The Democrats* (New York: McMillan, 1976), 36–92.

113. Ladd to Director, March 3, 1949.

114. Ladd to the Director, March 15, 1949, FBI file HQ 100–360261, section 1; "Truman Cancels UN Visit Here," *New York Times,* March 25, 1949.

115. Burton, *Bernstein,* 158, 160–61. Apparently anti-Bernstein feelings were so high that when Koussevitzky told the trustees he would resign if they did not approve Bernstein's appointment, the trustees accepted his resignation (171, 174).

116. Mitropoulos's biographer, William R. Trotter, claims that the trustees held against Bernstein his youth, his politics, his Judaism, and his Broadway career. But to Trotter, Bernstein was simply receiving his due. According to Trotter, Bernstein had betrayed Mitropoulos when Koussevitzky, who disliked Mitropoulos, asked Bernstein for any information that could damage Mitropoulos's candidacy with the trustees. Bernstein complied, informing Koussevitzky

that Mitropoulos was homosexual. *Priest of Music: The Life of Dimitri Mitropoulos* (Portland, OR: Amadeus Press, 1995), 240–41.

117. Aaron Copland Collection, box 211, folder 23, Library of Congress, Washington, D.C.

118. "Red Visitors Cause Rumpus," *Life,* April 4, 1949, 39–43. Bernstein was joined by, among others, Aaron Copland, Charlie Chaplin, Olin Downs, Albert Einstein, Lillian Hellman, Langston Hughes, Norman Mailer, Thomas Mann, F. O. Matthiessen, Arthur Miller, Clifford Odets, Dorothy Parker, George Seldes, Louis Untermeyer, and Mark van Doren. The same issue carried a photo story promoting Western recognition of Franco Spain. "Franco's Regime, Slightly Mellowed, Looks West for Friendship and Aid," 111–23.

119. Bernstein recorded nothing in 1948 due to the Petrillo ban—the musicians union boycott of the recording industry. In June 1949, however, he recorded three works in New York: (1) Copland's *Billy the Kid Suite,* with the RCA Victor Symphony Orchestra, June 23, RCA Studio RCA Victor, 33 rpm, LM 1031; and RCA Camden CAL 439. The recording was reissued as a RCA/BMG compact disc, 09026 609152. (2) Copland's *Statements for Orchestra: "Jingo,"* with the RCA Victor Symphony Orchestra, June 23; RCA/BMG, compact disc, 09026 616502. (3) His own *I Hate Music,* with Blanche Thebom, mezzo-soprano, and himself at the piano, June 15, RCA Studio RCA/BMG, compact disc, 09026 681012.

120. For example, at Tanglewood, in the summer of 1948, Edmund Wilson noted, "Bernstein, conducting Mahler, was better than I have seen him—showed delicacy as well as intensity, and there were only moments when he seemed to be doing an interpretive dance to the music rather than leading the orchestra." Edmund Wilson*, The Forties: From Notebooks and Diaries of the Period,* ed. Leon Edel (New York: Farrar, Straus and Giroux, 1983), 276.

121. *Counterattack,* February 24, 1950 (no. 144). According to an FBI writer, "The article said that Bernstein . . . cabled greetings to Dimitri Shostakovich, a Russian composer, before Shostakovich left Russia to attend a conference in New York and the fact that Shostakovich had debased his talent by producing musical paeans to Stalin's 'accomplishments' did not deter Bernstein." FBI Summary, December 13, 1950, p. 94.

122. *Red Channels: The Report of Communist Influence in Radio and Television* (New York: Counterattack, 1950).

123. Testimony of CBS producer Mark Goodson, in Griffin Fariello, ed., *Red Scare: Memories of the American Inquisition: An Oral History* (New York: Avon, 1995), 321, 325. In his discussion of the blacklist at CBS, Robert Slater mentions Bernstein only as one of those named by *Red Channels* and then notes that "to be

on *Red Channels* could prove devastating to one's career." He adds, "As a result of their appearance in *Red Channels,* the careers of these men and women were often seriously harmed." But he says nothing specific about Bernstein's treatment by CBS. *This . . . Is CBS: A Chronicle of 60 Years* (Englewood Cliffs, NJ: Prentice-Hall, 1988), 136. For Slater's discussion of the blacklist, see 135–38.

124. The following is a representation of the *Red Channels* Bernstein exposé.

| LEONARD BERNSTEIN, COMPOSER, CONDUCTOR: | REPORTED AS: |
|---|---|
| People's Songs, Inc. | Sponsor, Letterhead, March 1948 |
| Scientific and Cultural Conference for World Peace | Sponsor, Official Program, March 1949 |
| American-Soviet Music Society | Affiliated, Un-American Activities Committee, *Review of Scientific and Cultural Conference for World Peace* (hereafter *Review*), April 19, 1949, p. 43 |
| Hanns Eisler Concert | Sponsor, *Review,* p. 43 |
| Protest Against Deportation of Hanns Eisler | Signer, *Review,* p. 43 |
| Committee for the Re-election of Benjamin J. Davis, 1945 | Affiliated, *Review,* p. 41 |
| Progressive Citizens of America | Signer, Arts, Sciences and Professions Council, Statement in defense of Communist cases. *Review,* p. 37 |
| World Federation of Democratic Youth | Affiliated, *Review,* p. 36 |
| Voice of Freedom Committee | Affiliated, *Review,* p. 35 |
| Southern Conference for Human Welfare | Affiliated, *Review,* p. 34 |
| Progressive Citizens of America | Affiliated, *Review,* p. 33 |
| National Negro Congress | Affiliated, *Review,* p. 32 |
| Joint Anti-Fascist Refugee Committee | Affiliated, *Review,* p. 28 |
| Civil Rights Congress | Affiliated, *Review,* p, 25 |
| Committee for a Democratic Far Eastern Policy | Affiliated, *Review,* p. 24 |
| American Council for a Democratic Greece | Affiliated, *Review,* p. 22 |
| American Youth for Democracy | Affiliated, *Review,* p, 22 |

*Red Channels*, 16–17.

On the copy of this list in the Leonard Bernstein Collection, all entries from the Voice of Freedom Committee to the American Youth for Democracy, with the exception of the Southern Conference for Human Welfare and the Progressive Citizens of America, have a penciled *X* beside them in the right margin. The folder also has a penciled memo, in a hand unknown to Mark Eden Horowitz, the Library of Congress archivist of the Leonard Bernstein Collection, apparently denying membership in the Civil Rights Congress but adding the American Committee for Yugoslav Relief, the Action Committee to free Spain of the American Committee for Spanish Freedom, and the American-Soviet Music Society. "Memorandum 1 of 2," Personal Business Papers, LBC, box 1006 [box 21A in the older archival series].

125. Dean Acheson, Secretary of State, Outgoing Telegram Department of State Division of Communications and Records, Telegraphic Branch, December 1950. Supplemental Release. The U.S. embassy in Paris was warned not to use Bernstein for "Embassy's music program." Bernstein "had been affiliated with a number of Communist inspired activities and organizations" many of which are "dangerous because of their close control by the Communist element. The Embassy is [was] advised to be particularly cautious about its contact with Mr. Bernstein and under no circumstances to sponsor his performances or use his services in connection with the Embassy's program."

### 3. AMERICAN BIEDERMEIER

1. Felicia's lover, Richard Hart, died unexpectedly on Tuesday, January 2, 1951, while Felicia was waiting at the dock for Bernstein to disembark. Soon thereafter, Felicia agreed to marry Bernstein. See "Richard Hart, 35, Actor, Succumbs; Leading Player on Television, Stage and Screen Stricken with a Heart Attack," *New York Times,* January 4, 1951; Meryle Secrest, *Leonard Bernstein: A Life* (New York: Vintage, 1994), 177; and Humphrey Burton, *Leonard Bernstein* (New York: Doubleday, 1994), 208.

2. Hallinan would be the Progressive Party presidential candidate in 1952.

3. Office Memorandum from SAC [Special Agent in Charge], New York, to Director, April 30, 1952, FBI file HQ 100–360261–15, section 2. Morros's name (and for that matter, Hallinan's) is blacked out in this FBI file but not blacked out in the file in the Bernstein archive at the Library of Congress, where it is cited as "FBI, Memo from SAC NY to Director Jan 17, 1951, re: Boris Michael Morros— Espionage," Personal Business Papers, Leonard Bernstein Collection (LBC), box 946, folder 1, "Proskauer: FBI Files 1950–1970," Library of Congress, Washington, D.C. Years later, Morros revealed that he had been an undercover informant for the FBI since 1947. "Spy on a World Stage; Boris Mihailovitch Morros,"

*New York Times,* August 13, 1957; *My Ten Years as a Counterspy,* as told to Charles Samuels (New York: Viking Press, 1959).

4. Mitropoulos "would like to inform the members of the committee that he recommends as guest conductors for next year Bruno Walter, George Szell and Guido Cantelli." Minutes of the Executive Committee of the Board of Directors of the Philharmonic-Symphony Society of New York, Inc., January 3, 1951, 1, New York Philharmonic Archives, New York.

5. Serge Koussevitzky, handwritten note, December 1949, Koussevitzky Archive, Library of Congress, box 6, folder 5, General Correspondence, "Bernstein, Leonard, 1949–1951."

6. Bernstein to Koussevitzky, January 15, 1951, Koussevitzky Archive, box 6, folder 5.

7. Helen Coates to Nelly Walker, January 30, 1951. A carbon copy of this letter is on the back of Nelly Walker's letter of January 22, 1951, to Helen Coates. Personal Business Papers, LBC, box 990, file "Columbia Artists Management Inc. (1949–53)."

8. The dates and performances are listed in Howard Shanet, *Philharmonic: A History of New York's Orchestra* (Garden City, NY: Doubleday & Co., 1975), 561–65. The recording of Ives, *Symphony no. 2* can be heard on NYP Special Editions, compact disc, NYP 2003.

9. Bernstein led studio recordings of Copland's *El Salón México* and Milhaud's *La Création du Monde* for Columbia Records on March 21 and 23, respectively. He recorded the former with the Columbia Symphony Orchestra, Columbia, 33 rpm (ML 2203 and CL 920); and Sony released the recording on compact disc, SMK 60695, SMK 61697. He recorded the latter with the Columbia Chamber Orchestra, 33 rpm, Columbia ML 2203 and CL 920. Quote from Burton, *Leonard Bernstein,* 205.

10. Leonard Bernstein to Serge Koussevitzky, May 30, 1951, Koussevitzky Archive, Library of Congress, box 6, folder 6, General Correspondence, "Bernstein, Leonard, 1951–1974."

11. Minutes of the Executive Committee of the Board of Directors of the Philharmonic-Symphony Society, February 6, 1950, 3.

12. I discuss the events that led to Bernstein's removal from the CBS blacklist later in this chapter. In any case, Bernstein did perform with members of the New York Philharmonic, using the name the Stadium Concerts Symphony Orchestra, for performances in Lewisohn Stadium on the campus of the City College in the summer of 1953. They recorded the following series of 33 rpm releases for Decca that summer: Beethoven, *Symphony no. 3,* June 22, Decca DL

9697; Schumann, *Symphony no. 2 in C Major,* June 24, Decca DL 9715; Brahms, *Symphony no. 4 in E Minor,* June 29, Decca DL 9717; Tchaikovsky, *Symphony no. 6 ("Pathétique"),* June 29, Decca DL 9718; Dvorak, *Symphony no. 9 ("From the New World"),* July 28, Decca Mar-37. This set was reissued on compact disc: DG 00289 477 0002; it includes Bernstein's spoken commentary recorded for the Book of the Month Club in 1956.

13. "After this therefore because of this."

14. John Cogley, *Report on Blacklisting,* vol. 2, *Radio-Television* (New York: Fund for the Republic, 1956), 122–28; Sally Bedell Smith, *In All His Glory: The Life of William S. Paley* (New York: Simon and Schuster, 1990), 300–307. Papers of Bruno Zirato and William S. Paley, box 005–03–25, New York Philharmonic Archives.

15. Joseph Horowitz, *Classical Music in America: A History of Its Rise and Fall* (New York: W. W. Norton, 2005), 430–31. Judson, who didn't want his artists to offend the powers that be, was the person who had ordered Bernstein not to appear at the JAFRC dinner in February 1946, as noted in chapter 2.

16. Minutes of the Executive Committee of the Board of Directors of the Philharmonic-Symphony Society of New York, December 13, 1950, 4.

17. Ibid., November 19, 1953, 3. On March 31, 1953, Bernstein recorded the following 33 rpm releases for Columbia: Harold Shapero's *Symphony for Classical Orchestra,* ML 4889; Luigi Dallapiccola's *Tartiniana for Violin and Orchestra* with violinist Ruth Posselt, ML 4996; Nicolai Lopatnikoff's *Concertino for Orchestra, op. 30,* ML 4996; these works are available on Sony compact disc, SMK 60725. On May 27, 1953, he recorded Copland's *In the Beginning* with Martha Lipton and the Pro Musica Chorus, available on Sony compact disc, SMK 60560. On April 1, 1953, he recorded Edward Burlingame Hill's *Prelude for Orchestra,* Columbia, 33 rpm, ML 4996, available on Sony compact disc, 61849. All were studio recordings.

18. Minutes of the Executive Committee of the Board of Directors of the Philharmonic Society of New York, November 19, 1953, 5.

19. The Emergency Detention Act, Article II of the McCarran Internal Security Act of 1950, stated that in the event the president declared a state of national emergency, the attorney general was to order the roundup and detention in one of six camps of people expected to "conspire with others to engage in . . . acts of espionage or sabotage." Detainees could hire counsel, present evidence, and unless national security interests forbade their doing so, confront and cross-examine accusers, and examine the government's evidence. If the hearing officer appointed by the Justice Department found the detention legitimate,

the individual could appeal to higher administrative and judicial bodies. But these appeals could focus only on procedure. If the procedures were properly in place, the detention could be indefinite. However, Article II was never enforced. By 1957, Congress had ceased appropriating moneys to support the camps. In 1971, under pressure by Japanese Americans who had suffered detention during World War II and by African Americans worried about use of the detention camps by the Nixon administration, and in light of Warren Court decisions supporting the extension of civil liberties, Congress repealed the Emergency Detention Act. See Richard Longaker, "Emergency Detention: The Generation Gap, 1950–1971," *Western Political Quarterly* 27, no. 3 (September 1974): 395–408. Bernstein would probably have been interred in the camp set up in Allenwood, Pennsylvania.

20. Memorandum from Director, FBI, to SAC, New York, April 9, 1951: "It is recommended that a Security Index Card be prepared on the above captioned individual" namely, Leonard Bernstein, with other spellings in FBI files, Lenord Bernstein, Leonard Bernstine, Leo Bernstein. On April 20, 1951, Director Hoover notified SAC New York that a Security Index Card for Leonard Bernstein was to be included "in the Special Section—Prominent Persons of the Security Index." On March 10, 1952, the FBI dropped the Prominent Individuals Subdivision of the Special Section of the Security Index: "The Bureau is of the opinion that prominent and nationally known individuals should not be set apart from the general Security Index because of their prominence." Included in the list were Joseph Fels Barnes; Leonard Bernstein; [name blacked out]; Bartley Cavanaugh Crum; Olin Downes; [two names blacked out]; Stanley Meyer Isaacs; [two names blacked out]; Leon Pressman; [name blacked out]; Donald Ogden Stewart; [two names blacked out]. FBI file NY 100–360261, section 2.

21. Bernstein believed that these investigations aimed to halt ongoing anticolonial and anti-imperialist revolutions around the globe, but they were doomed to failure. As he wrote Helen Coates on April 30, 1951, he certainly did not favor victory by the "strong arm boys of China and Russia," but third world peoples would have to "work out their destiny." Roosevelt would understand, he wrote. "Oh where is FDR?" Correspondence, LBC, box 14, folder 1, "Coates."

22. Greg Lawrence, *Dance with Demons: The Life of Jerome Robbins* (New York: G. P. Putnam's Sons, 2001), 156–59. For more on Sullivan and witch-hunting, see Robert Slater, *This . . . Is CBS: A Chronicle of 60 Years* (Englewood Cliffs, NJ: Prentice-Hall, 1988), 137.

23. Quoted in Lawrence, *Dance with Demons*, 169.

24. Ibid., 170.

25. Leonard Bernstein to Shirley Bernstein, May 16, 1951, Correspondence, LBC, box 8, folder 6 of 6, Shirley Bernstein Papers.

26. Alvin Ludkoff, *Gene Kelly: A Life of Dance and Dreams* (New York: Back State Books, 1999), 79. Garfield was a guest at Bernstein's and Felicia's engagement party in 1947. See Burton, *Leonard Bernstein,* 157.

27. House Committee on Un-American Activities, *Hearings on Communist Infiltration of Hollywood Motion-Picture Industry—Part 2,* 82nd Cong., 1st sess., April 23, 1951, 357–58.

28. Kazan wrote, "When I saw Julie, the impression I had was that he'd begun to look seedy and to wonder what was most important in his life." According to Kazan, who had not yet testified and named names at the time of Garfield's testimony, Garfield was thinking about recanting his testimony before HUAC and seeking reinstatement: "He turned to a lawyer, Louis Nizer, for advice, and I suspected that Julie's feelings were shifting to a more 'reasonable' position. His wife, Roberta, had hints of Julie's evolving change of heart and disapproved of it. Julie told me that he was now uncomfortable in his own home, that his living room was always full of people who were scornful of him—friends of his wife. He said that when he came home he didn't feel welcome. He hadn't done anything overt, but the left was alert and quick to condemn." Elia Kazan, *A Life* (New York: Alfred A. Knopf, 1988), 441–42.

29. Leonard Bernstein to Shirley Bernstein, May 16, 1951, Shirley Bernstein Papers, LBC, box 7, folder 6 of 6.

30. An FBI file entry shows that the agency had a different interpretation of Bernstein's Tanglewood plans. "On March 6, 1951, an informant [name blacked out] in New York City, advised she was recently informed that AARON COPLAND and LEONARD BERNSTEIN, the composer will be 'kept underground' this year at the Tanglewood Concerts held each year in the Berkshire Mountains. . . . Informant believes that 80% of the faculty of the Tanglewood groups are Communists." FBI Summary, January 22, 1952, p. 68, FBI file NY 100–99895, section 1.

31. House Committee on Un-American Activities, *Hearings on Communist Infiltration of Hollywood Motion-Picture Industry—Part 3,* 82nd Cong., 1st sess., June 25, 1951, 671–718. Rossen left an interesting opening when, upon questioning, he said that he might reconsider his testimony at some point. In 1953, he did return to the committee, made a fascinating case for why people joined the Communist Party in the 1930s and, like him, remained members until revelations of Soviet anti-Semitism disillusioned them. He then named names. Within short order, he was off the blacklist.

32. Ibid., 725.

33. Helen Coates to Bernstein, September 19, 1951, Correspondence, LBC, box 14, folder 2.

34. Bernstein to Helen Coates, December 18, 1951, Correspondence, LBC, box 14, folder 2.

35. UNESCO is the United Nations Educational, Scientific and Cultural Organization. Bernstein to Francois Valéry, Correspondence, LBC, March 8, 1952, box 56, folder 10. The same day, Bruno Zirato, then vice president of Columbia Artists Management, noted that Bernstein had told him that the Rome conducting position was the only one he would take on full time. Bruno Zirato to Helen Coates, March 8, 1952, Personal Business Papers, LBC, box 990, folder 8, "Columbia Artists Management Inc. 1949–53."

36. Helen Coates to Nelly Walker, handwritten note on letter from Walker to Helen Coates, March 13, 1952, Personal Business Papers, LBC, box 990, folder 8, "Columbia Artists Management Inc. 1949–53."

37. Judy Holliday was lucky; not only had Columbia Pictures hired experts to clear its Academy Award–winning star of *Born Yesterday* before the witch-hunting groups, but Holliday's testimony (almost as if straight out of her "dumb blond Billie Dawn" role in *Born Yesterday*) convinced the committee that she had simply been a dupe of the Communists. Senate Committee on the Judiciary, Subcommittee to Investigate the Administration of the Internal Security Act and Other Internal Security Laws, *Hearings on Subversive Infiltration of Radio, Television and the Entertainment Industry—Part 1,* 82nd Cong., 2nd sess., May 21, 1952, 141–45. See John Cogley, *Report on Blacklisting,* vol. 1, *Movies* (New York: Fund for the Republic, 1956), 115–16.

38. Testimony of Clifford Odets, House Committee on Un-American Activities, *Hearings on Communist Infiltration of Hollywood Motion-Picture Industry—Part 8,* 82nd Cong., 2nd sess., May 19–20, 1952, 3483.

39. Testimony of Lillian Hellman, May 21, 1952, ibid., 3546. Hellman declined to answer questions about her own or others' politics.

40. Arthur M. Schlesinger Jr., *The Vital Center: The Politics of Freedom* (Boston: Houghton Mifflin Company, 1949), 35–42.

41. Ibid., 213–15

42. Ibid., 216, 217.

43. "Our Country and Our Culture," editorial statement, *Partisan Review* 19 (1952): 283–84.

44. Arvin is quoted by Stacey Olster, *Reminiscence and Re-Creation in Contemporary American Fiction* (New York: Cambridge University Press, 1989), 19.

45. "Our Country and Our Culture," 295–96.

46. Ibid., 316.

47. Ibid., 326.

48. Ibid., 302.

49. Ibid., 299.

50. Ibid., 300.

51. Ibid., 307.

52. Ibid., 308n.

53. Marc Blitzstein to Bernstein, August 15, 1952, Correspondence, LBC, box 8, folder 30.

54. Was Bernstein's use of his father's name merely a coincidence? We have no documentation that Bernstein intended *Tahiti's* "Sam" to replicate or otherwise stand in for his father. Elizabeth L. Keathley recently speculated that Sam and Dinah could be Bernstein's parents or even Bernstein and Felicia. "Postwar Modernity and the Wife's Subjectivity: Bernstein's *Trouble in Tahiti*," *American Music* 23, no. 2 (Summer 2005): 245.

55. According to Blitzstein's biographer Eric Gordon, this critique of American imperialism was "definitely a child of *Cradle*." Gordon, *Mark the Music: The Life and Work of Marc Blitzstein* (New York: St. Martin's Press, 1989), 343, 358. For an extended discussion of the expression of political criticism in this opera, see Keathley, "Postwar Modernity," 220–57.

56. Aaron Copland and Vivian Perlis, *Copland Since 1943* (New York: St. Martin's Press, 1989), 184–89.

57. See Volker R. Berghahn, *America and the Cultural Cold War in Europe: Shepard Stone Between Philanthropy, Academy, and Diplomacy* (Princeton, NJ: Princeton University Press, 2001), 74, 314n71. See also Frederick Kuh, "Top Composers' Works Barred at U.S. Libraries Abroad," *Chicago Sun Times,* April 26, 1953, cited by Howard Pollack, *Aaron Copland: The Life and Work of an Uncommon Man* (New York: Henry Holt, 1999), 454, 647n8.

58. Ruth McKenney had been a Hollywood writer and a radical labor activist and member of the Communist Party in Ohio. On October 30, 1947, FBI agent Louis J. Russell told HUAC that McKenney was a former member of the Communist Party who had been expelled "for revisionism." See Eric Bentley, ed., *Thirty Years of Treason: Excerpts from Hearings before the House Committee on Un-American Activities, 1938–68* (New York: Viking, 1971), 237. McKenney was also identified as a Communist by the writer Abe Burrows, who appeared before HUAC on November 12, 1952 (ibid., 548). The play attracted, among others, former president Harry Truman. See David McCullough, *Truman* (New York: Simon and Schuster, 1992), 934. Only a few years before, as we have seen,

Truman had gone out of his way to avoid being in Bernstein's presence. There was a further irony: According to the musicologist Carol J. Oja, Comden and Green had written some politically satirical lyrics about "Eric the Red," a Viking who is forced into perpetual exile, but the text was excised before the show opened. "Bernstein's *Wonderful Town* and McCarthy-Era Politics" (paper presented at the American Musical Society Meeting, Quebec City, November 2007).

59. See Secrest, *Leonard Bernstein*, 197–98.

60. Testimony of Jerome Robbins, House Committee on Un-American Activities, *Hearings on the Investigation of Communist Activities in the New York Area—Part 4,* 83rd Cong., 1st sess., May 5, 1953, 1318.

61. Testimony of Robert Rossen, House Committee on Un-American Activities, *Hearings on the Investigation of Communist Activities in the New York Area—Part 4,* 83rd Cong., 1st sess., May 7, 1953, 1454–1500.

62. Robert D. Dean, *Imperial Brotherhood: Gender and the Making of Cold War Foreign Policy* (Amherst: University of Massachusetts Press, 2001), 62–96.

63. See the interview with David Diamond in Aaron Copland and Vivian Perlis, *Copland: 1900 through 1942* (New York: St. Martin's/Marek, 1984), 243.

64. The poet John Ashbery described the anxiety of these days in this way: "I couldn't write anything from about the summer of 1950 to the end of 1951. . . . It was a terribly depressing period both in the world and in my life. I had no income or prospects. The Korean War was on and I was afraid I might be drafted. There were anti-homosexual campaigns. I was called up for the draft and I pleaded that as a reason not to be drafted. Of course this was recorded and I was afraid that we'd all be sent to concentration camps if McCarthy had his own way. It was a very dangerous and scary period." Quoted by Brad Gooch, *City Poet: The Life and Times of Frank O'Hara* (New York: HarperCollins, 1993), 190.

65. Testimony of Aaron Copland, Executive Sessions of the Senate, Permanent Subcommittee on Investigations of the Committee on Government Operations, 83rd Cong., 1st sess., May 26, 1953. Made public January 2003, U.S. State Department Teacher-Student Exchange Program, 1267–91.

66. Testimony of Lee J. Cobb, House Committee on Un-American Activities, *Hearings on the Investigation of Communist Activities in the Los Angeles Area—Part 6,* 83rd Cong., 1st sess., June 2, 1953, 2345–56. Cobb's testimony is available in Bentley, *Thirty Years of Treason,* 653–66.

67. Bernstein learned of the denial of his passport sometime before July 16, 1953, when his attorney, Abraham Friedman, wrote to ask whether the passport had arrived. Helen Coates wrote back to Friedman on the 19th that it had not. Personal Business Papers, Correspondence—General (1953–1958), LBC, box 991.

68. Leonard Bernstein to Burton Bernstein, August 15, 1953, quoted in Burton, *Leonard Bernstein,* 231.

69. This confessional procedure followed the pattern of "degradation ceremonies," as Victor S. Navasky has dubbed them, which aim to "reconstitute [and] reform" the deviant individual while reinforcing the orthodox ideology. See his *Naming Names* (New York: Penguin Books, 1981), 314–26 (quote on 319).

70. Bernstein's affidavit of August 3, 1953, can be found in Supplemental Release, FBI file HQ 100–360261.

71. L. Arnold Weissberger to Irving Moross, Columbia Pictures, March 15, 1954, Personal Business Papers, LBC, box 982, folder 12, "Affidavit on Communist Accusations—1954 in re." On the American Legion's high place in the blacklisting hierarchy, see Cogley, *Report on Blacklisting,* vol. 1, 118–43.

72. James McInerney to Leonard Bernstein, April 9, 1954, Personal Business Papers, LBC, box 1006, folder "McInerney."

73. Murray C. Bernays to Francis J. McNamara, April 9, 1954, Personal Business Papers, LBC, box 985, folder 26, "Bernays and Eisner (1953–55)."

74. James McInerney to Leonard Bernstein, May 14, 1954, and Leonard Bernstein to James McInerney, May 20, 1954, Personal Business Papers, LBC, box 1006, folder 5a, "McInerney."

75. Goodson's remarks are in Griffin Fariello, ed., *Red Scare: Memories of the American Inquisition: An Oral History* (New York: Avon, 1995), 325.

76. Robert Saudek, interview by Charles T. Morrisey, September 14, 1972, Ford Foundation Oral History Project, Ford Foundation Archives, New York, 28–32.

77. Ibid., 40–41.

78. See Schuyler Chapin's account in his *Leonard Bernstein: Notes from a Friend* (New York: Walker and Company, 1992), 22–38.

79. Shanet, *Philharmonic,* 316–24.

80. Harold Taubman, "The Philharmonic—What's Wrong with It and Why," *New York Times,* April 29, 1955.

81. Arthur Judson to the Board of Directors of the New York Philharmonic Society, April 1, 1952, New York Philharmonic Archives, box 009–11–05. In August, Thomas Shippers's name was mentioned by Dorle Jarmel, an EMI Records executive close to Columbia Records and Judson, with the interesting comment that Shippers "has what Lenny had when he started plus the asset of one talent instead of dozens." In other words, Shippers could be counted on to simply conduct rather than compose and involve himself in other extraconductorial matters. Dorle Jarmel to Arthur Judson and Bruno Zirato, memorandum, August 1, 1952, New York Philharmonic Archives, box 005–02–19.

82. Shanet, *Philharmonic,* 324.

83. According to Jerome Toobin, Bernstein stated sometime in late 1955 or early 1956 that "Judson . . . told some friends of mine that it was time for the Philharmonic to get a Jew there as conductor so that it can get out of the doldrums it was in. The old bastard said that he doesn't like me much, but that I was the only guy around that fitted the bill." Jerome Toobin, *Agitato: A Trek Through the Musical Jungle* (New York: Viking Press, 1975), 102.

84. According to William R. Trotter, by identifying himself as a married man with children, Bernstein was able to overcome the antigay bias that had ruined Mitropoulos. Trotter argues that the drop in orchestral discipline that apparently destroyed Mitropoulos's career at the Philharmonic was due not to his supposed shortcomings but to the bigotry of the players, whose lack of respect for the gay Mitropoulos led them to deny his authority. Trotter claims that Bernstein had been adding to the anti-Mitropoulos gossip while implying that as a family man, he was right for the job. *Priest of Music: The Life of Dimitri Mitropoulos* (Portland, OR: Amadeus Press, 1995), 394, 396.

85. Joseph Horowitz's *Understanding Toscanini* (New York: Alfred A. Knopf, 1987) is indispensable.

86. See, in general, Frances Stonor Saunders, *The Cultural Cold War: The CIA and the World of Arts and Letters* (New York: New Press, 1999). See also Berghahn, *America and the Intellectual Cold Wars,* 153–77.

87. Bernstein kept a clipping from *Variety* of April 3, 1957: "Gershwin, Bernstein, et al., Off USIA 'Blacklist' Since 1953, It's Disclosed." "On the eve of a new HUAC investigation into musicians and artists due April 9 in NY, a communication of the US Information agency discloses that there is no longer a 'blacklist' in operation against a group of top flight American composers whose works were reportedly banned for some time in US overseas libraries prior to 1953. The composers who came under the ban included such names as the late George Gershwin, Aaron Copland, Leonard Bernstein, Roy Harris, Roger Sessions, and Virgil Thomson. Arthur Larson, USIA director, in replying to an inquiry about the blacklist made by a NY publicist, Jesse Gordon, said that the situation 'has not been in effect since 1953.' The original disclosure about the blacklist was made by Frederick Kuh in a 1953 article in the *Chicago Sun-Times.* According to Kuh's 1954 article, the various composers were banned because information had been supplied the State Department about their reported contributions to various Spanish Civil War refugee groups and other organizations of a similar nature." Personal Business Papers, box 1006, folder "Memoranda 2 of 2." For an account of this episode, see Thomas C. Reeves, *The Life and Times of Joe McCarthy: A Biography* (New York: Stein and Day, 1982), 476–91.

88. Nicholas Nabokov to Bernstein, July 21, 1953, Correspondence, LBC, box 41, folder 10, "Nabokov, Nicholas." On Nabokov's role in the Congress for Cultural Freedom, see Mark Carroll, *Music and Ideology in Cold War Europe* (Cambridge: Cambridge University Press, 2003); Saunders, *Cultural Cold War,* 113–128; and David Caute, *The Dancer Defects: The Struggle for Cultural Supremacy During the Cold War* (Oxford: Oxford University Press, 2003), 381–414.

89. Saunders, *Cultural Cold War,* 221–24.

90. By 1955, the State Department had enlisted the New York Philharmonic to undertake cultural missions abroad. Shanet, *Philharmonic,* 318.

91. On the program were Tchaikovsky's Piano Concerto no.1 with Emil Gilels and selections from Beethoven's *Missa Solemnis* with Adele Addison. "U.N. Concert Marks Tenth Anniversary," *New York Times,* October 25, 1955.

92. Bruno Zirato to Bernstein, telegram, November 18, 1955, New York Philharmonic Archives, box 010–01–37; Shanet, *Philharmonic,* 324–25. This move was face-saving for Mitropoulos, who was soon on his way out. But more to the point in this narrative is Bernstein's rehabilitation.

93. Toobin, *Agitato,* 71–99.

94. Ibid., 99–100. Bernstein may have been trying to conjure up his sponsorship of a dinner celebrating the National Conference for Birobidjan on March 9 and 10, 1946. FBI Report, March 30, 1952, file NY 100–99895. Birobidjan was a Soviet republic in Asia set up for Jews.

95. Burton, *Leonard Bernstein,* 254.

96. "Leonard Bernstein, Security Matter-C Fraud Against the Government," FBI Office Memorandum, Director to Wm. F. Tompkins, Assistant Attorney General Internal Security Division, August 23, 1955, FBI file HQ 100–360261.

97. A reading of the FBI memoranda on Bernstein's case reveals a very frustrated Hoover. On **July 1, 1954,** Hoover sent a memorandum to the Internal Security Division of the U.S. Justice Department noting Bernstein's possible perjury in his passport affidavit when he denied that he "knowingly engaged in activities which supported the Communist movement." Hoover had the testimony of many informants that Bernstein had been a member of the Communist Party. Referred to in Tompkins to Hoover, Office Memorandum, October 1, 1954, FBI file 100–360261. On **October 1, 1954,** Assistant Attorney General William F. Tompkins requested that FBI agents "recontact" various informants and agents to ascertain whether their reports of Bernstein's membership and activities were based on hearsay or could be documented as evidence that Bernstein lied, thus making him indictable for perjury. Ibid. The case began to fall

apart, however, when on **April 7, 1955,** Hoover reported that many informants were now unavailable for recontact and noted that one informant had publicized, and sought to "capitalize" on, his relationship with the bureau. Director to Tompkins, "re: Leonard Bernstein, Security Matter-C, Fraud Against the Government," 100–360261–43, in FBI file 100–360261, section 2. On **August 22, 1955,** Tompkins wrote the FBI that there was only "hearsay rather than personal knowledge" of Bernstein's possible membership in the Communist Party and concluded, "As such it is insufficient to warrant prosecution" for perjury. SAC New York to Director, Office Memorandum, September 16, 1955, FBI file 100–360261. The FBI's interest in Bernstein seems to have ended with a memorandum of **April 2, 1958,** from SAC New York to Director, stating, "A review of [Bernstein's] file in the New York office reflects [that] no pertinent subversive information concerning [Bernstein] has been developed since . . . 3/18/55." FBI file HQ 100–360261, section 2. Hoover would try again to destroy Bernstein in 1970, as we will see later.

98. Lillian Hellman, Leonard Bernstein, Richard Wilbur, John Latouche and Dorothy Parker, *Candide* (New York: Random House, 1957), 37.

99. Ibid., 38.

100. Ibid., 39.

101. Ibid., *Candide,* 41.

102. Leonard Bernstein, *The Joy of Music* (New York: Anchor Doubleday, 1959), 179.

103. Brooks Atkinson, the longtime theater critic for the *New York Times,* wrote that during *Candide*'s run, "the bumbling Metropolitan Opera Company was presenting a sloppy, hokum production of Offenbach's *La Péricole,* much to the delight of its humorless subscribers. The situation was painfully ironic: Broadway did an opera with distinction, and it failed; the Met did an operetta badly, and it succeeded. *Candide* had a cast of forty-three singers, a full orchestra, and seventy-three performances. Broadway had no interest in a musical drama that lacked romance." *Broadway* (New York: Macmillan, 1970), 446.

104. Handel, *Messiah,* New York Philharmonic, Adele Addison, soprano; Russell Oberlin, countertenor; David Lloyd, tenor; William Warfield, bass; Westminster Choir; Director John Finley Williamson, December 31, 1956; Columbia, 33 rpm mono, MRL 242; Columbia, 33 rpm stereo, M2S 603 and MS 6928; Sony, compact disc, SM2K 60205.

Prokofiev, Sergei, *Violin Concerto no. 2,* New York Philharmonic, with Isaac Stern, January 21, 1957; Columbia, 33 rpm mono, ML 5243; Sony, compact disc, M4K 42003 and M3K 45956.

Beethoven, *Concerto no. 2 in B-flat Major for Piano and Orchestra, op. 19,* Columbia Symphony Orchestra, Glenn Gould, April 9 and 10, 1957; Columbia 33 rpm mono, ML521; Sony Classical, compact disc, SM3K 52632.

Tchaikovsky, *Romeo and Juliet Overture,* New York Philharmonic, January 28, 1957; Columbia, 33 rpm mono, ML 5182; Columbia, 33 rpm stereo, MS 6014, MG 33270 and MY 36723; Columbia, compact disc, MYK 36723; Sony, compact disc, SMK 47632.

105. Leonard Bernstein, "You the Public" Writings, LBC, box 72, folder 17.

106. Bernstein, *Joy of Music,* 40–51.

107. Ibid., 185.

108. Ibid., 190–91.

109. Testimony of Wellington Riegger, House Committee on Un-American Activities, *Investigation of Communism in the Metropolitan Music School, Inc., and Related Fields—Part 1,* 85th Cong., 1st sess., April 9–10, 1957, 651–58.

110. See McCullough, *Truman,* 969. Whatever had caused Truman to avoid Bernstein a decade earlier was now apparently all forgotten.

111. Bernstein, "Address to the National Press Club in Washington, D.C.," October 13, 1959, Writings, LBC, box 77, folder 11.

112. See Herbert Mitgang, *Dangerous Dossiers: Exposing the Secret War Against America's Greatest Authors* (New York: Donald I. Fine, 1988).

### 4. THE LONG SIXTIES

1. The term *long sixties* in the title of this chapter was coined by Arthur Marwick to cover the period of cross-Atlantic cultural changes that actually started in 1958 and terminated in 1974. The cultural explosion ongoing in Britain, France, Italy, and the United States in 1958 certainly justified Marwick's decision to place 1958 as the point of take-off. He quite properly selects 1974 as the termination date—the year in which the rise in the price of oil induced a recession that ended the great boom of the 1960s, Nixon resigned from the presidency, and American troops withdrew from Vietnam. *The Sixties: Cultural Revolution in Britain, France, Italy, and the United States, c.1958–1974* (New York: Oxford University Press, 1998), 7–8. For the purposes of this book, however, I consider 1960 to be the beginning of the era. Kennedy's run for the presidency, and his victory in November, seemed to liberals and progressives such as Bernstein to presage a revival of New Deal domestic and foreign policy principles. The civil rights movement seemed to gain new strength. That year also saw the introduction of the birth-control pill, so significant for the coming gender revolution. I reserve

1974 for the beginning of the "short seventies": the period of economic downturn and the rise of the conservative movement.

2. On February 17, 1960, Schuyler G. Chapin, then an executive at Columbia Records, asked Bernstein to come to Miami in June for a Columbia Records sales convention wherein he could promote the "New Bernstein Look" for the upcoming sales campaign. Personal Business Papers, Leonard Bernstein Collection (LBC), box 989, folder "CBS Records, 1949–1965," Library of Congress, Washington, D.C.

3. Tyler Branch, *Parting the Waters: America in the King Years, 1954–63* (New York: Simon & Schuster, 1988), 360–70.

4. Norman Mailer, "Superman Comes to the Supermarket," *Esquire,* November 1960, reprinted in *The Presidential Papers of Norman Mailer* (New York: Bantam, 1964), 40.

5. Humphrey Burton, *Leonard Bernstein* (New York: Doubleday, 1994), 320.

6. Victor S. Navasky, *Naming Names* (New York: Penguin, 1981), 326–29; David Caute, *The Great Fear: The Anti-Communist Purge Under Truman and Eisenhower* (New York: Simon and Schuster, 1978), 533–35.

7. Stanley Kauffmann, *A World on Film: Criticism and Commentary* (New York: Dell, 1966), 415–28.

8. Leonard Bernstein, *Kaddish: Symphony no. 3,* Vocal Score, rev. ed. for Orchestra, Mixed Chorus, Boys' Choir, Speaker and Soprano Solo, by Abraham Kaplan and Ruth Mense (New York: Boosey & Hawkes, 1980).

9. In his original 1962 text, Bernstein assumed that the narrator would be Goethe's "Eternal Feminine," "that part of man that intuits God." By 1977, he thought this restriction to the feminine voice "too limiting" and decided on a male voice to narrate. See the liner notes to Bernstein, *The Symphonies: Jeremiah, The Age of Anxiety, Kaddish,* Deutsche Grammophon, compact disc, 4452452, 14–15.

10. Andrew Bernard makes a convincing case that Bernstein derived his indictment of God from Levi Yitzhak's *Kaddish of Rabbi Levi Yitzhak of Berditchev,* and among others, post-Holocaust writers, who could not fathom how God could have permitted the Nazi tortures and murders of the Jewish people. See his doctoral dissertation, "Two Musical Perspectives of Twentieth-Century Pacifism: An Analytical and Historical View of Britten's *War Requiem* and Bernstein's *Kaddish Symphony*" (University of Washington, 1990), 196–204.

11. Leonard Bernstein, "The Skin of Our Teeth [Planning Note]," September 1, 1962, Writings, LBC, box 81, folder 4.

12. John XXIII, "Opening Speech to the Council," October 11, 1962, in *The Documents of Vatican II*, ed. Walter M. Abott (New York: American Press, 1966), 717.

13. The spirit of reconciliation extended to the production of Miller's *After the Fall*, the play that inaugurated the Vivian Beaumont Theater, where he declaimed about informers such as Elia Kazan even as he permitted Kazan to direct the play.

14. See Burton, *Leonard Bernstein*, 344–47.

15. Eberhard Bethge, *Dietrich Bonhoeffer: Man of Vision, Man of Courage*, trans. Eric Mosbacher, Peter Ross, Betty Ross, Frank Clarke, and William Glen-Doepel (New York: Harper and Row, 1970).

16. Hannah Arendt, *Eichmann in Jerusalem: A Report on the Banality of Evil* (New York: Viking, 1963; rev. and enlarged ed., New York: Penguin, 1964). Years later, Bernstein praised the work and the concept of banality of evil as "magnificent." Typed draft of manuscript 17, December 1977, 72, of film interview by the USIA, Writings, LBC, box 90, folder 38.

17. The play ran throughout Europe and in New York, with lines of demonstrators in front of theaters and heated debate in the press and in journals of opinion. To the church establishment, the play was an affront to the memory of the pope. Hochhuth argued, however, that the facts were undeniable. This debate marked a major turn in the pope's reputation. From the end of the war until he died in 1958, Eugenio Pacelli had been generally venerated for his courage in standing up to the Nazis when all other representatives of European civilization had been silenced by fascism and for his spiritual and organizational leadership of those Catholic clergy in France, Holland, and other areas of Nazi-occupied Europe who had protected Jews. (See Catholic Reform's collection of *New York Times* writings during the 1930s and into the war at its website, www.catholic reform.org/piusterenzio.html.) To be sure, many people were reluctant to honor Pius XII, claiming that he had failed to speak out directly against the ongoing holocaust, but these people were largely on the marginalized left wing. In the United States, where such sentiments were even more on the margins, mainstream Jewish groups, cooperating with Catholics and other Christians to promote toleration and universal brotherhood, had gone out of their way to praise the pope. Indeed, news of his death in October 1958 was met with virtually universal sorrow. Of the many commemorations, one stands out for present purposes: At the Philharmonic's October 9, 1958, performance, Leonard Bernstein asked the audience to honor the pope's memory with a moment of silence. *New York Times*, October 10, 1958. In this climate, we cannot be surprised that Hochhuth's play

was received with consternation and anger, not to mention vitriol, by Catholics and by Jewish groups that feared a revival of the old animosities.

18. David J. Garrow, *Bearing the Cross: Martin Luther King, Jr., and the Southern Christian Leadership Conference* (New York: HarperCollins, 1986), 383.

19. As far back as early 1963, Hoover had ordered that King be kept ignorant of death-threat letters that the bureau had intercepted. Taylor Branch, *Pillar of Fire, America in the King Years: 1963–65* (New York: Simon and Schuster, 1998), 197–98.

20. Garrow, *Bearing the Cross,* 372–74.

21. *New York Times,* March 25, 1965.

22. See U.S. Congress, Senate, Subcommittee on Public Buildings and Grounds, The Senator Gravel Edition, *The Pentagon Papers: The Defense Department History of the United States Decisionmaking on Vietnam,* vol. 1 (Boston: Beacon Press, 1971), 83, 87–88.

23. Both Gruening and Morse lost their next election.

24. Theodore Draper, *The Dominican Revolt: A Case Study in American Policy* (New York: Commentary, 1968).

25. Dwight Macdonald, "A Day at the White House," *New York Review of Books,* July 15, 1965.

26. Nora Sayre, *Sixties Going on Seventies* (New York: Arbor House, 1973), 329.

27. Helen Epstein, *Joe Papp: An American Life* (New York: Da Capo, 1996), 202–10. Papp staged Václav Havel's *The Memorandum* in 1967, but he shelved his plans for some other dramatic works so that he could produce the antiwar musical *Hair.*

28. Mary McCarthy, who had been a leading figure in the Congress of Cultural Freedom, wrote the following about her decision to take up the offer by the *New York Review of Books* to travel to Vietnam:

> As I look back, the chronology of those days telescopes. Nineteen sixty-five blurs with 1966. I thought it was in the summer of 1965 that I did an interview with Edwin Newman in Paris during which I said that if Americans did not act against the war, put down some real stake, our case would not be so different from the "good" Germans under Hitler who claimed to have disagreed with the Final Solution, offering as proof the fact that they had taken no active part in it. But my files assure me that it was in 1966. As late as that. So it took me a whole year to say on television what I had been muttering to myself about Vietnam. That is, that talking while continuing your life as usual was not enough. Still, I could not see what else to do.

Mary McCarthy, *The Seventeenth Degree* (New York: Harcourt, Brace Jovanovich, 1973), 10. For Denise Levertov's thoughts about her involvement, see her "Life at War," in *The Sorrow Dance* (New York: New Directions, 1966), 80. Levertov was hardly alone among American poets in being pulled into the political arena in these years. See Robert Duncan, *Passages 22–27 of the War* (Berkeley, CA: Oyez, 1966); and Robert Bly, "On Political Poetry," *Nation,* April 24, 1967, 523–24.

29. See Garrow, *Bearing the Cross,* 578–79. On the University of Wisconsin demonstrations, see David Maranis, *They Marched into Sunlight: War and Peace, Vietnam and America, October 1967* (New York: Simon and Schuster, 2003).

30. Norman Mailer, *An American Dream* (New York: Dial Press, 1965).

31. Norman Mailer, *Armies of the Night: History As a Novel, the Novel As History* (New York: New American Library, 1968).

32. Noam Chomsky, "On Resistance," *New York Review of Books,* December 7, 1967, and republished with revisions and "Supplement" in Chomsky's *American Power and the New Mandarins* (New York: Vintage, 1969), 367–404.

33. Writings, LBC, box 78, folder 2.

34. The evolution of Bernstein's discussion from the purely aesthetic to the increasingly political from 1960 to 1967 may have been due not to his own political preoccupations but to the fact that he was conducting and recording Mahler's later symphonies, which are darker and loaded with more angst and catastrophic episodes than the composer's earlier works. I do think that Bernstein, like so many others, was himself more angst ridden, for reasons that follow.

35. Writings, LBC, box 83, folder 2.

36. Bernstein, "Mahler: His Time Has Come," in *Findings* (New York: Garden City, NY: Anchor Doubleday, 1982), 260.

37. Ibid., 261.

38. John Gruen, *The Private World of Leonard Bernstein: Photographs by Ken Heyman* (New York: Viking, 1968), 26.

39. The publication of Gruen's book apparently caused some embarrassment to Bernstein, who accused Gruen of including remarks that were supposed to be largely off the record. Gruen shot back that he had given Bernstein the right to edit out anything he wished. See Burton, *Leonard Bernstein,* 377–78.

40. Gruen, *Private World of Leonard Bernstein,* 28.

41. Ibid., 29.

42. Ibid., 30.

43. Ibid., 149–67.

44. Ibid., 151. Note how far Bernstein had traveled from his earlier days as a propagandist for modernism. By 1967, he had lost touch with much of contemporary music. See the extended discussion of this point in chapter 5.

45. Ibid., 152.

46. Ibid., 153.

47. Ibid.

48. Ibid.

49. Ibid., 154.

50. Ibid., 166.

51. *New York Times,* January 8, 1968; Burton, *Leonard Bernstein,* 371.

52. Writings, LBC, box 83, folder 26.

53. Ibid., folder 28.

54. Evelyn Ames, *A Wind from the West: Bernstein and the New York Philharmonic Abroad* (Boston: Houghton Mifflin, 1970), 24.

55. Ibid., 51.

56. Oliver Daniel, *Stokowski: A Counterpoint of View* (New York: Dodd, Mead & Co., 1982), 835.

57. The work did not quite die but lay dormant until 1987, when Bernstein, Robbins, and Laurents gave it another try. See chapter 6.

58. Mahler, *Das Lied von der Erde*, Vienna Philharmonic Orchestra, James King, tenor; Dietrich Fischer, baritone; Decca, 33 rpm stereo, OS 26005; Decca, compact disc, 417783, 452301, and 466381; Deutsche Grammophon, compact disc, 00289 477 5187.

59. Burton, *Leonard Bernstein,* 387–88.

60. Writings, LBC, box 83, folder 36.

61. Ibid., folder 37.

62. Writings, LBC, box 83, folder 39. "Informant explained that along with 500,000 demonstrators . . . were Benjamin Spock, Dave Dellinger, Rev. William Coffin, Dick Gregory, Leonard Bernstein, and Pete Seeger. Entertainment was furnished by Pete Seeger, Arlo Guthrie and the cast from 'Hair.' The majority of the speakers were critical of Pres. Nixon, Vice Pres. Agnew or the Establishment." Office Memorandum, Pittsburgh, December 9, 1969, p. 3, FBI file NY 100–99895, section 3.

63. Murray Kempton, *The Briar Patch: The People of the State of New York v. Lumumba Shakur, et. al.* (New York: E. P. Dutton, 1973), 1–10.

64. Charlotte Curtis, *New York Times,* January 15, 1970; "False Note on Black Panthers," *New York Times,* January 16, 1970.

65. "False Note on Black Panthers."

66. Correspondence, LBC, box 32, folder 17, "King, Martin Luther, Jr. & Coretta Scott."

67. John M. Lee, "Bernstein Denies Shift on Panthers," *New York Times,* February 21, 1970.

68. Hoover to SAC [Special Agent in Charge], February 25, 1970, FBI file NY 100–161140:

Director, FBI (100–448006)

COUNTERINTELLIGENCE PROGRAM

BLACK NATIONALIST HATE GROUPS

RACIAL INTELLIGENCE

(BLACK PANTHER PARTY)

New York is authorized to direct correspondence to individuals known to have attended the 1/14/70 Black Panther Party (BPP) fund-raising function held at the home of Leonard Bernstein outlining the BPP's anti-Semitic posture. In accordance with your request, correspondence should enclose a copy of the article from the BPP newspaper of 1/3/70 authored by BPP Field Marshall Donald Lee Cox which clearly shows the BPP's anti-Jewish, pro-Arab position.

Contrary to New York's recommendation, the above correspondence should not bear the signature of a nonexistent individual alleging affiliation with the Jewish Defense League of New York City since it would appear such action might prove self-defeating in the event of an inquiry placed at that organization by any one of the recipients of this letter. It is recommended that New York sign this letter with an anonymous name with additional phraseology such as "A Concerned and Loyal Jew," or other similar terminology.

New York should insure use of unwatermarked bond stationary in connection with the above and utilization of mailing procedures which will not allow the Bureau's identification with the origin of this correspondence.

Personal Business Papers, LBC, box 946, folder 1, "Proskauer: FBI files 1950–70."

69. "[Name blacked out] in October, 1970, advised that Meir D. Kahane (103–207795) advised [name blacked out] in the Jewish Defense League (JDL) that he finally got Lenny [*sic*] Bernstein's home address and that soon they were going to ask JDL members to 'take over the entire building, sit in it, and see how much pressure Bernstein can take.' This sit-in at Bernstein's home, in NYC, was scheduled for 10/20/70." FBI file HQ 100–360261, section 3.

70. The situation could have been worse. In his biography of Hoover, Curt Gentry describes one of Hoover's meetings with Nixon at the White House in 1970, at which Bernstein's name came up almost at the outset:

"Who finances the Black Panthers?" he [Hoover] asked rhetorically. "They get their money from Leonard Bernstein and Peter Duchin and that crowd" . . .
"Leonard Bernstein, Peter Duchin and that crowd" was very much on the director's mind. Recently the symphony conductor had given a gala fundraiser for the

Panthers in his Park Avenue duplex. Tom Wolfe later immortalized the occasion in his hilariously funny essay "Radical Chic: The Party at Lenny's," but to J. Edgar Hoover there was nothing funny about it. The day after the party he had the social columns combed for the names of the attendees. Those who didn't already have FBI files now had, while the party's host was the target of a special COINTEL-PRO operation. . . . In an attempt to 'neutralize' Bernstein, the Bureau tried to plant items about the conductor's alleged homosexuality, with emphasis upon his reputed fondness for young boys, but, without an arrest record, even the Hollywood trades wouldn't touch the story.

Curt Gentry, *J. Edgar Hoover: The Man and the Secrets* (New York: Penguin, 1991), 646–47.

71. Tom Wolfe, *Radical Chic and Mau-Mauing the Flak-Catchers* (New York: Farrar, Straus and Giroux, 1970).

72. Burton, *Leonard Bernstein,* 386.

73. On the Berrigans up to 1970, see Francine du Plessix Gray, *Divine Disobedience: Profiles in Catholic Radicalism* (New York: Alfred A. Knopf, 1970), 43–228.

74. For a discussion of how Philip and Daniel Berrigan's antiwar action, conflict with Cardinal Spellman, and overall political and ethical engagement inspired their fellows, see du Plessix Gray, *Divine Disobedience,* 102–6; and James Carroll, *An American Requiem: God, My Father, and the War That Came between Us* (New York: Houghton Mifflin, 1996), 157–74.

75. See Daniel Berrigan, *Night Flight to Hanoi: Daniel Berrigan's War Diary with Eleven Poems* (New York: Macmillan, 1968).

76. Du Plessix Gray, *Divine Disobedience,* 47.

77. Bethge, *Dietrich Bonhoeffer;* Robert Coles, *The Geography of Fate: Conversations between Daniel Berrigan When Underground and Robert Coles* (Boston: Beacon Press, 1971).

78. Leonard Bernstein, 1971 Datebook, February 2 entry, LBC.

79. Daniel Berrigan, *Lights on in the House of the Dead* (New York: Doubleday, 1974), 213.

80. Berrigan claims he met with Bernstein on May 24, but Bernstein's Datebook entry has it May 25.

81. Daniel Berrigan, *America Is Hard to Find* (New York: Doubleday, 1972), 150–51.

82. "I hear Mr. Bernstein was listening to the 'Holy Outlaw' sermon (underground in Philly) and came on a title for his celebration of the Kennedy Center in D.C.—'A Mass for the Unborn.'" Berrigan, *Lights on in the House of the Dead,* 221.

83. Daniel Berrigan, "Sermon from the Underground, August 2, 1970," in *Witness of the Berrigans,* ed. Stephen Halpert and Tom Murray (New York: Doubleday, 1972), 141–43.

84. Berrigan, *Lights on in the House of the Dead,* 221.

85. Ibid.

86. According to the Church Committee report,

> Richard M. Nixon won his first Presidential election in 1968 by less than one percent of the total popular vote. The Presidential campaign that year had been accompanied by some of the most violent street demonstrations in the history of American elections.
>
> His first year in office provided the President with ample further evidence of the mood of revolt in the country. In March and April 1969, student riots erupted in San Francisco, Cambridge, and Ithaca; and in Chicago, ghetto blacks battled the police in the streets. By October and November, the anti-war movement was sufficiently well organized to bring to the nation's capital the largest mass demonstrations ever witnessed in the United States. The magnitude of the unrest was immense and, just as the nation was obsessed by Vietnam, so, too, the White House grew increasingly preoccupied with the wave of domestic protest sweeping the countryside.

Senate Select Committee to Study Governmental Operations with Respect to Intelligence Activities, *Supplementary Detailed Staff Reports on Intelligence Activities and the Rights of Americans, III. Final Report,* 94th Cong., 2nd sess., April 3, 1976, 924.

87. Jack Anderson, *The Anderson Papers* (New York: Random House, 1973), 171–72.

88. The government's case rested largely on the testimony of a jailhouse informer whose identity could not be divulged.

July 9, 1971

*To:* C. D. Brennan [Head of Domestic Intelligence]

*By:* R. L. Shackelford

*Subject:* Proposed Plans of Antiwar Elements to Embarrass the United States Government Information Concerning. [*sic*]

*Purpose:* To advise of information received from [name blacked out] which sets forth plans by antiwar advocates with the EASTCON movement to cause embarrassment to the United States Government.

*Details:* [Name blacked out] advised that he received the following information [half the page blacked out]. The basis of this project is allegedly a lengthy

Memorandum on prison reform by Daniel Berrigan, given the former Attorney General Ramsey Clark, which Clark reportedly has used in making public statements on this subject. An advisory board for the project reportedly includes Clark; Senator Edward M. Kennedy, Massachusetts; Senator Philip A. Hart, Michigan; Jessica Mitford, a female English author of "The American Way of Death"; Congressman William R. Anderson, Tennessee; former New York Senator Charles E. Goodell; and Attorney William Kunstler.

The source advised [blacked out].

The [blacked out] felt the information furnished by [name blacked out] if disseminated, would identify this sensitive confidential source. However, it is believed that this information is of such vital importance to the internal security of the country and involves also the violation of Federal laws that it must be disseminated to responsible officials concerned. Accordingly, letters have been prepared for such officials and the information furnished by the informant, suitably paraphrased to protect his identity, has been incorporated into a memorandum to be enclosed with these letters.

The matter is being closely followed and you will be advised of any pertinent information which develops.

*Recommendation:* If you approve: (1) The attached letters to the White House, the Attorney General and the Director, Secret Service, will be sent along with a copy of the memorandum containing the plans of antiwar elements to embarrass the United States Government.

(2) Information in the above memorandum of specific interest to the General Services Administration and the Bureau of Prisons will be extracted, paraphrased and furnished to those agencies under separate cover."

FBI file HQ 100–360261, section 3.

89. August 16, 1971

*To:* C. D. Brennan

*From:* R. L. Shackelford

*Subject:* Proposed Plans of Antiwar Elements to Embarrass the United States Government.

*Purpose:* To advise that information regarding a previously reported plot by Leonard Bernstein, conductor and composer, to embarrass the President and other Government officials through an antiwar and anti-Government musical composition to be played at the dedication of the Kennedy Center for the Performing Arts has been reported by the press.

*Background:* [Six or so lines blacked out]. The purpose of this action was to embarrass high Government officials, possibly even the President who might be present. This information was furnished to the White House, the Attorney General, Secret

Service, and Bureau of Prisons. Thereafter, on 7–14–71, Bernstein attempted to visit Berrigan at Danbury but was denied admission by prison officials after consulting Bureau of Prisons in Washington, D.C.

*Current Developments:* There is attached an article from the 8-7-71 issue of "Human Events" which discloses "rumors are sweeping Washington . . ." that Bernstein will embarrass the President with an anti-administration bombshell. The article referring to "administrative sources" as the basis for this information stated Bernstein had been in contact with Berrigan for ideas in connection with the dedicatory "Mass" he was composing for the Kennedy Center ceremony.

Also attached is an 8-11-71 article from "The Washington Post and Times Herald" which set forth an announcement by the White House that President Nixon did not intend to attend the dedication ceremony at the Kennedy Center as an act of courtesy to Mrs. Jacqueline Kennedy Onassis. The article indicates that Mr. Nixon felt the formal opening "should really be her night."

*Observations:* It would appear that the information disseminated to the White House resulted in the decision of the President not to attend the Kennedy Center ceremony and that the reported plan was purposely leaked by the administration to the press in order to minimize the effectiveness of Bernstein's plot to embarrass the administration.

*Recommendation:* None. For information.

FBI file HQ 100–360261, section 3.

90. Philip Berrigan with Fred A. Wilcox, *Fighting the Lamb's War: Skirmishes with the American Empire: The Autobiography of Philip Berrigan* (Monroe, ME: Common Courage Press, 1996), 126–31.

91. "In 1986," according to Joan Peyser, "[Conductor and Bernstein associate Maurice] Peress talked about the Celebrant: 'At first he is an innocent. He is Everyman. Then he becomes the Priest. Ultimately he faces the people. He tears his clothes off and has a midlife crisis. The people all lie there as he pours his guts out. Then he slams the door. He says, 'Fuck you!' That was the plan Lenny had and one he told us about while we were working on the show. He had a vision of Nixon and Congress sitting out there absolutely dumbstruck. The point of the piece is that the Celebrant suddenly abandons us, leaving us to bring peace to ourselves and to the world. I wanted to tell Lenny he couldn't do that. It was an antiwar piece. Nixon was in the White House. People were scared." Joan Peyser, *Bernstein: A Biography,* rev. ed. (New York: Billboard, 1998), 423.

92. September 8, 1971
*To:* C. D. Brennan

*From:* R. L. Schackelford

*Current Developments:* The New Haven Office has maintained a stop with the FCI [Federal Corrections Institution], where Berrigan is incarcerated, relative to any attempts on the part of the Berrigans to receive or to send out contraband which would include material relative to this plot. No such information has been brought to our attention; however, it must be noted that individuals connected with the Eastcon prosecution, defendants, unindicted co-conspirators and legal counsel have virtually free access to Daniel Berrigan and no check is made by prison authorities of brief cases or envelopes carried into or out of the FCI.

There have been two performances conducted to date, a dress rehearsal and a Congressional Night, and newspaper articles reporting this activity have been highly complimentary concerning the composition; but critics were asked not to publicly review the work before the opening night because of *possible changes* [underscore penned in] which may be made. One individual who attended the performance was quoted as saying "The 'Mass' shows the terrible, terrible tension of man today as he lives and as he prays. It is terribly contemporary." It was also noted that the performers were dressed in diverse garments such as hot pants and sweat shirts. In addition, Mrs. Edward Kennedy was interviewed and asked whether her mother-in-law, Mrs. Joseph Kennedy, "who will be in the Presidential Box tonight," would be shocked at some of the unorthodox passages in the "Mass" and she stated, "I hope not."

*Action:* None. This is for your information.

FBI file HQ 100–360261, section 3.

93. Bernstein could justify his apparent liberties with the traditional mass from the following text adopted by the church on December 4, 1963, the first major document to come out of the Second Vatican Council: "30. By way of promoting active participation, the people should be encouraged to take part by means of acclamations, responses, psalmody, antiphons, and songs, as well as by actions, gestures, and bodily attitudes. And at the proper times all should observe a reverent silence." *Constitution of the Sacred Liturgy (Sacrosanctum Concilium). Documents of Vatican II,* ed. Walter M. Abbot, trans. and ed. Joseph Gallagher (New York: America Press, 1966), 148.

94. Leonard Bernstein, *Mass: A Theater Piece for Singers, Players and Dancers: Text from the Liturgy of the Roman Mass. Additional Texts by Stephen Schwartz and Leonard Bernstein,* Vocal Score (New York: Amberson Enterprises/G. Schirmer, 1971).

95. "'The day they stop the war we can have Communion,' and the response, 'They don't deserve communion' were supplied by Father Dan Berrigan, a Catholic priest and anti-war protester whom Bernstein visited in prison during his work on MASS." www.leonardbernstein.com/research.html.

96. See, for example, Robert Craft, "Non Credo," *New York Review of Books,* October 17, 1971.

97. A postscript: on September 28, Nixon was in the Oval Office with his advisor Charles Colson discussing Nixon's decision not to appear at the premiere of *Mass.* Colson remarked that Bernstein or someone else—the tape is garbled—said that Nixon had stayed away because of Bernstein's association with the Berrigans. Nixon replied, "Bullshit," and then called Bernstein a "son of a bitch." In an ironic twist, both Colson and Nixon were delighted that the Knights of Columbus, Cardinal Cooke of New York, and much of the Catholic press considered *Mass* a "sacrilege"; they believed the issue could help swing more Catholic votes to the Republicans. Nixon Presidential Materials, University of Virginia's Miller Center for Public Affairs, http://millercenter.virginia.edu/scripps/diglibrary/prezrecordings/nixon/index.html, tape 579a at 1:17:30.

98. Why are we fighting? asks Undersecretary of Defense John T. McNaughton. "70%—To avoid a humiliating defeat (to our reputation as a guarantor); 20%—To keep SVN [South Vietnam] (and the adjacent) territory from Chinese hands; 10%—To permit the people of SVN to enjoy a better, freer way of life." *The Pentagon Papers,* Gravel Edition, vol. 3, 695.

99. Ibid., 700–701.

100. "List of White House 'Enemies' and Memo Submitted by Dean to the Ervin Committee," in *Watergate and the White House,* vol. 1, *June 1972–July 1973* (New York: Facts on File, 1973), 96–97.

101. Columbia entitled the album *Leonard Bernstein's Concert for Peace, Haydn's Mass in Time of War*; Liner Notes, Columbia, 33 rpm, M32196; Sony, compact disc, SM2K 47563.

## 5. NORTON LECTURES

1. Noam Chomsky, *Aspects of a Theory of Syntax* (Cambridge, MA: MIT Press, 1965); Arthur Berger, "Introduction" to *Aesthetic Analysis,* Apollo Edition, by D. W. Prall (New York: Thomas Y. Crowell, 1936), xxii–xxv. In his earlier book of 1929, Prall specifically stated, "Tonality is . . . a matter of convention." Prall, *Aesthetic Judgment* (Thomas Y. Crowell, 1929), 238.

2. Arthur Berger, *Reflections of an American Composer* (Berkeley: University of California Press, 2002), 45.

3. Indeed, the audience laughed in response to Bernstein's sardonic if not sarcastic remarks about this new music before the New York Philharmonic performance of Xenakis's *Pithoprakta* on February 9, 1964. In his introductory remarks,

Bernstein virtually likened some of the new music to "hoaxes," referred to works that have "reverted to a semi-idiotic simplicity," and described with rather a sneer a "neo-dada" work that has "no notes at all." He noted that while some of this music was the result of "sincere striving," much else was the product of "ambitious chicanery." Audience members laughed again when he spoke of György Ligeti's "writing a work for mass metronomes." Bernstein did claim that this new music was part of a "Copernican revolution" in which "man's ego is no longer the inner motor of a work of art"; but despite his insistence that not all this music is "ambitious nonsense," the damage had been done: he had educated his audiences too well. NYP Special Editions, compact disc, NYP 2012.

4. Leonard Bernstein, "Aaron Copland at Seventy: An Intimate Sketch," in *Findings* (New York: Simon and Schuster, 1982), 292–93.

5. Leonard Bernstein, "Varèse, Koussevitzky and New Music," in *Findings,* 216.

6. Leonard Bernstein, *The Unanswered Question: Six Talks at Harvard* (Cambridge, MA: Harvard University Press, 1976), 12; "Varèse, Koussevitzky and New Music," 216.

7. Beethoven, in other words, was following the classical idea as developed by Schiller: form stretched liberally by expressive need, but liberty checked by form.

8. Bernstein, *The Unanswered Question,* 265. Compare Bernstein with Copland, who wrote of Mahler's Ninth Symphony, "It was as if the composer knew, deep inside himself, that he was saying a farewell to the nineteenth century. All his music reinvokes the past glories of that golden age, but with an added note of regret for a wonderful epoch that was gone without hope of recall." Aaron Copland, *Our New Music: Leading Composers in Europe and America* (New York: McGraw-Hill, 1941), 30.

9. Bernstein, *Unanswered Question,* 359.

10. Ibid., 417.

11. Ibid., 270. Theodore Adorno, *The Philosophy of Modern Music,* trans. Anne G. Mitchell and Wesley V. Blomster (New York: Seabury, 1973).

12. For example, consider the four notes of the first movement of the Fifth Symphony and their pounding cadence at the finale of that movement as well as the coda at the end. Bernstein could have used this example to explain the compositional progress from ambiguity to resolution, but Adorno would use it to indicate Beethoven's expectations of reconciliation between individual and collective.

13. Adorno, *Philosophy of Modern Music,* 190.

14. See Theodore Adorno, *Mahler: A Musical Physiognomy,* trans. Edmund Jephcott (Chicago: University of Chicago Press, 1992), 5–14, 41–43.

15. Adorno, *Philosophy of Modern Music,* 143.

16. Ibid., 162.

17. Ibid., 211, 215, 208–9.

18. W. H. Auden, "The Poet & the City," in *The Dyer's Hand and Other Essays* (New York: Vintage, 1962), 78–80.

19. George Steiner, *In Bluebeard's Castle: Some Notes Towards the Redefinition of Culture* (New Haven, CT: Yale University Press, 1971), 81.

20. Theodore Adorno, *Prisms* (Cambridge, MA: MIT Press, 1981), 34; and *Critical Models,* trans. Henry W. Pickford (New York: Columbia University Press, 1999), 48.

21. Nor should composition be tailor-made for an audience. "The emancipation of music today," wrote Adorno triumphantly about atonality, "is tantamount to its emancipation from verbal language, and it is this emancipation which flashes during the destruction of meaning." *Philosophy of Modern Music,* 128.

22. In 1975, Bernstein noted that the theme of crisis of faith appears in virtually all his works, from *Jeremiah* and *Age of Anxiety* to *Kaddish* and *Mass,* with *Kaddish* "the biggest crisis piece of all." He argued that the "crisis in faith is tied up with the crisis in tonality." Philip Ramey, "A Talk with Leonard Bernstein," Writings, Leonard Bernstein Collection (LBC), box 90, folder 15, Library of Congress, Washington, D.C.

23. "Proportions . . . that are constituted of numbers, are almost like figures, not only because they are made out of lines and points, but because of their motion. Also with their movement the heavenly figures maintain themselves, and with their harmonies, their rays, their movements penetrating everything, they thus affect the spirit, in a hidden way, from day to day, as Music above all, can affect it in a more open way." Marsilio Ficino, *The Book of Life,* trans. Charles Boer (Dallas: Spring Publications, 1980), 143.

24. Ibid., 162–63.

25. D. P. Walker, *Spiritual and Demonic Magic from Ficino to Campanella* (University Park: University of Pennsylvania Press, 2000), 3, 18–19. Francis A. Yates, *Astraea: The Imperial Theme in the Sixteenth Century* (Routledge and Kegan Paul, 1975), 159–60.

26. Francis A. Yates, *The French Academies of the Sixteenth Century* (London: Routledge, 1988), 37–76, esp. 54.

27. Yates, *Astraea,* 149–72.

28. Bruno Walter, *Von den moralischen kraeften der Musik,* trans. Maryke Seldes, Vortrag Gehalten im Kulturband zu Wien (Vienna: Herbert Reichner Verlag, 1935).

29. Adorno, *Mahler*, 1–17, 119, 135.

30. Copland, *Our New Music*, 31. Copland did also write that along with Mahler's "histrionics" comes his "inner warmth, and the will to evoke the largest forms and the grandest musical thoughts" (32).

31. I depend for this calculation upon the Mouret Mahler Discography at http://gustavmahler.net.free.fr/us.html, with emendations and commentary by discographer and discophile Alan Lesitsky.

32. Datebook, August 1, 1948, LBC.

33. Donald Mitchell, *Gustav Mahler,* vol. 2, *The Wunderhorn Years: Chronicles and Commentaries* (Berkeley: University of California Press, 1977).

34. Precisely how the concept of genocide is conceptualized by the United Nations Convention on Genocide.

35. Bernstein, "Mahler: His Time Has Come." *Findings,* 255–64.

## 6. BERNSTEIN AT SEA

1. Indeed, Barbara Rose had already argued rather presciently in 1969 that the culture industry "neutralized any kind of critical or satirical charge pop [art] may have intended. Now conceptual and process art, originally motivated by moral revulsion against the baseness of American society, has been quickly assimilated into the existing structure. Its original negative stance has become diffused. It is utterly robbed of any critical sting." Barbara Rose, "The Politics of Art: III: Chaos and Entropy," originally published in *Artforum* in 1969, republished in *Autocritique, Essays on Art and Anti-Art: 1963–1987* (New York: Wiedenfeld and Nicolson, 1988), 241.

2. Susan Sontag, "Freak Show," *New York Review of Books,* November 18, 1973.

3. Pauline Kael, "On the Future of Movies" (1974), in *Reeling* (New York: Warner Books, 1976), 415–44.

4. The FBI memorandum "Name Check" of November 18, 1974, refers to, among others, Bernstein's participation in the Selma to Montgomery march and the Berrigan dinner party and concludes that "the central files of the FBI, including the records of our Identification Division, contain no additional pertinent information concerning the [Bernstein or other] captioned individuals based upon background information submitted in connection with this name check request." Memorandum, FBI file HQ 100–360261, section 3.

5. Arthur Laurents, *Original Story: A Memoir of Broadway and Hollywood* (New York: Alfred A. Knopf, 2000), 371.

6. Transcript of film interview by the United States Information Agency, 1977, Writings, Leonard Bernstein Collection (LBC), box 90, folder 38, Library of Congress, Washington, D.C.

7. According to Jack Gottlieb, the other titles were "An American Songfest," "The Glorious Fourth," and "Mortal Melodies, A Secular Service, and Ballet for Voices." Jack Gottlieb, "Leonard Bernstein: Songfest." Liner Notes for Bernstein, *Songfest.* Leonard Bernstein and the National Symphony Orchestra of Washington, Deutsche Grammophon 2531 044.

8. Frank O'Hara, *The Collected Poems of Frank O'Hara,* ed. Donald Allen (Berkeley: University of California Press, 1995), 174, 530n.

9. Writings, June 1985, LBC, box 97, folder 28.

10. At this time, Bernstein was going through personal upheaval: in 1976, he left his wife, Felicia, to live with a same-sex partner. He returned to Felicia the following year to care for her during her losing fight with cancer. She died on June 16, 1978, at age fifty-six, and he was left a profoundly saddened man at sixty.

11. With the exception of *Das Lied von der Erde,* which he filmed in 1972 with the Israel Philharmonic with Christa Ludwig and Rene Kollo, all the rest were with the Vienna Philharmonic. He conducted the orchestra in Mahler's Ninth in 1972; the First, Fourth, and Fifth in 1974; the Seventh and the Eighth with Judith Blegen, Edda Moser, Kenneth Riegel, Hermann Prey, and Jose van Dam in 1975; and the Sixth in 1977.

12. Leonard Bernstein, *Findings* (Garden City, NY: Anchor Doubleday, 1982), 114–22.

13. Cyrus Durgin, "Bernstein, Here for Two Concerts, Talks of War and Music in Israel," *Boston Globe,* December 10, 1948, photocopied in FBI file BS 100–17761.

14. Humphrey Burton, *Leonard Bernstein* (New York: Doubleday, 1994), 184–85.

15. This was the event, discussed in chapter 2, that occasioned Truman's request for Bernstein's FBI dossier, an event from which Truman subsequently backed out.

16. The Unitel performance was with Christa Ludwig and Rene Kollo. Deutsche Grammophon, DVD, 00440 073 4093.

17. Benny Morris, *The Birth of the Palestinian Refugee Problem, 1947–1949* (Cambridge: Cambridge University Press, 1987), 8, 16–17.

18. Not until 1987 did Israeli historiography discuss a darker side to the victory. The evidence revealed that during the 1948 war, the Israelis had made some profoundly difficult if not sordid choices. With too many Arab spokesmen long

calling for the annihilation of Jews, it was small wonder that even the left-leaning Jewish leadership worried that Israeli Arabs would constitute a fifth column. With thousands of Palestinian Arabs already having fled, the Israelis decided to induce as many more to leave, and they often resorted to terror to force Arabs into exodus. The authoritative text is Morris, *Birth of the Palestinian Refugee Problem*. See also Tom Segev, *One Complete Palestine: Jews and Arabs Under the British Mandate* (New York: Metropolitan Press, 1999), 378.

19. Ilan Peleg, *Begin's Foreign Policy: Israel's Turn to the Right, 1977–1983* (New York: Greenwood, 1987).

20. "Protests from U.S. Jews Stir Controversy in Israel," *New York Times,* June 21, 1979.

21. See, for example, Jonathan Mendilow, *Ideology, Party Change and Electoral Campaigns in Israel, 1965–2001* (Albany: State University of New York Press, 2003), 80–87.

22. Writings, LBC, box 95, folder 14.

23. Martin Duberman, *Stonewall* (New York: Penguin, 1994), 169–212.

24. Stephen Wadsworth, "'A Quiet Place': Librettist's Notes" accompanying the libretto for Leonard Bernstein and Stephen Wadsworth, *A Quiet Place*, DG 419 761-1/2, 1–13. This new opera, he told the National Opera Institute in February 1983, was "a very American one, in that it deals not only with American characters, but with the American language, the vernacular." Writings, LBC, box 95, folder 8.

25. Dinah's death in the story was of intense personal importance to Wadsworth, who had just lost his sister in an auto accident, and to Bernstein, who was still grieving over Felicia's death.

26. Bernstein is listed as an endorser in Edward M. Kennedy and Mark O. Hatfield, *Freeze!: How You Can Help Prevent Nuclear War* (New York: Bantam, 1982), 191.

27. Writings, LBC, box 95, folder 15.

28. Bernstein to Derek Bok, December 15, 1983, Writings, LBC, box 95, folder 24.

29. "Words for St. John the Divine," December 31, 1984, Writings, LBC, box 96, folder 21.

30. Writings, LBC, box 96, folder 29.

31. Bernstein's statement is in Harry Kraut, Revised Memorandum, Personal Business Papers, LBC, box 1002, folder 17, "Journey for Peace," 2.

32. Writings, LBC, box 97, folder 15.

33. Edward M. Kennedy to Leonard Bernstein, Correspondence, LBC, box 32, folder 1, "Kennedys."

34. Writings, LBC, box 98, folder 17.

35. Writings, box 99, folder 17.

36. Greg Lawrence, *Dance with Demons: The Life of Jerome Robbins* (New York: G. P. Putnam's Sons, 2001), 370–71; Laurents, *Original Story*, 369.

37. "45 of a total of 49 performances of seven of Bernstein's works took place with the Wiener Philharmoniker during the last nine years." See the website of the Vienna Philharmonic: www.wienerphilharmoniker.at/index.php?set_language= en&cccpage=news_detail&set_z_news=86.

38. Leonard Bernstein, "I'm a Liberal and Proud of It," *New York Times,* October 30, 1988, Section E.

39. Bernstein to Martha Graham, Correspondence, LBC, box 25, folder "Martha Graham."

40. Bernstein penciled onto p. 200 of his copy of the February 13, 1989, edition of the *Nation* his notes to an article by Darrel Yates Rist, "The Deadly Costs of an Obsession." He noted that homosexuals would become free only when they turned their feelings of victimization and sense of others' disapproval into anger and political action. They also needed to stop thinking that AIDS was somehow visited upon them as retribution for their sins. Personal Business Papers, LBC, box 982, folder *"The Nation."*

41. See Alice Goldfarb Marquis, *Art Lessons: Learning from the Rise and Fall of Public Arts Funding* (New York: Basic Books, 1995), 207–12; and Burton, *Leonard Bernstein,* 505–6.

42. According to the Vienna Philharmonic website, "The figures tell the impressive story of the Leonard Bernstein–Wiener Philharmoniker connection. There were a total of 197 concerts, 99 in Vienna, 6 in Salzburg, 1 in Bregenz and no fewer than 91 outside Austria." Wiener Philharmoniker, www.wienerphilharmoniker.at/ index.php?set_language=en&cccpage=news_detail&set_z_news=86.

43. The report of the diagnosis is attributed to Shirley Bernstein. See Meryle Secrest, *Leonard Bernstein: A Life* (New York: Random House, 1994), 401.

44. Writings, LBC, box 103, folder 37.

### 7. UNDERSTANDING BERNSTEIN

1. Jane Fleugel, ed., *Bernstein Remembered* (New York: Carroll and Graf 1991); Thomas Seiler, *Leonard Bernstein, The Last Ten Years: A Personal Portrait by Thomas R. Seiler* (New York: Edition Stemmle, 2000).

2. Humphrey Burton, *Leonard Bernstein* (New York: Doubleday, 1994), 136–37.

3. Leonard Bernstein, "Statement on choosing . . . conducting composing," October 15, 1946, Writings, Leonard Bernstein Collection (LBC), box 71, folder 19, Library of Congress, Washington, D.C.

4. Marc Blitzstein to Bernstein, May 19, 1950, Correspondence, LBC, box 8, folder 30.

5. William W. Burton, ed., *Conversations about Bernstein* (New York: Oxford University Press, 1995), 63–64; 123.

6. Virgil Thomson, *A Virgil Thomson Reader* (Boston: Houghton Mifflin, 1981), 431.

7. Burton, *Conversations,* 137.

8. Leon Botstein, "The Tragedy of Leonard Bernstein," *Harper's,* May 1983, 57.

9. David Denby, "The Trouble with Lenny," *New Yorker,* August 17, 1998, 50–51.

10. Hubbs explains that a colleague sent her these lines. Nadine Hubbs, *The Queer Composition of America's Sound* (Berkeley: University of California Press, 2004), 65.

11. Wilfred Mellers, *Music in a New Found Land: Themes and Developments in the History of American Music,* rev. paperback ed. (London: Faber and Faber, 1987), 434 (emphasis added).

12. Joseph Horowitz, *Classical Music in America: A History of Its Rise and Fall* (New York: W. W. Norton, 2005), 480.

13. Ibid., 481. Horowitz offers only one citation to support or elaborate on this idea of Bernstein's American crisis: Tom Wolfe's article on the Bernsteins' Black Panther fund-raising event (566n4). Horowitz also sees evidence of Bernstein's malaise in his deportment when he announced his retirement from the New York Philharmonic and at his Norton Lectures, a malaise that prompted Bernstein to leave for Vienna.

14. Leonard Bernstein, *The Unanswered Question: Six Talks at Harvard* (Cambridge, MA: Harvard University Press, 1973), 417.

15. Roger Sessions, "To Revitalize Opera," *Modern Music* 15 (March–April 1938): 150.

16. On the general diminution of critical expression and the concomitant rise of a culture of "banality," see Ellen Schrecker, *Many Are the Crimes: McCarthyism in America* (New York: Little, Brown, 1998), 359–403.

17. Arthur Miller, "On Social Plays," in *The Theater Essays of Arthur Miller,* ed. Robert A. Martin and Steven R. Centola, rev. and exp. ed. (New York: Da Capo Press, 1996), 53.

18. Hillary Mills, *Mailer: A Biography* (New York: Empire Books, 1982), 142–43. See the account of Robert Rossen in chapter 3 of this book.

19. Bernstein to Irving Fine, October 20, 1952, Correspondence, LBC, box 21, folder 44, "Fine, Irving and Verna."

20. Indeed, that these pieces lacked critical depth was precisely why Bernstein refused to consider them the kind of serious work he longed to create. See Arthur Laurents, *Original Story: A Memoir of Broadway and Hollywood* (New York: Alfred A. Knopf, 2000), 329.

21. Philip Roth, "Writing American Fiction," *Commentary,* March 1961, reprinted in *Reading Myself and Others* (New York: Farrar, Straus and Giroux, 1975), 117–35. Roth's dedication of this collection to Saul Bellow was fitting inasmuch as Roth described an America very much like that of Bellow's *The Adventures of Augie March.*

22. Ihab Hassan, "The Character of Post-War Fiction in America" (1962), in *On Contemporary Literature,* exp. ed., ed. Richard Kostelanetz (New York: Avon Books, 1969), 37.

23. Harold Clurman, *The Naked Image: Observations on Modern Theater* (New York: Macmillan, 1966), 162.

24. Norman Mailer, "The Argument Invigorated" (1966), in *The American Novel Since World War II,* ed. Marcus Klein (New York: Fawcett, 1969), 73.

25. Quoted by Helen Epstein, *Joe Papp: An American Life* (New York: Da Capo, 1996), 200. Epstein: "The contrast between the state of American society and mainstream American theater seemed, to both Papp and Brustein, obscene" (201).

26. In 1966, only a year before he wrote most of *Armies of the Night,* Mailer summed up the failure of American writers to produce social fiction: "No writer succeeded in doing the single great work which would clarify a nation's vision of itself as Tolstoy had done perhaps with *War and Peace* or *Anna Karenina,* and Stendhal with *The Red and the Black,* no one novel came along which was grand and daring and comprehensive and detailed, able to give sustenance to the adventurer and merriment to the rich, leave compassion in the ice chambers of the upper class and energy as alms for the poor." Mailer, "Argument Reinvigorated," 73.

27. Bernstein, *Unanswered Question,* 314.

28. Ibid., 315.

29. Years later, in his 1990 *Vineland,* Thomas Pynchon did locate human agency in a berserk, Reaganesque attorney general who invades a zone of free, mutually aiding, noncompetitive and non-capital-accumulative exiles and escapees from stifling conservative America. The liberal imagination was thus able

to compose a narrative of right-wing revanchism. But by the time of *Vineland*'s publication, Bernstein was dying, if not already dead.

30. Norman Mailer, *The Idol and the Octopus* (New York: Dell, 1968), 122.

31. Theodore Lowi, *The End of Liberalism: The Second Republic of the United States,* 2nd ed. (New York: W. W. Norton, 1979), 51.

32. Gerald M. Pomper, "The Decline of the Party in American Elections," *Political Science Quarterly* 92, no. 1 (Spring 1977): 40.

33. The political scientist Walter Dean Burnham, in his analysis of data about ideological shifts in the electorate between 1964 and 1978, wrote: "The relative swing toward a more 'conservative' position has been even more marked among liberals, Democrats, and lower-class elements than among conservatives, Republicans, and upper-middle to upper class elements." *The Current Crisis in American Politics* (New York: Oxford University Press, 1982), 295.

34. Gerald M. Pomper, "The Presidential Election," in *The Election of 1980: Reports and Interpretations,* ed. Gerald M. Pomper (Chatham, NJ: Chatham House, 1981), 70–73.

35. Melvyn Bragg, "A Murderer's Tale: Norman Mailer Talking to Melvyn Bragg," in *Conversations with Norman Mailer,* ed. J. Michael Lennon (Jackson: University Press of Mississippi, 1988), 259 (emphasis added). In 1959, Mailer had talked of "large literary works which were filled with characters, and were programmatic, and had large theses, and were developed, let's say, like the Tolstoyan novel." Steven Marcus, "An Interview with Steven Marcus," *Paris Review* 31 (Winter–Spring 1964): 28–58; *Conversations with Norman Mailer,* 83. His model for the great American novel was *USA* by John Dos Passos. Charles Monaghan, "Portrait of a Man Reading" *Washington Post Book World* July 11, 1971, reprinted in Lennon, *Conversations with Norman Mailer,* 189. He did write a work deep in the American character, *The Executioner's Song,* but it was a far cry from the great social-political novel that he aspired to.

36. Michiko Kakutani, "Mailer Talking," in *Conversations with Norman Mailer,* 291, reprinted from *New York Times Book Review,* June 6, 1982, 38–41 (italics added).

37. Ned Rorem, *The Nantucket Diary* (San Francisco: North Point Press, 1987), 244 (entry for May 22, 1979).

38. Burton, *Leonard Bernstein,* 502. Interestingly, Arthur Miller and Norman Mailer took much the same road; Miller had already done so in 1964 with his *Incident at Vichy* but later also wrote *Broken Glass* (New York: Penguin, 1995), and Mailer did so in *The Castle in the Forest* (New York: Random House, 2007).

39. Laurents, *Original Story,* 374.

## EPILOGUE

1. Bertolt Brecht, "To Those Born Later" ("To Posterity"), trans. John Willett, *Bertolt Brecht: Poems, 1913–1956* (London, Methuen, 1976), 318–20.

2. Hannah Arendt, *Men in Dark Times* (New York: Harcourt, Brace, 1968), viii-x, 17–23.

3. "Lenny was a socialist!" exclaimed his publicist Margaret Carson to me during a personal interview on April 25, 2001.

4. According to Ned Rorem, "Marc [Blitzstein] was an intellectual where Lenny Bernstein was not (although he tried to be and was, in fact, smarter than many an intellectual)." *Knowing When to Stop: A Memoir* (New York: Simon and Schuster, 1994), 317.

# INDEX

Text: 11/15 Granjon

Display: Granjon

Compositor: IBT Global

Indexer: Kevin Millham

Printer and binder: Maple-Vail Manufacturing Group